TRANSFORMATIVE
RELIGIOUS EXPERIENCE

Transformative Religious Experience

A Phenomenological Understanding of Religious Conversion

JOSHUA IYADURAI

◆PICKWICK *Publications* • Eugene, Oregon

TRANSFORMATIVE RELIGIOUS EXPERIENCE
A Phenomenological Understanding of Religious Conversion

Copyright © 2015 Joshua Iyadurai. All rights reserved. Except for brief quotations in critical publications or reviews, no part of this book may be reproduced in any manner without prior written permission from the publisher. Write: Permissions, Wipf and Stock Publishers, 199 W. 8th Ave., Suite 3, Eugene, OR 97401.

Pickwick Publications
An Imprint of Wipf and Stock Publishers
199 W. 8th Ave., Suite 3
Eugene, OR 97401

www.wipfandstock.com

ISBN 13: 978-1-62032-746-3

Cataloguing-in-Publication data:

Iyadurai, Joshua.

Transformative religious experience : a phenomenological understanding of religious conversion / Joshua Iyadurai ; foreword by H. Newton Malony.

xii + 254 pp. ; 23 cm. Includes bibliographical references and index.

ISBN 13: 978-1-62032-746-3

1. Conversion—Christianity. 2. Experience (Religion). 3. Phenomenology. I. Malony, H. Newton. II. Title.

BL51 I95 2015

Manufactured in the U.S.A.

To

Hema,

My wife, love, and friend

Contents

Foreword ix

Acknowledgments xi

Introduction 1

1 Visions 13

2 Dreams 34

3 Voices of God 57

4 Miracles 85

5 Prayers 101

6 Mild Experiences 120

7 The Mystical Turning Point 143

8 Transforming Effects 169

9 Hostilities 198

10 The Step Model 234

Bibliography 249

Index 253

Foreword

Not since William James's *The Varieties of Religious Experience* have readers been afforded such rich descriptions of the personal reports of conversion experiences. And, in addition, these experiences are recounted from within a cross-cultural context, i.e., India. James's reports were largely from within the English-speaking world. While dynamics across cultures may have similar features, there are qualitative dimensions of religious experiences that are different where conversions occur in environments where Christianity is not the dominant religious tradition. All the people the author interviewed came from non-Christian backgrounds.

Further, through the application of the phenomenological method and structured interview construction, the author has given us unequaled details of personal reflections in his case studies. He intended to allow each person to fully describe and reflect on the process of conversion as well as the impact of the experience in their lives—and he succeeded. While some may become frustrated with the detail in these accounts, he was nevertheless very successful in probing the process of religious conversion within daily life. It was rather remarkable that he was able to provide an interview atmosphere of trust that would result in such introspective openness.

The plan of the book is itself somewhat unique. It actually follows the author's intent to let these experiences speak for themselves. Many books on conversion fit examples into models that are superimposed on the events. This volume follows a sequence of experiences stemming from the reports themselves. Visions, dreams, voices of the divine, solutions to problems, answers to prayers—these are the ways all converts would speak of their experience. They would rarely, if ever, superimpose such constructs as friendship associations, anxiety, social groupings, assimilation, etc. on their conversions.

This does not mean that the author was unaware of the various social/psychological models that have been used by scholars in understanding such experiences as conversion. Such models include my personal

Foreword

conviction that conversion is an example of *psycholinguistic labeling*.[1] The final chapter of the book summarizes these models and illustrates how these anecdotal reports from India could be understood from within them. The author does a worthy incorporation of this literature into his own unique taxonomy of the conversion process that still retains his intended "phenomenological" flavor.

I predict that this volume will take its place as a notable contribution to our continuing efforts to understand religious experience as grounded in the conversion process.

H. Newton Malony, PhD
Senior Professor
Graduate School of Psychology
Fuller Theological Seminary
Pasadena, CA

---

1. H. N. Malony, "Conversion as Psycholinguistic Labeling: A New Model for Church Ministry," *Theology News and Notes* (Spring 2003) 19–21.

Acknowledgments

First of all, I am profoundly thankful to the converts who opened their lives to me so I could explore the complex phenomenon of religious conversion in India. Their fascinating narratives sustained my interest in this field and resulted in the present volume. I thank Dr D. Christopher, Mrs Mary Philip, Mr G. Richard, Mrs Christina, and others who introduced the converts to be part of my study.

I am grateful to Dr. Joe Mannath, my doctoral supervisor at the University of Madras, Chennai, South India, for his guidance, encouragement, and his keen interest in bringing the fruit of the research to publication. I thank Dr. Henry N. Malony for his foreword and his insights in shaping the research from the beginning, along with Dr. Richard Peace of Fuller Theological Seminary. I am indebted to Dr. Peace for his continued interest in my research all these years and his valuable comments on my book proposal. I am fortunate to have Dr. Lewis R. Rambo, editor of *Pastoral Psychology*, interested in my research ever since my article appeared in his journal. I thank him for his comments on the book proposal and his support in finding a publisher, along with Dr. Robert Johnston of Fuller Theological Seminary.

A special thanks to Global Research Institute (GRI) at Fuller Theological Seminary for the grant to write this book. I thank Dave Scott and Rachel Paulus for their warmth and support in making my time at GRI profitable. The Langham Partnership (formerly John Stott Ministries) financially supported the initial stage of my research at Fuller and Langham Literature made a publication grant; I am thankful to Langham. I am happy to express my gratitude to those who provided financial support: my mother, Mrs Susily Iyadurai, Chris and Irene, Pento, Sathyabalan *annan*, Beula *akka*, and someone who never disclosed his/her identity. I appreciate the prayer support of many for my research and the publication. I am grateful to John Wipf for his keen interest in getting my book published by Pickwick Publications. My special thanks to Nathan for copyediting the manuscript, and I record my appreciation to Jim, K.C., and others at

Acknowledgments

Wipf and Stock for their role in bringing out this volume. I thank Springer for giving me permission to use the material that appeared in *Pastoral Psychology*. I thank Hema for her comments and corrections.

I am extremely thankful to my wife, Hema, and my daughters, Jedidah, Jerusha, and Jemimah, for their inspiration, support, and cooperation. All these years, they had to put up with my preoccupation with the research and my long spells of absence, especially when I was away in the USA in 2004 and 2012. I am enormously grateful to them, and the debt I owe Hema is too great to express.

Introduction

> Would you ... preach the Gospel to a cow? Well, some of the untouchables are worse than cows in understanding.
>
> —M. K. Gandhi (1999, p. 77)

> Unfortunately, I was born a Hindu untouchable—there was nothing I could do to prevent it. However, it is well within my power to refuse to live under ignoble and humiliating conditions. I solemnly assure you that I will not die a Hindu.
>
> —B. R. Ambedkar (quoted in Das, 1980, p. 108)

Religious conversion is a political act in India that comes with multiple backlashes. Gandhi was interested in a change of power from the hands of the British to high-caste Hindus (Ambedkar). But group conversion to Christianity by the Dalits, the oppressed people in India, and the announcement to convert by B. R. Ambedkar, a messiah of the Dalits and the one who drafted the Indian constitution, rattled Gandhi's dream of controlling the majority of the indigenous people in the name of religion after the British. The Dalits found the gospel to be real good news that provided a new identity and dignity as human beings, that were denied them by the caste Hindus. Gandhi could not tolerate this upsurge and Ambekar's determination to liberate the Dalits from the high-caste Hindus by leaving Hinduism amass, so he compared the Dalits to cows. Gandhi even threatened to introduce legislation to prevent conversion when India attained independence. However, later Ambedkar did convert to Buddhism on October 14, 1956, along with 500,000 Dalits. Recently, legislation similar to what Gandhi threatened to introduce has been proposed in India with the emergence of right-wing Hindu political forces.

In this context, conversion studies in India have been largely preoccupied with the sociopolitical dimension of the complex process of group conversions or conversion movements. The spiritual dimension has been ignored in the heat of political debate on conversion. Some studies, in order to avoid the conflict of religions over the problem of conversion, have attempted to portray group conversion as a means of liberation and social emancipation, minus the spiritual or religious dimension. But this perspective undermines the Dalits, as if they were impotent spiritually.

Further, there is hardly any rigorous academic study on individual conversions in India. While conversion studies in India have been preoccupied with the sociopolitical aspect, conversion studies in the West have been primarily from the field of psychology, dealing with individual conversion within Christianity or to cults. Recently, sociology and anthropology have stepped into the study of conversion in various cultural contexts. Sathianathan Clarke (2003, p. 290) pointed out, "If the phenomenon of conversion should include the psychic structure, developmental stages, and overall well-being of converts, there needs to be much more work in the area of psychology of conversions [in India]." Both in the West and in India, I find that conversion is not studied from a phenomenological perspective to bring to light converts' own perspective on conversion. A phenomenological understanding of conversion takes the actors' understanding of their experience into consideration in defining the process of conversion.

The purpose of *Transformative Religious Experience* is twofold. The primary purpose is to demonstrate that religious experience—in other words, the *divine–human encounter*—is central to religious conversion and triggers personal transformation, because converts attribute great significance to this factor. The secondary purpose is to let the reader hear the voices of converts in their own words, as the subtitle, *A Phenomenological Understanding of Religious Conversion*, indicates. In the West, conversion studies are largely based on Judeo-Christian samples and, in recent times, on conversion to Islam in the West. Contrary to this trend, this book deals with conversion experiences to Christianity from different religious traditions in India. It carries rich narratives of conversion as data for researchers to explore further in this area, and for others these narratives have inspirational value. The unique multicultural and religiously pluralistic context of India makes this book unusual and challenges some of the present understandings of religious conversion. For the Indian audience, this may be the only book to promote converts' own perspectives on the burning issue of religious conversion in India. Some narratives in this book expose the cultural and familial hostilities to conversion in India and show how converts handle such hostilities. *Transformative Religious Experience* also highlights the role of religious practices, such as prayer and reading the Bible, in the conversion process. The continued interaction between converts and the divine, through prayer and reading the Bible, signals an intimate relationship between converts and the divine that sustains them in their newfound faith.

Defining religious conversion is a challenge for scholars who study it. I prefer the term "transformative religious experience" instead of "religious conversion," as it keeps the focus on the religious experience in conversion. However, both terms are used interchangeably here. Transformative religious experience is a complex phenomenon. Many definitions are proposed; however, they lack coherence in presenting a comprehensive view of religious conversion. William James in the *Varieties of Religious Experience* (1902/2004, p. 171) defined conversion by saying, "a self hitherto divided, and consciously wrong inferior and unhappy, becomes unified and consciously right superior and happy, in consequence of its firmer hold upon religious realities." James's definition was based on his analysis of conversion experiences in Christianity that were primarily regenerative spiritual experiences. His definition does not address the aspects of converting from one religion to another or the absence of a "divided self" before conversion. Rambo (1993, p. 5) defines conversion as "a process of religious change that takes place in a dynamic force field of people, events, ideologies, institutions, expectations, and orientations." Rambo considers the surrounding world while defining religious conversion. He acknowledges the presence of the divine, in line with other studies (James, 1902/2004; Ullman, 1989; Zinnbauer & Pargament, 1998). However, these studies, except James's, have not analyzed explicitly the divine–human encounter in the conversion process. From a phenomenological perspective, we can understand that transformative religious experience or religious conversion is both a complex process and an event—the divine–human encounter—that triggers personal transformation, an ongoing process that is sustained by religious practices and socialization that leads to the integrated well-being of a person and a change of religious beliefs.

Many psychological and sociological studies on conversion are reductionistic in nature, explaining away the religious or spiritual elements in conversion. Other studies, though acknowledging the presence of the divine in the conversion process, fail to give a significant place to religious experience even though converts attribute great significance to it. Existing studies on religious conversion approach the phenomenon from their discipline's boundaries. Theology might tend to ignore the psychological, sociological, and cultural elements in the conversion experience. Psychology views conversion only from its vantage point and ignores the religious dimension. Sociologists treat conversion as a social issue while ignoring other dimensions. The need is to have a multidisciplinary approach to understanding the conversion process (Rambo, 1993). As a scholar trained in theology, I designed a study from a phenomenological perspective while drawing insights from the disciplines of psychology, sociology, anthropology, and theology.

Transformative Religious Experience enables us to understand religious conversion from a phenomenological perspective. The phenomenological method takes the experience of a person as it appears and as a whole, "examining entities from many sides, angles, and perspectives" (Moustakas, 1994, p. 58). Phenomenology looks for the meaning of an experience while staying committed to "thick" descriptions—detailed descriptions of the phenomenon as it appears. Wulff (1995) asserts that phenomenological psychology redeems *experience* to the center stage in psychological studies. Rambo and Reh (1992) suggest six elements of phenomenological approach to conversion: observation, description, empathy, understanding, interpretation, and explanation. Observation in phenomenology is seeing something as it appears. Description is taking the experience as genuinely experienced with its details of context and process. Empathy is seeing the phenomenon from the participant's perspective or entering the world of the experiencer. Interpretation means seeing the phenomenon from a researcher's perspective, which may be different from the participant's perspective but not necessarily superior. Explanation is viewing the phenomenon from existing theoretical perspectives. I have adopted these elements in seeking to understand the complex process of conversion.

Bracketing or *Epoche* is an important step in phenomenological research. It means identifying one's own prejudgments, biases, and preconceptions. "In the *Epoche*, the everyday understandings, judgments, and knowings are set aside, and phenomena are revisited, freshly, naively, in a wide open sense" (Moustakas, 1994, p. 33). By identifying the ideological position, it helps a researcher look at things as they appear. In the phenomenological study of conversion, Rambo and Reh (1992) suggest that researchers should set aside their ideological convictions in order to see conversion experience in a new light. They argue that recognizing and expressing one's biases will contribute to objectivity.

Let me state my theological journey so you will know my position. I grew up in a Protestant Christian home as member of the Church of South India (CSI). CSI is a unified church of several denominations that came together to form an Indian identity in 1947. It is close to the Episcopal Church in structure. During my college days, I was associated with an evangelical student movement that shaped my basic theological concepts. These concepts were reinforced when I later joined the movement as staff. My theological education in a leading evangelical seminary influenced me toward a rationalistic approach to Christianity. My higher education under Catholic scholars in a prestigious state university opened my mind to other perspectives on theology. This exposure enabled me to see various theological positions from their perspectives and appreciate their merits rather than simply disapprove of them. Interactions with people from various traditions and my readings on conversion helped me recognize many ways of looking at conversion. Nevertheless, I was skeptical about Pentecostal or other claims of supernatural experiences. As I ventured into my research, in order to see conversion experience as a true phenomenologist I tried my best to set aside the rational bent of my evangelical orientation and my skepticism of Pentecostal and supernatural experiences. On the other hand, hearing converts speak of their conversion experiences and the price they paid for their conversion drew me closer to believe them. Though I do not identify myself as a Pentecostal, towards the end of my research I became sympathetic to considering Pentecostal or supernatural experiences favorably. I believe I have moved closer to the participants of my study. I say this so you will be able to identify my biases popping up here and there. I strongly agree with Rambo and Reh (1992, p. 245) that "no researcher can attain perfect, detached objectivity."

I have developed an interdisciplinary model of transformative religious experience by giving due significance to the meaning converts attach to the divine–human encounter in religious conversion. I call it the Step Model of transformative religious experience, which carves a space for the religious experience and religious practices in the conversion process, while accommodating the psychological and sociological factors. The Step Model is flexible enough to accommodate various types of religious conversions. The phenomenon is so complex that the steps cannot be precisely demarcated to a definite, clear beginning and end. However, the steps enable one to make sense out of the complex reality of the conversion process.

The Step Model of transformative religious experience has seven steps: Exposure, Disenchantment, Crunch, Pursuit and Test, Hostilities, Participation, and Maturation (see the Step Model figure in chapter 10). They indicate different phases in the conversion process. They are usually sequential, however, there is a possibility of skipping some steps in the conversion process. The Spark—the divine–human encounter—is central in the conversion process. Unlike the steps, the divine–human encounter is the event or moment in the conversion process. The two axes in the model provide the supportive roles in the conversion process. The x axis indicates the social psychological dimension and the y axis indicates the religious dimension. These two axes provide the context for conversion, or an interface between the social and religious dimensions. These factors have constant interaction throughout the process and cannot be restricted to a single step. Transformation begins at the Spark and moves towards maturation independent of the steps.

The divine–human encounter in conversion is the turning point that occurs in the mystical states of consciousness. Converts are not initially ready to follow Christianity, but when an encounter with the divine occurs, the divine is identified with Jesus and converts gain a certainty of experiencing the truth and claim a special knowledge of God based on this personal experience. The experiential evidence is forceful in converts' articulation that the divine–human encounter is personal and unparalleled to any other experience that comes with the knowledge of God. This knowledge gained is not a rational understanding of religious truths. This knowledge is possible only through direct experience of God, which cannot be imparted or articulated in verifiable philosophical propositions. This knowledge is given to converts at the divine–human encounter despite their antagonism against Christianity. Similar to Paul's conversion, converts from different religious backgrounds find their religious belief is replaced with a belief in Jesus. I find a suspension of volition in the moment, and when one returns to normal waking consciousness the previously held religious belief is discarded with a strong conviction that the newfound knowledge of God is real and true. Some converts might agitate for some time over leaving their previously held religious belief; however, there is a sense of excitement that God came to meet them. So the previously held religious beliefs eventually are discarded to embrace the new knowledge of God because the new knowledge is gained through direct revelation of God.

At the divine–human encounter, an informal conversation takes place between the divine and the convert. In this encounter, converts find unconditional love and acceptance from the divine, who is invisible, but in every other count converts begin to relate to the divine as a close companion as if one were relating to a close friend in a social relationship. The intimate relationship with the divine is a vital factor that makes converts hold on to their newfound faith.

When converts meet God in the divine–human encounter, they are terribly struck by the consciousness of sin. Suddenly, converts gain a new sense of sin in the presence of the divine. The sins they become convicted of are not usually terrible sins like adultery or murder, but even small habits, like watching movies or being proud, etc., are viewed as great sins. The moment converts realize their sins, they have no hesitation to confess them and at once gain a sense of being forgiven by the divine. The divine–human encounter creates a sense of sin and a sense of being forgiven simultaneously. Though converts feel miserable about their sins during the encounter, when the encounter is over they are filled not with remorse but long-lasting joy, peace, and happiness.

The fruit of religious conversion is the integrated well-being of a person. The effects of religious conversion encompass all aspects of the convert's life. It effects a change in the spiritual, psychological, behavioral, physical, social, and economical dimensions of the convert's life. Religious conversion cannot be restricted only to the religious or spiritual dimension, because most often it begins at the psychological level with a crunch as the context and permeates all dimensions of life. The effect is that converts experience a sense of well-being not only in the spiritual dimension, but in other dimensions too. Therefore, conversion results in integrated well-being that includes one or several aspects of the person. Any religious conversion that results in integrated well-being of a person can be termed a genuine conversion. The individual's or community's right to convert is the right to have access to integrated well-being. Denying the religious or spiritual dimension in the conversion process, or restricting conversion only to the religious or spiritual dimension, is erroneous. A phenomenological understanding of religious conversion brings us to this understanding of religious conversion.

Transformative Religious Experience is the outcome of my passion for the study of religious experience, on the one hand, and my concern for the perennial issue of religious conversion in India that bedevils the Indian church, on the other hand, which kindled my interest to explore this phenomenon over a decade ago. The seminal research for this book is my doctoral study of religious conversion at the University of Madras in Chennai, India. My continued interaction with the literature on religious conversion, religious experience, and spirituality from the fields of psychology, sociology, anthropology, theology, and missiology resulted in this volume.

This book deals with individual conversion experiences to Christianity in India. The converts are from many different walks of life. They come from different caste groups, from Dalits to Brahmins and tribal communities. In education they range from school dropouts to doctorates. Their economical status varies from poor laborer to rich businessperson. They converted from many different religious traditions—Hinduism, Islam, Sikhism, and tribal religions—to follow Jesus, but not necessarily with the intent to adopt Christianity as their religion.

I have designed the book to let you hear the voices of converts themselves about their conversion experiences. Each chapter will carry conversion narratives, mostly in converts' own words, followed by my reflection in light of literature pertaining to the theme of the chapter. Some conversion narratives could fit under more than one theme and I have used my discretion to place them under a particular theme. I have also split some narratives to fit into the themes of more than one chapter. However, as far as possible, I have given the complete narratives in order to enable you to understand the life story of each convert and the effects of conversion in his or her daily life. Some interviews were conducted in English and others were in Tamil. They lasted for one to two hours. Verbal communication differs from written form. The interviews in English have the idiom of Indian English. The extracts are not the verbatim of the interviews, however, I have not attempted to polish the language to make it very formal. Whether in Tamil or in English, I have taken care to retain the sense of the narrator while translating them and making them readable. I have tried to preserve the tone, hesitation, emotion, and struggle in articulation. The names are changed and identifiable information is either omitted or changed to protect their identities. Original names are retained in the conversion narratives that have been taken from the public domain. I have consciously reduced disciplinary jargon and references to scholarly literature so as to make the text approachable to both specialists and the general public.

Chapter 1 deals with experience of visions that led to conversion. It begins with a story of Sania, a businessperson from a Muslim family.

Introduction

She had a vision of Jesus during her college days. Being a devout Muslim, she wondered why Jesus appeared to her and was troubled by the vision. Sekar, a Hindu, had a vision of Jesus and was liberated instantly from his addiction to alcohol. The story of Selvi revolves around a vision of the crucifixion she saw as a teenager. All three of them never did anything to seek Christianity, but were faithful followers of their prior religions. These visions were given to them and they received them gladly.

Chapter 2 presents the dreams of three women in extreme anxiety owing to family situations. Everything changed in their lives after the dream. Komala hails from a Brahmin family, but was disenchanted with her religion and could not find peace, so she prayed and asked to know who the real God is. She had a dream that same night in which she received an answer to her question. The next story is about Vinodha, who suffered at the hands of her husband, who neither understood nor loved her. She was going through intense anxiety due to the situation in her family. She had a dream in which the divine called her "Daughter." Thereafter she felt that she has someone who loves her, and she began a lasting relationship with the divine. Lastly, I present the dream of Sarala, who lost her husband and had a dream of Jesus that connected her to the divine. She found this new relationship offering strength to face the harsh reality of her life. These women became connected to the divine through their dreams and have cultivated an intimate relationship with the divine ever since.

Chapter 3 focuses on experiences in which converts claim that God spoke to them while reading the Bible or listening to a sermon. These kinds of divine communication are not auditory, but consist in a sudden realization or a feeling that someone spoke to them from within, directly addressing their crises or needs. I first present the story of Inban, an assistant professor in a technical university. He was a faithful follower of his religion of birth, Hinduism, but when he attended a Bible study he experienced that someone within him spoke to him about his private life. Secondly, Rekha, a college student, experienced the divine love by hearing a sermon, and she narrates her faith journey in which she had to walk out of her house because of her conversion. This is followed by the narratives of a husband and wife who are from a Brahmin family. The husband, while reading the Bible, heard someone within him tell him to be baptized. His wife, Praveena, had a thought repeatedly flashing in her mind that her gods were not real while she was chanting their names. These narratives contain descriptions of converts' struggles and the resolution that led to a sense of peace and joy from the communication they received from God.

Chapter 4 presents the stories of converts who experienced dramatic relief from their troubled situations. They claim that these deliverances were miracles and they attribute the cause for such changes to God, which led them to believe in Jesus. This chapter begins with the story of an actor being saved from drowning in a sea, which is followed by the story of a woman who escaped death after her attempt to commit suicide. Then I present two conversion narratives of businessmen, which involve miraculous healing and miraculous resolution of a serious crisis in the family. In these narratives we see that converts test the workability of the new religious option before accepting it. Converts perceive such divine interventions as proofs for them to believe in Jesus.

Chapter 5 deals with experiences of prayer. It opens with excerpts from interviews of converts who had prayed to a generic God, without using a name or religious symbol, as they were not sure who the true God is. To their surprise, they claim that their prayers were answered by Jesus, which convinced them to believe in Jesus as the true God. Jemmu Bai, a tribal man, prayed to God asking him to heal him and reveal who the real God is. He had a vision that led to his conversion. This is followed by the stories of Nathan, a charted accountant, and Balan, an engineer, who both prayed to God without using any name. This chapter also carries other stories of answered prayer by Jesus and some that were not answered in a manner converts expected. Despite this, they found that Jesus gave them peace and the ability to face difficult situations in life. Such experiences convinced them to believe in Jesus.

Chapter 6 explores mild experiences, those that are without any sensory or dramatic elements. Such experiences include being struck with a consciousness of sin, a sense of personalizing the message of the gospel, and the feeling of the presence of God. Though these experiences are considered mild, the divine–human encounter in them is clearly significant. Converts claim that believing in Jesus is like falling in love with someone and cannot be explained. The story of Karan presented here is a typical conversion story in which he struggled with his sinful life and found peace and joy in surrendering to Jesus. This is followed by the narrative of a Hindu teenage priest who found his deep thirst to experience the Supreme God met with finding Jesus. The stories of Vinitha and Vinay show how they experienced the presence of God.

Chapter 7 analyzes the mystical turning point, that is, the divine–human encounter. This is the religious experience or the event in the conversion process. The changeover from one faith to another occurs at this point. This chapter examines the narratives of conversion experience and traces the point that triggers personal transformation. I argue here that conversion is an act of God, not simply a rational choice, because the turning point occurs in the mystical states of mind while normal waking consciousness is suspended. A rational choice is made only after the religious experience. The conversion of Ganga is very simple. When she got up from her sleep one morning she felt that Jesus is the true God. Nithya, a medical student, describes her conversion experience as similar to falling in love. Besides these narratives, I draw examples from other chapters to show how the divine–human encounter occurs in the mystical states of consciousness. The mystical turning point has the following features: *revelatory, conversational, noetic, ineffable, transient, passive,* and *intimate*.

Chapter 8 traces the transforming effects of conversion. This chapter shows that the conversion experience has great impact on various aspects of converts' lives: spiritual, psychological, behavioral, physical, social, and economic. To illustrate the transforming effects of conversion in various dimensions, I pick up particular aspects from the narratives presented in other chapters. This chapter demonstrates that the fruit of conversion is the integrated well-being of converts.

In Chapter 9, converts narrate the torments they have gone through because of their conversion. This chapter highlights the hostilities associated with conversion in India. These narratives will enable you to grasp the intensity of persecution from family and friends that converts faced because of their conversion to Christianity. Here, I continue the story of Sania from chapter 1. She had to flee her home because of her conversion and moved to twenty-six different places to evade her father's pursuit. I then pick up the story of Mohan, the teenage priest presented in chapter 6. He faced a life-threatening situation, humiliation, and torture at the hands of his friends and family. The stories of Janaki and Kushbu in this chapter will show how difficult it is for women to practice their newfound faith. For thirty years Janaki was not allowed by her husband to practice her Christian faith publicly, however, eventually he became a Christian. This chapter also discusses how converts handled such situations by drawing strength from God through prayer and reading the Bible. Here I also present the role of agents and the religious community in the conversion process, especially during persecution.

Chapter 10 presents the Step Model of transformative religious experience. This chapter elaborates on the steps involved in the conversion process. Though it is impossible to demarcate the precise beginning and end of each step, the flexibility of the Step Model can accommodate different aspects of this complex process. Unlike other models of conversion, the Step Model emphasizes the religious experience in conversion while incorporating the role of religious practices like prayer and reading the Bible in the conversion process. This chapter demonstrates that conversion is both a process and an event.

The goal of this book is to enable readers hear the voice of converts to Christianity in India that the divine–human encounter—the experience of Jesus—sparks off personal transformation, for which many have had to pay a heavy price owing to persecution. Furthermore, converts testify that they have been sustained their newfound faith through an intimate relationship with the divine, practiced through prayer and reading the Bible.

As you hear converts speak in the following pages, I am confident that you will be inspired, enriched, and challenged.

1 Visions

> I have never seen the slightest scientific proof of the religious ideas of heaven and hell, of future life for individuals, or of a personal God.
>
> —Thomas A. Edison (n.d., p. 8)

> If … personal experience cannot serve as evidence for religious truth, then we have every reason to doubt the veridicality of orgasms.
>
> —Gwen Griffith-Dickson (2000, p. 135)

Religious experiences involving a vision have visual, auditory, and automatic elements that involve the sensory organs. In automatism, one does something apart from conscious thought. While having a vision, the convert is passive, however, some sensory organs are active during the vision and the convert returns to waking consciousness after the experience. Though prior knowledge is a tool to interpret the vision, prior religious belief is redundant. In conversions to Christianity, converts identify the divine with Jesus in the their vision. Converts' prejudices against or enmity toward Christianity disappear at this vision of Jesus. Fervor and pride in their religion of birth also vanish at the religious experience, and then they follow Jesus without hesitation. I present three visions in this chapter. The converts are ordinary people who did nothing to induce their religious experience, but still they had a vision of Jesus.

I first present the conversion narrative of Sania, a wealthy businessperson from a Muslim family. Sania had a vision of Jesus at the age of eighteen when she was studying engineering. She had to flee her home and move from one city to another for about ten years to evade her father's pursuit owing to her conversion to Christianity. I tried to contact her through various sources to have her as part of my study but failed. She never responded to my communication as she was reluctant to give an interview to a stranger. Finally, through a common friend I was able to get her to agree to meet with me. I introduced myself to her as a cross-cultural missionary working in North India, though I hail from South India and was then doing research on conversion. Once she was convinced that I was not simply an academic, but also one who serves the Lord, she was willing to share her life story. After this introduction and clarification about me, I was able to establish a good rapport with her and asked her to narrate her conversion story.

Sania: Actually, I am from . . . a Muslim family. From a very young age, we were taught Quran . . . My father is well-known in the business circle in the city. He treated me like his son [he has only two daughters] for educating me with a modern worldview. I grew up with a strong belief in my religion; however, we practiced tolerance towards other religions. I was good at my studies. I had to go to another city . . . for my engineering studies. That was the first time I left my home and stayed in a hostel.

My conversion happened dramatically. I never went to a church or read the Bible then. I never even had a Christian friend—no, I had only one Christian friend, but she never told me anything about Christ. She herself did not know anything about Christianity. I never had any idea about Christianity. All I knew about Christianity was that there was a religion called Christianity and Jesus was their God. My understanding of Christianity was based on whatever I had seen—mass or church—in the movies. My understanding of Christianity was very limited.

During the second year of my engineering studies, suddenly I was going through some kind of depression. I felt that I should be alone. I did not feel like talking to anybody. Otherwise, I was very active and also active socially.

Visions

  This happened during Ramadan. We women continue the fast if we cannot complete it during the month of Ramadan. [When women have their periods, they carry over the fast.] Women can complete the fast later. So my mother told me, "Why don't you fast and pray? You can get peace of mind." They felt I should consult a psychiatrist. Because I was having exams I could not go. I asked the warden for a corner room where I could be alone and prepare for my exams. She gave me a room in the basement where no one else stayed. So literally I used to go to classes and come back and stay in the room and do my studies.
  I forgot the exact date, but it was sometime in 1993. It was the coldest season. In the afternoon I left the window open. Sunlight was coming in. My table was in front of the window, and I was writing an assignment. I locked the door from inside. As I was writing, suddenly I heard a voice calling me by name and saying, "Pray." I felt as if someone were standing behind me. I heard a man's voice . . . I just turned back only to see none. The door was locked. I felt much wearied. I really felt as if I were hallucinating or going mad. Already the talk of consulting a psychiatrist was considered by my parents . . . As I started reading, again . . . the same voice was saying, "Pray." This time it kept repeating, "Pray, pray, pray" . . . I really thought, "I am gone mad." I thought I was really becoming mad . . . I really felt something was wrong with me. I closed the book as I could not concentrate; just sat there. I looked at my watch, and it was 1:30 p.m. The Muslim prayer time had passed in the afternoon. Really, I did not know how to pray; we were taught to pray only at that time. I was thinking, "How will I pray now?"
  So I just closed my eyes, sitting on my chair. I said within my heart—I remember very well, I said, "I do not know who this is asking me to pray. If there is a God, then I want to see that God. I have done all that my parents have told me to do. But I have never felt or seen you." I prayed as if it were a routine. "If I am not mad, then I need to see who is calling me." I was saying this in my heart. I just closed my eyes.
  I was eighteen then. For the first time in my life, never had I seen such a thing. I saw with my eyes closed; I saw the whole room and everything. Near my table, I saw one person was standing—a huge, tall person—but I could not see the face. His face was bright, very bright . . . mmm, very bright. The garment itself was very bright. I do not know what he was wearing; it was like a *kurtha* [a long top

men wear in India], a very bright thing. I knew it was a person, but I could not see the face. I knew *instantly* that it was Jesus. Now he did not say, "I am Jesus"—nothing! I knew in my heart immediately that it was Jesus. I did not have any doubt. I never had any doubt. I did not even question myself. I cannot explain . . . that feeling! I just knew it was Jesus.

The next moment, I was on my knees. I just fell down . . . I just fell, on my own; I fell down. I was sobbing and crying and crying and crying and crying because I felt very dirty. The brightness—whatever the bright thing was, the brightness around me . . . I looked at myself in my vision. I was seeing; I was looking at myself. I was fully black and full of dirt. The light gave such feeling about me. I felt I was so poor inside of me. Since I come from a rich family, I never lacked anything. I never had such kind of feeling. But that day I felt I was very poor. I felt I had too much of pride. I never knew that I had all these things. But I was crying and crying, sobbing and sobbing on my knees. I remember saying, "I do not know who you are, but Jesus, I need you. I know I need you in my life because I am very poor—I cannot handle it. I am very poor on my own. I cannot do anything. I need you." I did not realize at the time that I was born again. I was crying and then the vision disappeared.

Sania was a righteous person and never felt that she was sinful before her vision. She never struggled to overcome sin, but only the vision made her feel that she was sinful, dirty, and poor. It appears that the vision brought in her a sense of sin and created a need to depend on the divine. A crisis was created and a resolution offered at the religious experience. She continued her narration:

Sania: When I opened my eyes, it was about 2:15 or 2:45 p.m. It lasted for a long period. Then a fear gripped me; I felt very scared. I felt, "What has gone wrong with me? Why was I crying like this?" I felt like running out of my room. I was terrified and opened the door and ran out. Then I was very disturbed. I did not know what to do. Who do I talk to? I cannot tell anyone. I was thinking, "Where to go? What to do?" Then came to my mind a Christian girl who was in another branch of study and was in the same hostel. But I never talked to her in the past. She was very different. She never used to hang around with others. But her name came to my mind.

I went to her room and woke her up. She was napping—it was in the afternoon. I woke her up. I had never spoken to her earlier. I told her what I said [in response to the voice asking me to pray]: "If there is a God, I need to see you." Then I saw Jesus. I questioned her, "Why did I see Jesus? Because I am not a Christian! I am a Muslim! Why did I see him?" I think my eyes were red; I was quite . . . you know. She might have been scared. She did not know what to do. She had a Bible with her and gave me the Bible and said, "I do not know!" She opened to the Book of John and put a slip of paper there and said, "You read this." She also said, "If you have seen Jesus, he would speak to you." [Laughs.] I think she was taken aback. She did not know what to do!

I took the book and went to my room. I started reading. That day I read and read and read. I read the Bible from John to Revelation, then from Genesis. I was reading till 3:00 in the morning. I kept on reading and reading, just like that. I never read a book like that; it was very alive, as if the words were popping out of the pages and speaking to me. As I was reading, I was crying at that time. The words were alive. I never read any book in my life like that, a different kind of a book. So I kept reading. Next morning I went back to her . . . No, it was not the next day; I kept reading the Bible; after two days . . . I do not remember; I was reading the Bible for a few days.

During these days, there was a battle in my mind. Throughout my life, I have been a science person and quite logical. I was taught that Islam was true. I was thinking of all that I believed. I really looked up to my father and what he taught me. I had a feeling that he could never be wrong. How could what I believed all these days become all false suddenly? In a fraction of a second, it goes off. I was not sure what I was doing all the time. How come it was wrong all of a sudden? All of a sudden, I found out that all I believed was wrong. I questioned, "If Jesus is the true God, if all religions are same, if all roads lead to one God, why did not I see Allah or Shiva or someone else when I prayed?" All kinds of questions were coming up in my mind; it was like a battle. After some time, I could not deal with it by myself. Because I knew I needed to speak to somebody. I was going deeper and deeper and it was troubling me very badly. I went back to this girl and asked her to tell me more about Jesus.

She then took me to one church and that was the first church I went to... No, it was not a church, it was an African Students' Fellowship. I never had gone to any church, even to a Catholic church that is so silent. That was my first visit. I did not understand a thing. They were jumping and dancing. [Laughs.] I was wondering, "Why are they doing like this?" For me, worship is a very somber and solemn kind of thing and very personal—not like this. But I knew one thing... from their faces: it was real; they were not faking. Then the preacher, a Nigerian, started speaking. He was very loud. He was speaking in English, but I did not understand anything. I should have understood, but I did not understand. At the end he said, "All close your eyes." But I did not close my eyes, and then he loudly said, "All eyes must be closed." I was looking at him, and he came near me and loudly said, "Close your eyes." Then I got scared and closed my eyes. After this, I did not realize when people sat down [after the prayer]; my friend had to pull me down to make me sit. That was my first experience in a church. After the meeting, someone asked me, "Are you born again?" I did not know what it was and I said, "I was born in [a state in India]." Absolutely, I had no idea! I slowly understood as I read, going to church, and understood the Word of God.

Later in the interview I probed her more on the person she saw in the vision. Since she was a faithful Muslim, how come she did not see anything related to her religion of birth? So I asked her, "In your vision, you couldn't see the face, but you were convinced that it was Jesus. Did you ever reflect on it later whether the person might be someone else?" She was emphatic in her reply:

Sania: *Never* [emphatically]. I cannot... I cannot explain how. I just knew. It is not—it is *instant*. I looked at him, Jesus, *instantly*. How to explain? [Whispers and pauses for a moment.] I never had a doubt, then or even later. It is my own... it is like my own personal thing. I feel when a human meets God, he or she knows his or her God. You know, because I never had any doubt. You have asked a very nice question. Because I never ever doubted; I never doubted that it could be someone else. *From that day till today I never doubted.*

Q: Did not you think of your religious symbols . . . then?

Sania: At that moment I did not think about my religion. Later on when I went to meet the girl, I asked her, "Why did I see Jesus?" I had this question, "Why didn't I see Allah?" But I was sure that it was Jesus and the assurance was one hundred percent. I cannot explain. I never doubted it. I just knew it was Jesus.

For one week, since the vision, there was a war in my head. Because I cannot doubt the fact; I knew it. Never before I had something like that for sure. You know I was so sure [that it was Jesus]. But the question was, "Why Jesus?" That was the question—"Why Jesus?" That meant all that I believed was wrong. All that I believed was wrong? It shook the foundation and was a very shaking thing. I went through a struggle. But the doubt that it could be someone else never ever occurred to me.

Q: As a Muslim, what was your religious life like?

Sania: I was not deeply religious, but whatever I was supposed to do—reading [Quran], *namaz*—not five times a day, whenever I got time, at least once a day or twice a day—I did them. We were taught to read the Quran from a very young age. It is in Arabic, so I learned Arabic when I was three years. I used to read Quran very regularly. We used to have prayer meetings at home. My father comes from an Imam family and is very religious. He cultivated those habits in us. I really believed my religion was true; I believed this. Not because I had my own conviction, but because my dad told me. He did say that Islam was the truth, the only truth, and I really believed; I really believed. I did everything—fasting, prayer, and how a normal Muslim would do that—by fully believing Islam was the truth.

Q: How do you differentiae your newfound faith with the former?

Sania: When I found Jesus, I have my own way of praying. I close my eyes and talk to him—just talking. In the Islamic way of praying, I followed a set of rules, like, say this and bend down, etc. We just do the entire ritual, just that. No one talks to God, and there is no relationship [with God]. But here, I can hear Jesus speaking to me. That is the biggest difference. I speak to him; I hear him speak back. I speak to him; I hear him speak back. Earlier, I never heard anyone speaking to me. Here, I hear him speak back. Over the years, I learned to differentiate the voices and am still learning. Now I learned to differentiate all other voices [from the voice of Jesus]. That is the major difference.

If you have noticed, we find a tone of disappointment in Sania's words that she did not see something related to her religion in her vision. She says there was a *war* in her mind, but at the same time she was so certain that the person in the vision was Jesus. The conflict between allegiance to her religion and the vision is very obvious in her narration; she struggled to come out of it. But never wanted to give up the person she saw in the vision.

She also described the transformation in her life and the subsequent religious experiences she had that enabled her to increase her knowledge of Christianity.

Sania: At eighteen, all of a sudden . . . all of a sudden I felt I was enlightened. I never knew that I had pride or I never knew that I was self-righteous. I saw my heart changed. In the sense, I cannot say that I did wrong things like alcohol or all those bad things . . . On the whole, I realized that there is something more to life. How would I say? It's like a vacuum; you feel the vacuum. Earlier, I was thinking, "Okay if I study and become highly educated and become like my father"—my father was my role model and I wanted to become more than he—"then I will achieve some things." [Laughs.] I had that kind of idea [about life]—always wanting something. But since the moment I saw the vision of Jesus, suddenly everything was changed.

Since then, Jesus was speaking to me directly because I did not know the Bible. So every time I used to pray in my own style—just go into my room and close my eyes and talk, as I did that day. I simply talked. I would see a vision through which he would show me various things. My friend introduced me to a Pentecostal church. I would call up the pastor and tell him a vision. He used to come and explain to me from the Bible exactly what I had seen in my vision. So I asked him, "Why does it happen to me?" The pastor would say that he himself did not know! The basic thing is that God loves me and died for me, you have to be like a child to enter heaven . . . and he showed me all those things.

Q: Any examples?

Sania: For example, you have to be like a child. One day as I was closing my eyes and talking to him [Jesus], you know, I fell in love with him and was always talking to him. I used to close my eyes and talk to him. I say everything to him. Closing my eyes only, I could talk to him. That is my pattern. [Laughs.] I do this as if I cannot talk to him otherwise. I could talk to him only if I close my eyes, in my room alone with no one around. I just—I do not know what to call this—a prayer or what . . . whatever it is.

I saw another vision of the same person whom I saw on that day. This time he was holding a small girl by hand and was showing as he was going up on a mountain, kind of nice valleys, rivers, and animals, those kinds of things. He was showing as if they were hers but not without him. He was holding her hand and showing her. I felt that the little girl was I. So I asked the pastor, "Why did I see myself as a little girl? I am a big girl now. Why as a very small girl? It was a small baby." The pastor explained to me from the Bible, "Unless you become like a little child you cannot enter the kingdom of God. God is showing you this. For him, you are a little kid. You are a little kid to him. He is showing you all that he has for you and given you." I was experiencing those kinds of things. But I would say God's love for me is more than anything.

After a month, one night I had a dream. I saw myself under the water and was coming out in the dream. Something like a rubber stamp coming and hitting me here [showing her forehead]. I called up the pastor, and he explained me about baptism. Then I asked him to baptize me. But he said, "No, no, wait. You are going too fast. Take time. No, no, you wait. You think about it." He was telling me about baptism and its meaning. After a week—no, after three or four days—I had the same dream again. I knew in my heart, this time I had to do it. By then I knew what baptism was. I took my friend and some clothes to change, and went to the pastor. I told him, "You have to baptize me." He said, "[This time] I have to do this!" Only his wife and my friend were there. It was a nice experience. Jesus was directly talking to me and actually I needed that.

I experienced transformation. The way I started looking at my life, in terms of inner meaning of life, brought about a huge difference in me. Earlier I was not like that. The biggest transformation is that I have discovered meaning in life, and I got a new heart.

I drew her attention to the depression she had before the religious experience. I asked her whether she was able to come out of her depression after the vision.

Sania: Again . . . for me, I see it as a miracle because the depression simply went away. What happened on that day was, when I was sobbing, I felt very warm within me. I did not feel . . . I did not feel somebody was pointing a finger at me. I was crying and was feeling very dirty. I did not feel . . . did not feel someone telling me . . . I did not feel the person in the vision was telling me, "You are dirty." I cannot express it. All the while I was crying, I felt physically warmth around me. It was a different kind of love; I never felt something like that.

It appeared that her depression was in order to have the vision. In our conversation she was pointing out that she used to be socially very active, but all of a sudden she felt that she was depressed and wanted to be alone and got her room changed in the hostel where she could be on her own. After the vision, she never went into depression, despite the ordeal she went through for more than ten years owing to her conversion to Christianity.

To bring out what makes people change from one religion to another, I almost always asked them what caused them to hold on to their newfound faith and to describe God based on their experience.

Q: What is the most significant thing that holds you to Jesus?

Sania: [Silence.] Mmm . . . if I pinpoint, for example, I cannot even think of a life without him now. Why could I not think of a life without him? The most significant thing is to be alive inside; I need Jesus to be alive within me. I am not saying physically dead. What happened was I became alive on that day when I saw him. The feeling—something that is not tangible—I cannot explain to you. The most significant thing is I am alive; my inside is alive. That is the one thing that keeps me in Jesus.

Q: How do you describe God based on your experience?

Sania: Mmm ... to me, for me, the first thing, if you ask me, based on my life and based on what I have discovered: God is real. That is the first thing. Earlier I never realized whether God is real or man-made. But now I know that he is real. Second, he loves his creation. For me, God is real; he is my Father and loves me unconditionally. His love is not going to change or grow more or grow less. I cannot do something that would make his love grow more or do something that would make his love grow less. I understood this great truth. My religion was based on deeds—God loves you more if you do something good or he loves you less if you do not do something good. With Jesus, there is nothing that I could do to make him love me more or less. This is something different.

That was Sania's dramatic story of conversion, and I reserve the rest of her story to discuss later in chapter 9, on "Hostilities." We will move on to the next vision.

Sekar, a businessman, was struggling with his addiction to alcohol. He had tried his religion to get deliverance from his addiction, but there was no result. Sekar has a furniture showroom in Chennai. I met him at his showroom and he was busy entertaining the customers. I requested an appointment to interview him, but he refused and was reluctant to meet me elsewhere to discuss his vision. But he opened the drawer in his table and pulled out a sheet of paper and handed it to me. It was a handwritten photocopy of his testimony that he kept readily available for distribution to his customers. I quote a section from his testimony here:

Sekar: I was an alcoholic for many years and tried my best to leave the habit, but I could not. I visited various temples like [a famous temple in South India and other temples in Tamil Nadu], praying for deliverance from the addiction. But there was no change. I drank all the more even after returning from [a famous temple], after offering much prayer that I should leave this habit. On August 26, 2000, I drank so much of alcohol and went home at 11:00 p.m.

While I was in deep sleep, I felt someone patted me at the back and called me by name, "Sekar! Sekar! Wake up, wake up." He took hold of my hand and woke me up and said, "You come with me. From today, I will lead you on a good path." He led me for about two hundred feet from my bedroom to outside on the street. I was left at the gate outside my house. A bright light from the sky fell on me. I shouted, "Jesus save me!" and became conscious. I wondered, "Why am I here in the middle of the night?" I entered my house and saw both the doors were left open. I looked at the clock and the time was 3:00 in the morning. Since then, I could feel the bright light always appear before my eyes. Since then, the name Jesus . . . Jesus comes often in my mind. Since August 27, 2000, I do not know how the habits of idol worship and desire for alcohol left me! This happened by the glory of the Lord Jesus.

Sekar was struggling with sin before he had the vision. He tried his religion of birth to liberate him from his addiction to alcohol but was not successful. However, he neither prayed to Jesus nor considered Christianity to resolve the crisis. Nevertheless, the vision of Jesus instantly transformed him and liberated him from his addiction to alcohol.

Let me introduce you to Selvi, a businessperson from a Hindu family. She had a vision of the crucifixion during her school days. Though she studied in a Christian school, she was against Christianity. But after the vision, she feels that she is touched by the love of Jesus.

Selvi: I am from a Hindu family. I studied in a Christian institution. I was far from the Lord. Towards the end of my school days, I had a vision of Jesus while I was on my bed. I saw the Lord face to face in my vision. I saw Jesus hanging on the cross in my vision. The vision was very vivid and lasted for about three hours. At that time, all my sins that I had committed from my childhood days were appearing before me. Earlier, I had felt some kind of emptiness within me. But the day Jesus met me and forgave my sins, the first thing happened to me was his love filled my heart. His loving eyes had filled my heart. Since the moment I had seen the Lord—for three hours—my life was changed totally. I left my former pattern of worship and was convinced that the Lord Jesus Christ is the true God. I committed my life totally to God.

Q: Did you ever pray to Jesus earlier?

Selvi: No, I never prayed to Jesus. I studied in a Catholic school, so I liked Mother Mary. But later I studied in another school . . . that was a Protestant school. Many elders used to come to tell about Jesus. I had lot of Brahmin [the priestly caste in Hinduism] friends, and we used to sit at the back, as it was compulsory. We made fun of those who told about Jesus and criticized them very badly. The lives of many Christians were stumbling blocks to me. They talked so much, but they didn't show it in their life. I did not like the way they lived their lives. Earlier I used to like Mother Mary very much, but after coming to this school, I started hating Christianity. I was against Christianity.

In this situation, the Lord himself came in search of me. When I was an enemy to him, when I was speaking against him, and doing things against him, Jesus came in search of me. I never thought about Jesus and never prayed to him, nor did I call on him. I had nothing to do with him. I had seen some movies in which Jesus was carrying a cross, like *Annai Velankanni* [a Tamil movie based on a Catholic shrine in Tamil Nadu] and Bible-related films. But those days I never prayed to Jesus. The Lord himself came in search of me and showed me the crucifixion. But I could recognize him as the Lord Jesus Christ.

The Lord told me, "Daughter, you follow only me." The Lord spoke to me on that day. That day, all my sins from my childhood days appeared to me like a movie. I could see the cross as well as all my sins. Sins do not mean big sins, but small things like arguing with my parents, disobeying them, and things that grieved Jesus, etc. I was crying and praying. My tears wet my pillow. I did not know how to pray. But I felt that somebody was praying for me, from within myself. The whole of my pillow was wet with my tears. The vision lasted from 2:00 a.m. until 5:00 a.m., and it disappeared when the clock rang at 5:00 a.m. I was filled with great joy in my heart. All those days I was carrying a burden in my heart, but on that day there was a great joy in my heart. At that moment only I realized that Jesus is the true God. Since that day, God gave me the grace to worship him alone.

Q: Did you face any crisis prior to this?

Selvi: I did not face any crisis. But during my childhood days I felt that there was some kind of emptiness within me. I used to long for friends' love and was longing for worldly love. Those days, I did not realize that all those things were vain. I started realizing that my friends' love was not complete and not true. I did not have any problems or tragedy or anything. One thing I know: Jesus's love filled my heart. He is the God who gave his life for me. He gave his life for me. He is the God who loves me greatly despite my sins and limitations. Even today his deep love for me is a great surprise to me. He is the loving God who gave his life for me. His unlimited love is incomprehensible. I was drawn to him only because of his love.

Though Selvi was against Christianity, the vision of crucifixion changed her enmity against Christianity instantly. Selvi was not struggling with her sin as Sekar did. Only in the vision did she realize that she was sinful. So I asked her, "Did you consider those things that came as sins in your vision as sins earlier?"

Selvi: I realized my sins only on that day. I was crazy for movies. I sing nicely, so I pretend to study my subjects, but I would be singing movie songs. I did other things like disobeying parents, arguing with them, and fighting with my brothers and sisters. I did not consider these things sins then. Only on that day, when the Lord convicted me, I realized they were serious sins. I felt as if they were like big mountains and serious sins against God. Only on that day I realized; otherwise everyone does all these things. So I never felt they were sins. Only on that day the Lord convicted me of my sins.

I wanted to know the nature of the vision and her state of mind during and after the vision, so I asked her, "Were you conscious for the three hours?"

Selvi: I was very much conscious. It was not a dream. I am sure it was not a dream. Though I was on my bed, but I am sure that it was not a dream. It was not a dream, but I saw him face to face. I saw a vision and was surprised! I remember that our house was small. My parents were also sleeping in the same room. Still it was a big surprise for me!

I could not understand. I was on my bed—how I saw the Lord? But . . . I saw him face to face. The crucifixion scene was still in front of my eyes. I could not see his face, but I saw his suffering on the cross. The crucifixion is still fresh in my memory. I am sure that it was not a dream because I was fully conscious.

Q: What was your feeling immediately after the vision?

Selvi: I felt great happiness! I was filled with great and incomprehensible joy! I told my parents that day, but they did not take it very seriously, thinking that I was childish. I told my friends. I told my Brahmin friend whose father was a temple *pujari* [priest]. She was the same girl who was with me in making fun of people who preached Jesus. Later, she also accepted Jesus and is now a high official in the government.

Q: How was the whole day for you after the vision?

Selvi: I did not realize then that it was going to be a big turning point in my life. I did not realize that my life was going to change upside down because of this! But something significant happened. I thought I had known the true God. I never expected any great changes on that day. I was filled with great happiness and incomprehensible joy. I do not know how to express. I received great happiness and peace on that day. I was longing for love from my friends, but since then I never had anyone else in the first place. Christ's love filled my heart, neither the love of my husband nor my children—not even my parents' love.

We find a mixture of feelings here. In one sense, Selvi realized her sin and struck by the guilt of her sin. On the other, she was excited about the love of Jesus. She claimed that she was filled with incomprehensible joy. Our discussion moved on to the next phase of her conversion.

Q: After that how did you grow in the Lord?

Selvi: During the last days of schooling, they [teachers in the school] gave me the Bible. I was surprised the way the Lord guided me. Initially, when I started reading the Bible, my parents did not object. But when

I got completely changed, stopped worshiping Hindu gods, stopped going for movies, and stopped doing any of their practices, I began to face opposition at home. I faced problems at home. Especially, my mother opposed me. My father studied in a Christian institution, and he had a little faith in Christianity. So my mother blamed him that he had spoiled me. My father neither did anything to make me a Christian nor did he oppose me. We even had a Bible in our house. My parents were of the view that all religions are the same. But when I accepted Jesus Christ, only my mother was very much against me. She became very much agitated. No one else opposed me like my mother did.

My teachers and another Christian leader guided me nicely. My teacher only told me about the Holy Spirit. In one of the prayer meetings in a small group, I received the anointment of the Holy Spirit. It was a different kind of experience. I did not realize that experience would be a turning point! I was told that I need to take baptism. But I did not know what it was. I thought baptism was some kind of blessing from God that I needed to get. I went to a church for baptism, but the pastor told me that he would not give baptism for Hindu converts, saying that they need to grow more. When the pastor was not willing to baptize me, I felt all the more eager to receive it. I thought that this was something important, and I needed it. So I started praying that I should get it. However, on the day of baptism service, the pastor baptized me. Since then, I faced lots of problems at home. I faced many struggles because of Christ. Sometimes, I was beaten up and told that I should leave the house because of my faith. I used to cry and stand outside the house.

As soon as I joined college, I started a prayer cell. I faced opposition from the college authorities, as it was a Hindu college. I was publicly humiliated for my faith and was ridiculed that I would fail in my studies. My movements were closely observed by the authorities. The authorities confiscated all my spiritual books and my Bible. But one of my seniors gave me a Bible. I used to hide it inside a book and read. The Lord used to speak to me every moment. The Lord was using me to spread the gospel to others. At the end of the year, I could shine in my studies; the warden returned the Bible and other books to me.

Then I went to a Christian college where I thought that I would enjoy more freedom to grow in the Lord. But I was denied permission to go to church as my certificate showed me a Hindu. However,

I managed to go to church sometimes without the knowledge of the authorities. Jesus guided me graciously those days.

Later, Selvi married a Hindu, and her mother-in-law made her practice all the Hindu rituals. In a Hindu family, the daughter-in-law is expected to fulfill all the responsibilities with regard to the religious life of a family. Selvi did them all, as she was afraid of her mother-in-law. She was frustrated a lot, but never thought of giving up Jesus.

When they went through some problems in their business, she began to assert her right to practice Christianity. She started refusing to participate in the family rituals. Her husband slowly began to see her prayers being answered with regard to their business problems, and he also started reading the Bible. In the meantime, her mother-in-law suffered from cancer and asked Selvi to pray for her. After many years, Selvi could see a turnaround in her family believing in Jesus. I present our conversation on her understanding of God in light of her experience.

Q: How do you describe God in light of your spiritual experience?

Selvi: I cannot describe him in words. His love is incomprehensible. I praise God for his love. I worship him in tears. We cannot understand his love. His love protected me while I was facing all the troubles and sustained me. I am the worst sinner in the world, but he loves me so much. I am nothing, I am weak; still he loves me! He came to this world for me. He died for me! He gave his life for me. He shed his blood for me. His love filled my heart. God is love only. I have tasted his love in a deeper and deeper manner. I wondered why he still loves me!

Q: Who was instrumental in leading you to Christ?

Selvi: No one was instrumental in leading me to Christ. The Lord came in search of me. Earlier I had despised him, but the Lord came to me.

Selvi was emphatic in saying that no human agent was involved in leading her to Jesus. Though she acknowledged that her teachers and others played a role in guiding her since the vision, she claimed that Jesus came in search of her. The vision of the crucifixion dramatically transformed her life.

In all three visions, we find the element of automatism. When Sania saw the person in the vision, immediately she knelt down and started crying. In Sekar's vision, he got up from his bed and walked all the way out of the house into the street. When Selvi saw the vision, she was crying and her pillow was wet with her tears. This is something similar to a hypnotized person who would obey the command of the hypnotizer; however, in such cases, when consciousness is regained they do not remember anything they did. But in religious experiences, people remember everything, and the experience has a profound impact in their lives. William James (1902/2004, p. 412) observed, "Beliefs are strengthened wherever automatisms corroborate them . . . Motor automatisms, though rarer, are, if possible, even more convincing than sensations. The subjects here actually feel themselves played upon by powers beyond their will. The evidence is dynamic; the God or spirit moves the very organs of their body." Converts to Christianity perceive Jesus as the cause of their behavior in their religious experience. However, their religious beliefs are not strengthened by automatism, as found by James, but replaced with a belief in Jesus. The dynamic evidence of automatism in conversion to Christianity makes a lasting impact in the lives of converts that results in a change of religious faith.

We also find auditory element in these visions. Sania, Selvi, and Sekar heard a voice speaking to them in their visions. Both Sania and Sekar heard their names called and were spoken to by the divine. In Selvi's vision she was addressed as "daughter." Selvi points out that her parents were also sleeping in the same small room; however, they never heard anything, nor did they see anything that Selvi saw. These features are similar to the vision of St. Paul in the New Testament. Richard Peace (1999, p. 83) analyzed St. Paul's vision and claimed, "The result of Paul's encounter with Jesus was the restructuring of his theological understanding." For converts to Christianity, it is not simply a restructuring of their theology, but a replacement of their religious belief. This replacement of religious belief is not due to rational exercise, but due to their sensory experience in their encounter with Jesus. Sensory experiences of Jesus are not unique only to converts. Luhrmann (2012, p. 216) finds similar experiences among evangelical Christians. She calls them *sensory overrides* and defines them as "moments when perception overrides the material stimulus." She observes that though sensory experiences have all the features of hallucinations, they are not hallucinations. She asserts, "The moments did meet psychiatric criteria for hallucinations . . . Yet the pattern and quality of the experience was quite different from that in psychosis, and there was no associated pathology" (2012, p. 231). She claims that believers are trained by Vineyard Fellowship, and prayer training makes people have more such sensory overrides. She demonstrated her claim through her experiment with a group of Christian volunteers. However, it was not out of any training that converts to Christianity experienced sensory experiences of vision, hearing voices, the felt presence of Jesus, or touch. Prayer training cannot be the cause of sensory experiences of a religious nature, but it might enhance the frequency of such experiences. We cannot brush aside converts' claims that the cause of their sensory experiences in conversion is Jesus because the religious experience was spontaneous.

In all the visions, converts either saw a bright light or brightness was otherwise evident. Many studies show the association of brightness or bright light with religious experience, much like Paul's vision in which he saw a bright light that blinded him. Converts could not see the face of the one they saw, but identified him as Jesus. Selvi's vision was a crucifixion, so we can understand that she was able to recognize that it was Jesus. Sania and Sekar never did anything to seek Jesus nor did anything Christian, but they were able to recognize the person in their vision as Jesus. They instantly recognized that it was Jesus without being told so or given something to indicate that was Jesus. This is something perplexing. Sania claimed that she could not see the face because it was so bright, but instantly she recognized that it was Jesus. I questioned Sania about how she could be certain that it was Jesus. She emphatically said that it was Jesus, and she was certain of what she saw in the vision. Sania even claimed that she saw the person in the vision with her "eyes closed." She claimed that it was her "personal thing" that cannot be expressed in words. When Sekar came out to the street in his vision, he saw a bright light and immediately cried, "Jesus save me." He did not elaborate how he, a devout Hindu, could identify the bright light with Jesus. However, they were conscious while having their religious experience. Sania believes that only the individual knows when he or she meets God and that cannot be described. This particular dimension indicates the revelatory nature of the divine–human encounter, which will be discussed in detail in chapter 7.

Despite converts not seeking a solution to their crisis from Christianity, they saw Jesus in their vision. Sania wanted to consult a psychiatrist for her depression. Sekar tried his religion of birth for deliverance from his addiction to alcohol. Both never considered Christianity as an option to solve their crisis. They never had any association with Christianity; however, the vision of Jesus gave them the absolute certainty of knowing the truth, and they felt its positive effects immediately. The vision gave them relief from their crisis. Sania claimed that she never had any depression after her religious experience. Sekar felt that he never had any urge to take liquor ever since his experience.

While seeing the vision, converts felt that they were sinful before the divine. They had a sense of being sinful, dirty, poor, incomplete, and so on. Since then, they feel that they cannot think of a life without Jesus; they feel the need of him in their lives very strongly. They were captivated by the divine presence and love. For both Sania and Selvi, we find that their religious experience created a sense of sin that had never been there earlier. We also find that it was resolved then and there, and they felt they were accepted and forgiven at once. Religious experience creates a crisis of sin and resolves the same instantly.

A relationship with a human agent is not a prerequisite for initiating the conversion process. No agent was involved in these conversions. The converts claimed that God himself came in search of them. They felt privileged at having a vision. However, they went in search of someone who could help them to know more about Christianity only after they had their vision. In such cases, agents appeared only after the religious experience.

Visions makes people zealous and passionate about sharing what they have experienced. Both Sania and Selvi claimed that they converted many of their friends within a year. Selvi married a Hindu. As a daughter-in-law, she had to fulfill all the responsibilities related to the religious life of her family, and her mother-in-law forced her to practice all Hindu rituals. Selvi did them all, as she was afraid of her mother-in-law. She was frustrated a lot, but never thought of giving up Jesus. Eventually, she was able to win over her husband and mother-in-law to Jesus.

Converts are certain of experiencing the *true God*. Their experiences gave converts the certainty of experiencing the true God, and their crises were solved. Sania, Selvi, and Sekar did nothing related to Christianity before they had a vision, but still they saw a vision of Jesus. However, all those who had a vision were certain of finding the truth or felt that the truth was revealed to them.

Studies show that such visions are not scarce. Alister Hardy (1979/1984, p. 33), based on his extensive research on religious experience in Britain, claimed, "There can be no doubt that such experiences are more common than many people suppose." Phillip Wiebe did a detailed study of Christic visions and made a similar claim. He (1997, pp. 212–13) observed, "The visions often occur quite spontaneously, rather than being generated by deliberate efforts to produce them through fasting, oxygen deprivation, focused meditation, or other similar techniques." A vision of Jesus can occur to anyone, irrespective of their interest in Christianity. However, when it occurs they adopt Christianity despite their indifference or animosity to Christianity. In my study, some never expected such an experience, and never searched for the truth or ever raised any existential question, but still they saw a vision of Jesus. On the other hand, some were eagerly waiting for an answer to their existential questions and they also saw a vision of Jesus. No matter what was the context in which they had a vision, they all identified the person in the vision with Jesus, contrary to their religious beliefs and expectations. Some were anti-Christian and some were prejudiced against Christianity, however, after their religious experience all their enmity and prejudices against Christianity vanished. They moved from one extreme to other, similar to St. Paul, and were certain of experiencing the truth. We will move on to discuss conversion experiences associated with dreams in the next chapter.

2   Dreams

> Dream is the dreamer's own psychical act.
>
> —SIGMUND FREUD (1914/2010, P. 1)

> Dreams can bring a dreamer closer to the sacred...the sacred becomes a more vital, immediate presence in his or her life.
>
> —KELLY BULKELEY (1999, P. 16)

DREAMING IS PART OF human nature. People have different kinds of dreams: some are pleasant and some terrifying; some dreams that can be recollected while others can only be vaguely remembered; some dreams make a lasting impact for the rest of their lives. Many dreams are simply about what preoccupies one's mind the most: excitements, anxieties, daily activities and so on. Some dreams are life changing. Here I present the dreams of three women who claim to have encountered the divine in their dreams and identified the divine with Jesus. All three went through intense anxiety prior to their dreams.

I present first the story of Komala, a retired government employee from a Hindu Brahmin family who experienced conversion at the age of forty:

Komala: My name is Komala and I am from an orthodox Brahmin family. I got married in 1976 and we lived in a joint family. I am from a village. I was working for the government and got transferred to

Chennai city after my marriage. Three years after my marriage I had my first child, and had the second child two and a half years later. We had lots of problems that were mainly related to money matters because of the joint family. I found it difficult to get acquainted with the new situation. Everything was new: the workplace, the city, and friends. Our basic needs such as food and clothing were taken care off, but I never had peace of mind. I worried a lot about my family because there were many of us living in the house and we often quarreled.

I used to go to several temples in search of peace. Whoever suggested me to do something to get peace, I did them all sincerely. I visited many temples and offered special *pujas* [prayers] and fasted on Fridays. In spite of all this, I was never satisfied. I could never find real peace. I had no peace in my heart though we had our own house, two children, and a good income. I did not have peace of mind and I felt emptiness within me.

One day, on my way back from the office, I was sitting near a window in a bus, with a heavy heart. I did not even realize that tears were rolling down from my eyes. I was saying in my heart, "I have visited many temples and done everything required, but I have no peace. Tonight I must know by which name I should call God. Otherwise, by tomorrow morning, I will become an atheist. If I do not come to know anything by tonight, I will stop worshiping any god." I made this decision.

I reached home and I did everything that I normally do. I fed my children. As usual, after completing my chores, I went to bed late. In the early morning, around 2:30, maybe between 2:30 and 3:00—I did not know the exact time—I had a dream. It was as bright as midday in my dream. There was a slope from a hill and a large crowd waiting for a VIP, and I was also one among them to see the VIP. I did not know who was to come, but I was eager to see the person who was to come. I was eagerly waiting to see the VIP. On both sides of the path, barricades were put up so that the VIP could walk freely, and people would not crowd him.

Suddenly, I saw Jesus walking slowly and coming between the barricades. He was so fair in complexion and had long hair. He was like a shepherd with a staff. As he was crossing by me, he turned towards me and said, "Read five and six of the Sermon on the Mount." His lips were not moving, but I could hear him say that. I had no confusion that it was Jesus. I was able to identify him easily because I had watched a few movies like *Ben Hur*, I had seen pictures of Jesus, and I had studied in a Christian school. I was so sure that it was Jesus. It was a pleasing scene. I was thrilled and excited that I had received an answer to my question.

In the morning, I did all the household chores as usual. Later I went to office and shared with my Roman Catholic friend about my dream. She was so happy and said, "People are longing to see this king, but you are privileged to see him." Earlier, she had given me a Catholic Bible. She asked me to read the book of Matthew [indicating to read the Sermon on the Mount]. I read that. My friend also introduced me to a fellowship near my house, so I could clear my doubts in the Bible. She also introduced me to another lady . . . I started attending the church [nearby], and I was baptized. I did not tell any of our family members.

My heart was after the Lord. I started knowing many things through visions, and I also heard the voice of the Spirit of God and he would guide me. And when I would sit for prayer, I would feel a kind of white dress covering or enveloping me. I started changing slowly and internally. After that, with my husband's permission, I started going to church regularly. I found peace. Whenever my sisters shared their problems with me, I would tell them to say, "Victory through the blood of Jesus," and "He would help you." They also believed and accepted Jesus Christ and started coming to church. In 1999 my daughter was saved by the Lord.

I did not know how to pray, but in the night, along with my children, we would say the Lord's Prayer. As I read the Bible and listened to the messages, I was filled and anointed with the Spirit of God. I started sharing about the true God, who gave his life for us while we were still sinners; he gave his life for us and lifted us. No one told me about the Lord. He revealed himself to me. I have decided to follow him at any cost.

Q: Was it a dream or a vision?

Komala: It was a dream, not a vision. I saw it in the night while sleeping. It was a dream only.

Q: What was your feeling after the dream?

Dreams

Komala: I was so excited, but I could not tell anyone at home. I did not express it until I went to the office. I was unable to concentrate till I met my friend in the office and told her about the dream. She told me that I was fortunate.

Q: Why did you not have peace of mind?

Komala: We lived in a joined family, you know, so even for small matters we ladies would quarrel among ourselves. I used to feel bad. I am the last child in my family and was a pet child. I was free totally, and I did not like to work at my home. But in our tradition, here in my husband's house, the daughter-in-law has to do all the work and bear all the burdens. We were four or five ladies at home and often we had arguments.

Q: Then what happened?

Komala: After the death of my in-laws, we divided our property and came out separately. That was the time I was saved. After that, I did not have much problem because we both [she and her husband] were planning and maintaining the family, and we were relieved. Then God blessed us, and we bought a single-bedroom flat and moved to our new house. The Lord has been continuously blessing us. Even though we went through lots of problems, I was having peace in my heart because I would tell myself, "I have prayed about this and the rest God will take care of." Sometimes I did not even realize how a crisis was solved, but it would be solved. I had the problem of piles. One day I was unable to bear the pain and I cried, "Lord, hereafter it should not trouble me." And it never came again; I was healed. In the beginning I enjoyed the love of God and now also.

Q: What were some of the changes in your life after coming to Jesus Christ?

Komala: Earlier, whenever we got some free time I would chat with others or watch some movies or plan some outings. But now, I feel, I can read the Bible more, or I can spend more time in meditating on God's Word. Now I am retired. While I was working, I had to work both at the office and at home, so I would feel tired and I could not spend much time on this. At the same time, even if I were simply chatting with others, he [Jesus] would remind me, "Do not sit there;

do not sit with the mockers as it is written in Psalm 1." [She laughs.] Even if I happened to sit with other ladies, I would slowly excuse myself by saying, "I have some work to do." I also started praying for my friends and a lot of problems were solved through prayers. Even the way I speak with others has changed, and I have become soft-spoken. I am not saying that my total personality is changed, but slowly, day by day, I am changing. I can feel that.

Q: What were your relatives' reactions then?

Komala: They did not object me directly, but they inquired my husband. I think he had explained my dream to them. Sometimes my husband also scolded me saying, "Because of you, I am ashamed; everyone speaks ill of me." Sometimes I would answer him back and sometimes I would pray, "Lord you handle this problem for me. You have chosen me. These problems should leave just as they came." One or two days I had to face such problems, then on the third day things would be back to normal.

The very first thing I came to know from the Bible was about Naaman. Somehow from somewhere, I heard that he said, "When my master enters the temple I will bow down in the temple, the Lord should forgive me for this." Similarly, I also decided that I would go to temples when my family members call me. When I happened go to a temple, I tell Jesus, "You are only everything for me." I tell this always. Then I will be satisfied and would not feel guilty. So I would take part in all our family functions and go wherever I was expected. I would pray, "Lord, you are with me and I will not have any problem." Sometimes I could not refuse, so I would go along with them. Though I was physically present there, I was trying to avoid eating food offered to the idols. With prayer I would participate in all things.

As the days went by, I told them, "I will not be participating in all these things because I have taken a baptism." I let them know this and also told them that I love them too. I told them openly, "I do not eat the food offered to idols, but I will come another day to eat with you." Now they do send food to us, but they make it clear that it is not offered to idols. God has given me favor among my own relatives and he has kept me high in front of them.

In 2000, I stopped wearing *bindhi* [a sacred red dot on the forehead of a married Hindu women to indicate her marital status; without that a woman is identified as a widow] because I felt uncomfortable in my heart. I told the Lord, "Lord I remove this for your sake and for no other reason. You are the head of this family, and you know how to solve if any problem arises out of this." For a few days it was all right, but again a problem would reappear.

My daughter was unmarried then. My husband was saying if I remain like this [without a *bhindi*], "No marriage proposal will come for our daughter and she will never be able to get married." But I always take my problems to the Lord in fasting and prayers because without fasting and prayer we cannot win such battles. The problems would disappear as they came. I would tell the Lord, "Father I do not know anything, but I should glorify your name in this." I could overcome all my problems through prayer in this way.

My relatives would say something to my husband about my faith that would create problems between us. However, the Lord gave good understanding between us. Because of God's Word, I could see some changes happening in our home. I prayed for my family's salvation because I had no strength to go through these problems. I asked for a prayer partner and the Lord enabled me to start a family prayer. The change was not big, but in due course there were changes. Now all are at peace and they have accepted me saying, "Okay, if you like, you do as you like." Even those who hated me are now at peace with me. After my daughter's wedding, all are friendly with me.

Q: How do you differentiate praying then and now as a Christian?

Komala: Earlier I would go to temples, give offerings, and observe fasting. Those days, I felt that God was somewhere far away and we could not go near him. I received some blessings, I cannot deny it. But generally prayers were like undelivered letters and sent to wrong address. I understood the difference only after I raised the question, "Who is the true God?" When I was a small girl, I never had such a question, but after marriage only I had that sort of question. Even after doing many *pujas* [prayers], I felt emptiness. Only then this question came to my mind.

Now I am confident that Jesus is listening to my words, our conversations, and our prayers. I can feel his presence in early-morning prayer. He is with us, and he answers us. If I told him to wake me at 3:00 a.m. for prayer, I felt sometimes he woke me. He has assured us that he is in us and with us. He is with us even when no one is with us. Often I think of a song, "Whoever may leave, but Jesus will never leave me." I love the songs sung by . . . Even while doing my work I would sing those songs and they are like tonic to me. I always feel his presence with me. He dwells in my house always. As it is written in Psalm 132:14, "This is my resting place forever and ever; here I will sit enthroned, for I have desired it." He dwells in my house.

Q: How do you describe Jesus?

Komala: He is full of mercy, because there were times when I forgot to pray . . . but Jesus is forgiving. What I love the most in him is that he is forgiving whether it's a small mistake or a big one. I cannot be perfect, without making any mistake. No human can be, but if we tell him, "I am sorry, by mistake I have done this," the next moment he forgives and we also feel forgiven. So I like his forgiving nature.

The next thing is that while we were still imperfect and sinners he came in search of us. Earlier, I would take revenge and argue like a lawyer; otherwise I would be restless. But now, my nature is changed by thinking, "If God started taking revenge like this, where would I be?" I could not even imagine the consequences. I am scared to think about the consequences, but he did not do that. He had taken all our sins on him, that too for sinners. Suppose if I am hurt with the bell-pin, how much pain it would cause. But without saying anything, he endured everything and shed his blood for us. If we are injured a little and if it bleeds, we create a big scene. But he gave his life for us. I like this nature in him. The main attraction for me is his crucifixion. I always meditate on it thinking, "You suffered so much for me; how am I going to repay?" As long as I live, I will always ask, "Lord, I need your forgiveness." I like his forgiving nature.

He is compassionate. When we call on him, his heart melts. He has given us the birthright to call him *Appa* [Dad in Tamil]. That is marvelous. Sometimes when I meditate on his nature, I am stunned and burst into tears. I love his nature of compassion. He is very gracious . . . I have asked him to forgive others as he has forgiven me . . . I like that. He is almighty God and nothing is impossible for him. We may be poor in asking him, but he is willing to give us abundantly. I like his loving nature. His love has enslaved me. I love to be like him. His love is in incomparable. I love to meditate on his love. I like all these qualities in him.

Q: Will you return to your previous faith?

Komala: I had the dream when I asked, "Who is God and what is his name? Otherwise, I will not believe in any god." On that day, I did not even think of Jesus and never talked about him with others. So I believed that the dream was not accidental, but was from God! So I believed very strongly that I got an answer to my question and it came from heaven. I also had this determination that once I asked and got an answer from God, so I should not go back. However, I pray, "Lord, You protect me till the end. You have anointed me with your Spirit. Help me run the race successfully till the end, towards the goal." Like a small child and without knowing the danger, I might leave him and run away, but I ask him to hold my hands tightly so that I will not return to my previous faith.

Q: Why?

Komala: Because I have known the truth and I know what is true. After knowing the truth, if I go back it will be like one may leave, but seven will come in, [meaning to say what Jesus said about when one demon leaves, it brings back seven]; then it will be very bad. So we should read the Bible every day and ask his grace to follow his words. God also gives us grace and trains us. When the Spirit of God comes in us, he will strengthen us and reveal himself to us. The Bible says, "You have known the truth and the truth will set you free." He will not change his words and definitely he will save me. I am sure he will take care of me till the end.

You know what I ask of him? Whether he comes first or I go early [die], I should be with him always. I ask him only this gift: that whether here or there [heaven], I want to be with him only. People are casting out demons, they ask and get it [the gift of casting out demons], but what does he want us to do? We are told that we should ask for the gifts, but I want him to be in me and me in him. He said, "If you remain in me and my words in you, the Father and I will dwell in you." That's what I need. Even last month also I prayed like that and I want to live like that.

Q: Who is Jesus to you?

Komala: I love to talk to him as a friend. We both talk now as close friends. Like Enoch [in the Bible], I converse with him like a close friend. As Enoch could walk with God, we could also be like him. He might also have had a family, children, and grandchildren, but still he walked with God.

Q: Who was the key person in leading you to the Lord?

Komala: It was Jesus only. That helps me hold on to him. Even now when I am disturbed, I read Matthew chapters 5, 6, and 7 because he gave everything in this passage that I needed.

Komala prayed to a generic God, as she felt her religion had failed her. The disenchantment with her religion led her to raise ultimate questions. She questioned whether or not her religion was true. If not, which one was true? She prayed, "I should know on whose name I should call." She also decided that she would not believe in any god if she did not get an answer that night. To her surprise, she got an answer from Jesus. She strongly believed that it was an answer from heaven to her question.

Another woman, Vinodha, put her religion to the test to solve a crisis in her family, but she was unable to find any solutions. She was a victim of domestic violence; on occasions, she had considered committing suicide. Some of her friends were converts, and her neighbor was a Christian. She was exposed to Christianity through them. However, only when she had a dream did she fully accept Jesus, her *Appa* ["Dad" in Tamil; she fondly referred to Jesus throughout the interview in this manner]. Unlike Komala, who did not do anything related to Christianity before her dream, Vinodha was exposed to Christian songs, prayer, and churches with her friends. These things came to help her at the time of crisis.

Q: Could you please tell me how you came to Jesus?

Vinodha: First I want to thank my *Appa* for changing my life to give a witness like this. By his grace I am alive today. In March 2006 I faced lots of problems in my family, and there was no peace in my family. I always had some problem or the other. I was in a condition of not knowing how to handle these problems. Only after my marriage I was facing such kinds of problems.

Basically, I am from a Hindu family and I belong to [a certain] caste. My parents are very religious, and I used to pray to all Hindu gods. I would observe all the rituals, like full-moon day, new-moon day, etc. I used to practice all sorts of religious rituals.

At the end of February 2006 we had some problems in our family. My husband and I never had good understanding. Within a few days of our wedding, misunderstanding started. He is loving but adamant. I did not like that. I am the last child in my family, so my words carried value in my home. At the end of February, there was a misunderstanding between my family and my sister's family [her sister is married to her husband's brother]. I said something that led to conflict between our families. I felt very bad and I thought that I should leave everything and commit suicide. I was unable to understand my situation. There was no one to help me.

I would always share my problems with my neighbor, a Christian. On March 13 I shared with her, and she prayed for me. At that time, I felt encouraged, and I felt that I have *Appa* who could save me.

Then on April 18 we had gone out. I had lost some things. I left my bag in the autorickshaw and came home. My husband scolded me very badly saying, "You are irresponsible. You will never change, etc." I was crying all the time. In the night—actually, early morning—I had a dream.

In my dream, I heard a voice from *Appa* calling me, "Come to me, my daughter." I could not see any figure, but I heard a voice. I fell prostrated at his feet and was crying and asking him to forgive me for not going to him all these days. Since then whatever problem came, I would ask *Appa*, and he would give me solutions, whether it be a financial or a family problem. Now I am bold. No god came to my rescue when I was in trouble. I had visited many temples and worshiped, but no one helped me. There is no other God like Jesus . . .

Even today my husband is without a job, but we lack nothing because of God's grace. Every morning while praying, I ask *Appa* for my needs; somehow I would get it. My *Appa* has done this for me till now and he will continue to do the same.

Q: Could you please describe your dream?

Vinodha: Actually, that day we had gone to see, with our neighbors, the Doulas ship operated by Operation Mobilization. In general, I am careless. Even at home I break things, and I do not handle things carefully. I do not know why. My husband does not tolerate this. He would always advise that I should be a responsible woman. Whenever he did that, I would get angry because I could not take it because of my inflated ego. On that particular day, my two-wheeler gave some problem. I left the vehicle and returned home by autorickshaw. I forgot to take my bag that had my son's new dresses and left it in the autorickshaw. Even though it was a careless mistake, I could not accept when my husband scolded me. I was so upset about it because the loss was great at that time. I was down because I could not afford to buy another set of dresses for my son as my husband was jobless . . .

On that particular day, when I went to bed I was full of sorrow because my husband had scolded me very badly. I was also expecting that the Lord would somehow get me the things back, but I did not take any effort. Around 4:30 in the morning I had a dream. I was disturbed in the night because my husband scolded me the previous day.

I heard a song in my dream that was sung by my friend. It goes like this: "Very soon your burdens will be taken . . . and the Lord loves you . . ." I do not even know this song fully. She was singing that. I could hear her singing—her voice only. At that time I heard a voice saying, "Daughter, come to me." I could not see anyone, but I heard a voice. I fell prostrated at his feet and crying and asking him to forgive me for not going to him all these days. I do not know whether it was a dream or what, but I was strengthened.

In the morning when my husband had gone out, I shared this with my neighbor. I do not know what it was, but it gave me the strength that I do have *Appa* with me who can bear my burdens and pains. Since then, I believed in him very strongly. If any problem comes now, I consider that it is allowed by *Appa* so that I could grow closer to him. After this incident, I have full faith in him.

Q: You did not see anyone. How can you say it was Jesus?

Vinodha: I did not see anyone, but no one could call out, "Daughter, come to me" other than *Appa*. That is why I am telling you. Because I went to bed after prayer and felt pain in my heart—that pain was removed. Even though it was a dream, I have *Appa* for myself and I heard his voice.

Q: How was your feeling when your friend prayed for you?

Dreams

Vinodha: I felt strengthened and that I had someone to lean on. Literally, I fell on her lap and cried because when I shared everything with her, I was broken and cried. I told her, "I cannot bear any more and everybody is blaming me, and I feel I have no one for me." When I was abandoned, *Appa* received me. As he said, "He is the savior of the destitute," and he had received me. When I was crying, I had a feeling that I have someone for me. I also felt whatever problem may come I don't have to tell others.

I am a short-tempered person. I do not know why; maybe because I am the youngest in my house. If my husband says one word, I would reply him with ten words. I always tried to prove that I was right, and I would argue with him. My husband does not like arguing, but now, whatever he says I just keep quiet. This change happened only after I started reading the Bible.

Every morning, I would watch some Christian programs on television and read the Bible. I feel the portion that I read in the Bible or the message I hear from the television program is meant for me. Likewise, I wish to follow the sayings in Psalms and Proverbs. Earlier, I would do the house chores for the sake of doing and was fed up. But now I do not have that feeling. Now I feel this is my responsibility, and every morning I ask *Appa* to help me work happily. Whenever I felt dull, he would give me strength for each day. Even this morning, I told *Appa*, "I do not have money," and that he should provide. I am sure before evening he will meet my need. I believe it. If I ask my husband for money, he will create a problem because he is jobless. Money is very much needed for the family. He also feels that there is no one to help him. I am also unable to support my family.

Q: What difference do you find in praying to Jesus?

Vinodha: Earlier I had no peace. The problems were never solved . . . problems, problems in the family. Always confusions, but now it is not like that. Whatever happens, I have strength within me. Now when I face a problem, I ask, "So what?" because I have the confidence that I can always tell *Appa* to take care of it. This was not the case earlier.

I had visited many temples and not missed any temple or *pujas* [prayers]. I had not withheld any offering; I did everything. Now only I am changed. Almost for a year, I accompanied my friend to a Catholic church to give her company. But I also started praying sincerely. But I did not know how to pray. Now I can pray to *Appa* without any distractions. At times of trouble, I cry and pray. Earlier I did not know how to pray, but now I can pray. I pray for others who are in trouble and for the people who are around me. Earlier I never had these feelings. But now, because my Lord and his love are with me, I pray for others.

Earlier I did not feel bad to trouble others by taking much of their time, but now I think twice before asking someone for each and every thing. Now I am conscious of taking others' time. I always go to [a friend's] house. I used to talk with my friend's mother for hours together, but I hardly helped her. But now I can talk to her and listen to her problems and pray for her. Earlier I was self-centered, but now I help others. I was selfish and always thinking about myself. Now it is not like that. Now I can give my time to others. Of course, I'm not able to help anyone financially, but I can give moral support. I am sure one day God will make me to help others financially too. Now I can counsel and encourage my friend who is also facing a problem in her family. Four months ago I was seeking for peace of mind and had none to comfort me. Today, because *Appa* is with me, I can pray for peace in their families.

Q: For the past year you have been going to church, is there any difference in the way you now pray? Did anyone teach you how to pray?

Vinodha: The very first person who prayed for me was my neighbor. She told me, "You can pray along with me. You can ask Jesus whatever you want, and he will give you." At that time I was unable to ask openly because I was used to praying in my heart. But after some time, through [watching television] I learned to pray. Initially I was listening to them praying, and later when they prayed I started praying along with them. I started reading the Bible. On March 21, Tuesday, I went to church. [She had visited church now and then, but had never attended a worship service nor been part of the congregation.]

Before going to church I prayed, "If you [Jesus] have really accepted me, you should give me a Bible today." But I didn't tell this to anyone. As I was accompanying my friend, I didn't know what she felt. She gave me a New Testament and said, "*Akka* [elder sister], you please keep this, read this, and you will have peace of mind. But it is in English; if you can't understand, you ask me and I can tell you in Tamil." I thanked her and told her this is what I asked from the

Lord. The Lord always blesses us doubly. When I returned home my neighbor gave me a Tamil New Testament. I was so glad. This is one of the assurances that *Appa* had accepted me. He wanted me to read and gave a Tamil version also. I can't spend a day without reading the Bible. If I don't read, that day is not peaceful.

My husband doesn't know that I have fully converted. I don't know whether he will accept this or not because it's only been four months since I have accepted the Lord. But I hope he will not restrict. Whenever he was not at home, I would read the Bible. Whenever I was down, the Lord would give me comforting words and I would feel happy. I am yet to complete the Bible, and before I can do that God will give me the opportunity to be his witness.

Q: Have you ever felt disturbed that you were leaving your own religion?

Vinodha: Initially I had that feeling. I was childish to think that my gods might get angry with me. But now I don't feel that way. Now I feel I get more problems if I follow the former pattern of worship. But for my husband's satisfaction I do observe all the special days and light the [sacred] lamp for namesake. But nowadays I am avoiding that also. My husband is not a staunch Hindu, but he believes in God. So far, I was doing everything for his satisfaction. Maybe for about a week initially, I had the feeling that my gods might get angry, but not now. I don't have that feeling anymore. For me, no other god helped me except *Appa*, so I don't bother.

All I pray now to my *Appa* is to give me an opportunity to attend a prayer meeting. Yesterday I visited my friend and she told me about a prayer meeting. If *Appa* is willing, he will give me the chance to attend. Earlier I went to church regularly, but in between my husband told me not to go. So I stopped going to the church and started praying at home because *Appa* is everywhere. Still I feel it would be nice if I could go to church. I feel now that it is very much needed for me. Maybe *Appa* will give me a chance to go.

Q: What are the changes in your personal life after coming to Jesus Christ?

Vinodha: I was a short-tempered person. Whether it was my father or my husband, I would argue with them. Generally when my husband returns home, I can't understand his feeling. If he comes home late, I would suspect him. But now I don't have those kinds of feelings. If he says something, I used to argue and irritate him, and that would eventually led him to beat me. In between, once there was an argument and he was very harsh. Generally, I wouldn't keep quiet. I would always fight back for my rights. Now nothing happens like that.

Because I was a pet girl in my family my parents gave me full freedom. My father had always considered me a son and he would say, "This is my son. She is going to be with me always and I will not give her in marriage." So after my marriage I always had a feeling that my husband had separated me from my father. I was so adamant in nature; now I have learned to be patient. Not only that . . . if God had given someone to us and if he [her husband] is his choice for me, then God will change him and give him back to me. And I hope this will happen.

I always wanted others to listen to me and do as I wish. That nature is completely changed. Now I have started thinking about the feelings of others. For example, I will tell you a small incident. Yesterday I went to my friend's house and my husband returned home early and was very hungry. He was irritated because I was not at home and called me over phone and scolded me badly. Earlier, I would have definitely argued with him, "Why shouldn't I take time for myself?" But because I have given my life to *Appa*, I didn't do that. I was jealous, but now that is changed. I would always compare myself to others, but now whenever that feeling of jealousy comes, I pray and ask *Appa* to remove such feeling.

Sometimes unknowingly I would verbally hurt others, especially my mother-in-law. These days before going to meet her, I just pray that I should have control over my tongue. Last week I visited her and without any problem I returned home. I wish the Lord should help me change completely as a loving wife. I wish he [God] should bind us together with love. I am sure the Lord will do so.

I can tell so many things like this. Once I had little petrol in my scooter, but I managed to reach a petrol station. After reaching there, I realized that I had no money in my purse. I was standing helpless because I could neither go home nor fill petrol. But fortunately a small boy who was working at the pump saw me. I don't know what he understood, but he told me that I could fill the petrol and later pay him. Even through the small boy God showed me favor.

In these four months and through every small incident he has proved that he is the true God. I struggled a lot; I was confused and doubted my husband whether he loved me or not. But now I am free from all this. Now God has given me the faith that whatever happens to me it's for my good. Now I am completely a transformed person.

Q: Who is Jesus to you?

Vinodha: He is my dad, friend, and everything. He is the first love in my life and all the others are next—even my husband. I don't ask money from my husband but I only ask *Appa*.

Q: How would you describe God in the light of your experience?

Vinodha: God loves me and he cares for me. He knows what I want—even food. We hadn't cooked non-vegetarian food for long time. Two weeks ago, my husband went to his friend's house; while returning he brought *Biriyani* [a South Indian special food, in which rice and meat cooked together with spices] from their house. God knew that I like *Biriyani*, so Jesus sent it through someone and I ate on that day. I only thought of it, but I didn't even ask him and didn't tell anyone either. Yet, my *Appa* knew that I should be given it and gave it through someone. Like that, so many small, small incidents have happened. Even though it is a small matter, when such things happen I feel very happy. Many times I cried and prayed to *Appa*.

Q: Will you return to your old religion?

Vinodha: No chance.

Q: Why?

Vinodha: I will not go back because when my *Appa* is with me, how can I go? I cannot go back. There is no room for returning. If possible, I will persuade my husband to follow Jesus. I am praying for that. I have chosen on my own, consciously, not for others. But I may have to do some of the Hindu rituals at home to satisfy my in-laws. But before doing that I would let *Appa* know that I am not doing this wholeheartedly, but only for the sake of the elders in the family. Even last week, when I went to my in-laws home I had to do it, but I did not do it wholeheartedly.

Q: What is the major difference in your life since coming to know the Lord?

Vinodha: Peace. Peace at heart. It wasn't there earlier. I had visited many temples. Many times I cried because of the problems in my family, but *Appa* has given me peace now and that is enough for me. Now I have the feeling that for anything and everything *Appa* is with me. He has confirmed many times that he is with me. He is enough for me. Even if something happens to me, it is his responsibility and he will take care of me and eventually it will be for the good.

Vinodha only needed assurance that she had someone to lean on to face life's realities. Her husband did not give her the needed support, and she could not have a fulfilled relationship with him. She never felt secured in her relationship with her husband. Constant conflict with him made her look for divine support, but she felt that her religion did not extend such support to her. When her neighbor prayed, she was encouraged, however, she did not fully adopt Christianity. Her dream gave her the conviction that Jesus was there for her. She described her relationship with her father as a positive one. She cherished her relationship with him before marriage. She would have expected such fatherly treatment from her husband, but unlike her father, her husband was neither loving nor understanding; instead he was violent. When her expectations were not fulfilled in her marriage, she searched for a secured relationship in her religion by visiting several temples, but the religion of her birth did not help her. The disenchantment she had with her husband and the religion of her birth drove her to contemplate suicide. In this situation, the dream connected her to the divine, who was willing to accept her, as her father did. The person in the dream said, "Come to me, my daughter." So she aptly calls him *Appa*. Besides resolving her crisis, her dream initiated a secured relationship between her and the divine. She was happy that her eight-year-old son started showing interest in Jesus. She was very confident that her husband would follow soon, but unfortunately he died suddenly a few years ago. Though he did not convert, he began to show some interest in Jesus before his death. She reconciled to the tragedy by claiming that except for Jesus she would not be alive today, as she lost her husband at a prime age.

Another woman who had a dream on the third day after her husband's death saw Jesus traveling in a car, and she became a Christian. I call her Sarala. She and her two daughters are her husband's lone survivors.

Dreams

Sarala: In the year 1995, my husband died when he was abroad. We were left like orphans. One Christian family visited us and prayed for us. On that night while I was sleeping, I had a dream. In that dream, I saw a car with glass doors and a man sitting inside who resembled Jesus. Others were saying, "This is *Arul Raj* ["King of Mercy" in Tamil]," but I was insisting, "No, this is Jesus." That dream was a witness to me. I started loving Jesus and going to church. Whenever I was sad, I would cry at his feet and the Lord has led us thus far. We have no problem for food and clothes. We live in a rented house and we do not have any problem with our house owner. The Lord is graciously taking care of us.

Not only that, we were able to conduct my elder daughter's wedding without any debt. All the people wondered and asked, "How could you do all this?" But I told them, "I did not do it. It is the work of my Lord." Somehow, I managed the whole year. She came for her delivery a year after. By God's grace, everything went on well and I sent her back home with her five-month-old son. After she had gone, I had only 800 rupees [US$ 16] left in my hand. I gave that to my house owner, saying, "I have only this much to pay for this month's rent. Unless the Lord gives me some more money, I will not be able to pay you."

Actually, I had asked some friends to find a job for my second daughter. Many promised to find one. One lady came and told that there was a job offer for my daughter. Then my second daughter started working. She was paid 1200 rupees [US$ 24] per month and we managed with that. Now she is earning 2000 rupees [US$ 40] and with this we manage everything. My Lord has never let us down and is taking care of all our needs. Next thing is to get my second daughter married, but I believe my Lord will do that also. We do not have much money, but we have committed our lives to God and we also tell others about our God.

Q: When did you have the dream?

Sarala: I had the dream on the third day after the death of my husband. My husband died on May 7, 1995, and on May 10 I had the dream. I was lying on my bed filled with sorrow because there were lots of debts to be paid. I was wondering, "We do not even own a house, and having two daughters [In South India getting daughters married involves a lot of money], how will I manage?" When I was filled with sorrow, the Lord showed himself to me in the dream. On that day I accepted him.

Q: When was the first time you heard about Jesus?

Sarala: I heard of him in 1994. A Christian meeting was conducted in our street. We were teasing them because we never worshiped him. I told them, "We will never pray to your god. We will worship only our god." One of our neighbors, a Christian, told me, "One day you will meet God." I replied her, "I will never meet your god." My elder daughter argued with her, "Our god is great. We will never come to your god." But within a year the Lord met us. He is so great; that is why he came in search of me.

We knew one Christian family. One of their relatives helped my husband go abroad. They wanted to help our family and arranged for his trip. When they [the Christian family] heard about the death of my husband they felt very bad. So they came to see us and pray for us.

Till that day I was opposing the Lord, but on that day I prayed along with them. I got up from my bed, knelt down, covered my head and prayed. On that day everybody was telling me, "You look like a Christian."

Q: What was your feeling after the dream?

Sarala: My heart, my mind, and everything was in the Lord. From that day until now, I have been leading a life without any problem. We earn a little and are living by his grace. We are living without borrowing money from others.

I felt that hereafter everything was in the Lord's hands only. The one who had gone is gone. So hereafter, for me, everything is God only. I was strengthened by this confidence in God.

Q: Why did not you think of seeking help from your religion?

Sarala: I had worshiped my gods all along, but they did not help me. But the moment I accepted Jesus, each and every moment I am living successfully. I have given him myself fully.

Q: How was your religious life before the tragedy?

Sarala: Before that, I went to many temples. What have I not done! I did all sorts of *pujas* [prayers]. Even a day before my husband's death, I went to [a nearby temple] and offered a *puja* and bought firewood for the ritual, "fire walk." I dressed nicely with a *bindhi* on my forehead and wore lots of flower in my hair. [In South India women have flower in their hair, but Hindu widows are forbidden to have flower. She says these things to bring out the contrast. Her husband died on the next day, and she could no longer have the *bindhi* and flower.] The person who took my husband abroad had returned. So I went to meet him to inquire about the welfare of my husband. He told me that my husband was doing well and everyone over there liked him so much. And he also commented that I look good [meaning to say, religiously and culturally a woman of dignity].

The following day, I heard the news of my husband's death. I started hating the god from that day onward. I felt that I have done so much to that god, and in return he did not do any good thing to me. So I had decided that I do not need him anymore. I kept him away from me.

Q: You say that now you are happy in the Lord. How?

Sarala: I am happy because of good things. In a sense, my elder daughter is married and happily settled, even though I did not give her much [dowry]. My pastor would tell my younger daughter that God wants her to work for the family. Though she is physically very weak, as the pastor said, she works and maintains our family. It is God's will and really a miracle. Today we live in a city and our house owner is a gift of God to us. We pay only 1200 rupees [US $ 24] as rent. If we vacate the house they can rent it for 2500 rupees [US$ 50], but still they are asking us to stay there. This is God's grace, you know! This is an evidence for God's provision!

Q: Did you experience any change in your life?

Sarala: I have developed a helping tendency. I cannot help financially, but physically I can lend my hands. I can help others up to some extent. My children also are changed. Earlier when we were Hindus, they would often get angry. But today they are very patient.

Q: When did your children come to know the Lord?

Sarala: They loved the Lord, but did not take baptism till 2001. They stopped going to temples; since 1995 none of us went to any temple. At the time of my daughter's marriage, there were some obstacles regarding the match in the horoscope. Even though they [the groom's family] are our relatives they said, "If they get marry, they might face problems. They will live together only for one and a half years." I thought to myself, "We are children of God. There will not be any problem. I was so sure that they will not face any problem." Boldly I gave her in marriage. Now five years have gone and nothing has happened to them. They are living happily. It's a big testimony.

Q: Did you face any problem from your relatives because of your conversion?

Sarala: I faced some troubles . . . They said that I should not have converted because we are from a high caste. But I did not listen to them. I told them not to disturb me because until now, only the Lord took care of me. So they did not say anything thereafter. They visit us even now; they have not rejected us. They told us, "If that God is so good to you, it is okay; we will not bother you." We are very happy now.

Q: Who is Jesus to you?

Sarala: He is my father. He is the one who is leading us, caring for us, and protecting us till now.

Sarala was stricken with tragedy and poverty but living with a radiant hope, all because of a dream she had that gave her courage and confidence to face life's hardships. This dream caused her to depend completely on the divine for everything and resulted in her conversion to Christianity.

The deep conviction of these women that they had received an answer from God caused them to forsake the religion of their birth and adopt Christianity. In Vinodha's dream, the person in the dream assured her that she was not alone in handling extreme anxiety. Sarala lost her husband and the dream enabled her to cope with the extreme anxiety and assured her that Jesus was with her to face life's realities. They all felt assured through their dreams and were determined to hold on to Jesus.

They experienced extreme anxiety before their dream. The dream came as an answer to their crisis and removed their anxiety. This is in line with the psychological theories that claims dreams help the dreamer to overcome different types of crises and anxieties. We find that dreams enabled these women to face their crisis with a new strength and confidence.

Each one gave religious meaning to their dream by identifying the person in the dream with Jesus. The divine in the dream assured them that they could rely on him at times of trouble. They felt that no one came to their aid, including their gods. When they were introduced to Christianity, they felt they should give it try as nothing else had worked.

Alister Hardy (1979/1984, p. 79), based on his study of religious experience, points out the significance of the religious dimension of dream experience: "Of the importance of dreams to many of the individuals concerned as a channel of religious experience there seems to be no doubt." Dreams are not simply psychic phenomena; some dreams have greater significance in the life of the dreamer.

When converts went through crises, sometimes they found solution to their crises through dreams. Religiously significant dreams offer greater energy and resources to face life's realities. Though sometime the situation remains the same, converts' outlook about their situation is completely changed due to the dream, because "such dream experiences bring the renewing powers of the sacred into the dreamer's present, conflict-ridden life" (Bulkeley, 1999, p. 22). He (Bulkeley, 2003) further claimed that such dreams radically alter the perception of the life and world of the dreamer. Bulkeley (1995, p. 143) observes, "Conversion dreams work to *integrate* psychological, cultural, and spiritual elements in such a way that the dreamer is thoroughly transformed. By means of these dreams, the sacred becomes a more vital, immediate presence in the dreamer's life" (italics original). This is true of conversion dreams that lead to Christianity. These women adopted Christianity as their religion since their dreams provided a solution to their crises. In such dreams, when the person awakens, the conceptual system is readjusted in the light of the dream. One finds a new energy to manage the crisis in the light of the new relationship established with the divine. The solution is the belief that the divine is present in real life, not just in the dreams. This belief gives dreamers relief from anxiety and courage to face any crisis.

Converts attribute the source of their dreams to the divine. Bulkeley (1999, p. 28) observes, "Religious and psychological approaches to dreams are logically compatible: both agree that dreams connect us with realms that extend beyond—and in some cases *far beyond*—the reach of ordinary waking consciousness. To their credit, many psychologists do acknowledge the limits of their theories, and recognize that at least some dreams escape naturalistic analysis and explanation" (italics original). Psychology cannot reject out right the spiritual dimension of life-changing dreams.

Converts' descriptions of their dreams were sometimes paradoxical. Komala reported that she could not see the face of Jesus, but she recognized the person in the dream as Jesus. Vinodha had similar expressions that she did not see anyone, but only heard a voice; however, she knew it was Jesus who called her. Sarala reported that others were calling the person in her dream *Arul Raj* [King of Mercy], but she was insisting that it was Jesus—in her dream, as well as when she awoke. Komala pointed out another paradoxical element in her dream: Jesus did not speak, that is, his lips were not moving, but she heard his voice. Even though it appears illogical, they were certain that they knew who he was and what he had spoken to them in their dreams. This is discussed further in chapter 7. We now move on to the next chapter, which deals with experiences of hearing God's voice.

3   Voices of God

> Intuition and inspiration would be such, if they existed; but they can safely be counted as illusions, as fulfilments of wishes.
>
> —Sigmund Freud (1932)

> When evangelicals speak of hearing God, they do not in general have an audible voice in mind.
>
> —T. M. Luhrmann (2012, p. 232)

Some converts receive divine communication that causes them to leave the religion of their birth to follow Jesus. The communication is not auditory, but they feel the message is from God and is specifically meant for them and appropriate to their situation. They hear God's voice while reading the Bible or listening to a sermon, in the form of a realization of a truth or personalization of a message. The messages vary: being convicted of sin, forgiven by Jesus, helped by Jesus in a crisis, convicted that a former pattern of worship is wrong, or sensing the need of accepting Jesus personally. These converts are certain that God spoke to them through the Bible or through a sermon. They have a feeling that someone from within communicated to them.

Let me start with a student who said, "I went to a church just for fun, as it was a newly built church, but God spoke to me that day and I accepted Christ." Converts often talk about a moment of realization that they are sinners and they need Jesus as Savior while reading the Bible. For the next example, I introduce Inban, who has a PhD in engineering and teaches in a prestigious technical university in Tamil Nadu. He hails from a Hindu family and narrated his experience of attending a Bible study during his college days where he felt someone other than himself was present within him.

Inban: At the age of twenty-one, I came to Chennai to study engineering at [the same institution where he now teaches]. When I was doing my first year, one of my seniors invited me to attend a Bible study. Through the Bible study, I began to know about the Lord Jesus Christ and the Bible.

When I was attending the Bible study, I got impressed. I felt as if someone knew all my crooked life and was talking to me. I felt those words were meant for me, and I found some happiness and peace of mind in the Bible study. So I started attending the weekly Bible study regularly. I found something that gave me joy and peace. I found the truth. I started reading the Bible and slowly started praying to the Lord Jesus Christ.

I could see my life being transformed. My old habits . . . a lot of sinful habits got changed. Whenever I prayed, the Lord answered my prayers. Then I found the reality in my life. In all the twenty-one years of my life, I did not find something like this in my former religious life. I never had these kinds of experiences. After knowing the Lord, after approaching him, after reading his words, after praying to him, I found a real change in my personal life. I could feel the presence of God—his happiness and his peace.

Then I realized that there is one God, Jesus Christ. I understood the purpose of Christ's coming into this world to bring salvation. Then I surrendered my life to him totally. So I experienced his salvation. I got the assurance from the Lord that the Lord has cleansed all my sins by his precious blood. I understood that he came to this world for this only. He died for me and he shed his blood for me and through his blood my sins are washed away.

Not only was I assured, but the Lord has given me spiritual power to overcome the temptations in my daily life. I can really feel it. Because of this, there is a real change in my life. I can say very boldly that Jesus is the Lord and he is the creator of the whole universe. I have the personal conviction that Jesus is God and his love is abundant. I could feel his love and presence in my daily life. I can talk to him as if I were talking to a friend. With all these experiences, I have decided to follow the Lord Jesus Christ wholeheartedly. I have put an end to all my old habits, like my former pattern of worship, etc. I stopped all those things. I found that Jesus is God and that he died for me. I worship only one God, the Lord Jesus Christ. He opened my eyes. I stopped the former pattern of worship and doing sins. I can say boldly that I am following Christianity because of my personal experience. This is a brief experience of my conversion.

Q: Could you please elaborate on the changes in your life?

Inban: For example, I was addicted to some sins of youth like watching movies, reading bad books, and talking with my friends unnecessarily. And the Lord has completely delivered me from these youthful lusts and all worldly pleasures like watching movies, reading novels, reading bad books, and listening to movie music. The Lord has completely delivered me from all these. I could feel it. Then only I understood, okay, there is some power in the Lord and he has delivered me from the clutches of sin. Earlier I tried my best, but I could not overcome. By the power of the Lord, I could overcome the sins.

Q: Before accepting Christ, did you feel that you were doing something wrong? Or were you enjoying them?

Inban: Before accepting the Lord Jesus Christ, I was like others, and I never felt guilty because everyone does those things. So I also just did it. I never felt guilty about doing those things. I enjoyed worldly pleasures . . . but it was only temporary. Afterward, I found a vacuum in my heart. I did not find real satisfaction in them.

I got the salvation experience only after coming to the Lord and after realizing that Jesus is God. So after my conversion whenever I committed a sin or when I messed up my behavior, I found a sting of guilt. Sometimes I could not even sleep. I understood the cruelty of sin's nature and my bad habits. It really pricked my heart, unless I reconciled with the Lord . . . unless I confessed . . . unless I came out of that situation, I would be restless. But I am not saying that after my salvation I have never fallen into sin. I do make mistakes, but then, I am not dwelling in that all the time. Again I pray to the Lord and the Lord delivers me. The great difference is that earlier I was doing everything without any shame and guilt. I was just enjoying worldly pleasures. Now, I am enjoying the presence of the Lord and I really have peace and happiness in my life. But unknowingly, by mistake, when I do something wrong, it pricks me and leaves me with a strong guilty conscience. When I confess, the Lord is merciful to forgive my sins once again and cleanses me. I press on toward the Lord Jesus Christ. I am leading a wonderful life.

Q: Did you feel bad for leaving your own culture and religion?

Inban: Yeah! When I initially started attending the Bible study, I never knew that I should not worship idols and other things. I was worshiping the Hindu gods as well as attending the Bible study. I was also praying to the gods. Initially . . . for a few months, I was doing both together. But after sometime, I got a strong realization that Jesus is God, and because of this knowledge I could not worship other gods.

At the depth of my heart there was some kind of realization because of God's touch. I could not raise my hands to worship the idols and I could not worship as I did earlier. Earlier I was worshiping the idols with all fear and zeal. I did everything. After my salvation experience, I looked at an idol, but I could not worship. And I never felt bad that I was coming out of my religion; instead, I felt very happy. I felt that God had delivered me from the clutches of my sins. I never thought that my family might oppose. Of course, I knew that there would be some opposition from my family . . . Yeah, it was there in the initial stage. Then they did not disturb me, and let me have my way. So I never felt any guilt for coming out of my old tradition; rather I felt really happy about it.

Q: How do you differentiate your life then and now?

Inban: I enjoyed worldly pleasures for three or four years prior to my conversion, but it was a miserable life. I mean, I cannot explain the kind of feelings I had. I was miserable. It was not a good life, and I was confused. Sinful habits were pulling me down all the time and ultimately it gave lots of sorrows in my life. And I really could not get any kind of feeling to lead my life for God.

At times I thought, "What am I going to achieve in this world? There's nothing to enjoy in this world and it is better to end my life." On one occasion, I also thought of committing suicide because I was examining, "What is life? I am studying now, then I will get a job, then I will get married, then I will die after sometime. What is there in this life to enjoy? It was a miserable life and full of difficulties.

Money may be there and other things may be there, but again this is a temporary life. Anyway, I am going to die one day and there is nothing to enjoy in this world. Everything I like is vanity. Instead of spending time and struggling with these things," I thought, "let me end my life." I decided like that. I was in a miserable condition before my conversion.

After my conversion, I have the greatest hope. I believe in eternity and a life after death. Very strongly I believe in heaven. So I got some hope in life. Maybe when I leave this earth I will enter into heaven—that kind of hope I have now.

Not only that, the Lord had delivered me from my sins. It was the greatest relief in my life and I became lighthearted. I have gotten the assurance that the Lord has forgiven my sins and once for all forgotten; he will no longer remember my sins. After my conversion the Lord has blessed my personal life, my education, and my carrier. In 2003 I had a severe sickness in my body and I had to undergo a surgery and the Lord protected me. Above all, I have a hope of life after death.

So after my conversion I have a meaningful life. I have a strong hope in the Lord. Day after day, I know what I am doing and where I am going. I have complete assurance about my life. Earlier, there was no hope, no assurance, no surety, and it was miserable . . . Now I know what life means, how to spend my future, and where to spend my future; everything I know, what I have achieved, etc. It gives lot of happiness and courage and strength.

Q: In light of your experience, how do you describe Jesus and what he means to you?

Inban: Jesus is God and a very good friend of me. His love is rich. More than anything, I enjoyed his mercy and long-suffering. He was so patient with me and did not reject me. Whenever I failed, he never rejected me. Whenever I approached him, he just embraced me. So I have tasted my Lord Jesus. He is full of mercy and compassion. He is always forgiving, patient, and long-suffering. I have experienced all these in my life. I am not saying this because I read these things from the Bible. I am not saying it because someone said this . . . I have understood these things from my personal experience. I know that Jesus is like this. I realize in my life that his love is unchanging.

Transformative Religious Experience

Q: How do you feel now about worshiping Jesus?

Inban: When I pray in the morning or in the night, I can really feel the peace of God ruling in my heart. Whenever I am in tribulation or persecution or under pressure, I pour out my heart at the feet of the Lord Jesus Christ, and I really find great peace ruling in my heart. When I pour out everything to him, I feel all the burdens are removed from my heart. I feel real joy and peace. I also feel his power, his encouragement, his strength, and his intimate fellowship. I feel the presence of God, real peace, and happiness. I really enjoy it.

Those days I enjoyed worldly pleasures. But they gave me very temporary . . . you cannot say that there was joy. Worldly pleasure was a passing thing. When I compare both, no way does it come near to the happiness our God gives. Those were all very temporary and after that it created a vacuum in my heart. But what I enjoy in the Lord is really overflowing and sparkling. Really it is unspeakable joy!

Q: Will you go back to your religion?

Inban: No . . . no way, no way, no chance, not at any cost. I cannot look back! I cannot think of going back, because I know what is right and what is wrong. I know what is real. I know what is . . . I cannot even imagine going backward. No way. Not at all!

Q: What is the one thing that holds you to Jesus?

Inban: I hold on to Jesus Christ for various reasons. He blessed my education, he gave me healing at the time of my sickness, he has lifted me up . . . up to the assistant-professor level in this prestigious university. And he has given me a good background and . . . has given me wealth and everything. Above all, I hold on to Jesus Christ because I am experiencing his salvation in my daily life. The Lord delivered me from the clutches of sin . . . from the clutches of Satan. The Lord delivered me from the clutches of worldly pleasures and sinful attitudes. He has given me peace that nobody could give. I am holding on to the Lord Jesus Christ because of these reasons. More than any of these benefits, I mean, I give priority to my salvation. Because my salvation is real, my repentance is real, and because my deliverance is real. So I hold on to Jesus Christ.

Inban felt that someone who knew his life was talking to him. That gave him a sense of exposure as well as joy and peace. He was able to see the changes in his life when he started attending a Bible study and reading the Bible. The presence of the "Other" within him is a vital element in his conversion experience. Though we do not find any sensory elements involved in this religious experience, the presence of the "Other" and the realization that his life was miserable is the result of his encounter with the divine. I questioned him about his feelings towards sinful acts. He responded by saying that everyone did them and so did he, but he felt the enjoyment was temporary and at times he felt a vacuum in his life. As we have seen in the previous chapters, a sense of sin is the result of the divine–human encounter and this guilt is removed instantly at the religious experience. Let us move on to another example.

Maharasan Vedamanickam, a devout Hindu who lived in the late eighteenth century, went for a pilgrimage to a famous temple in Chidambaram, Tamil Nadu, South India. Contrary to his expectation of fulfillment to his spiritual quest, he was greatly disenchanted with what was happening in the temple premises. While he was in the temple, he had a vision urging him to leave the place. This vision gave him a new hope of finding the truth elsewhere. In obedience to the vision, he left the temple and began his journey. Instead of going home, he took a journey to one of his relatives' house. They were converted Christians living in Tanjore, Tamil Nadu. After hearing his vision, they invited him to attend a church. He reported his experience of hearing a sermon in a church for the first time in his life: "The first time I heard the words of life, which the Lord revealed to me by his servant in Tanjore, my heart was cloven and the blessed news of salvation was to me as if the light of heaven had suddenly shone in upon one who had long been groping in darkness. I was unwilling to leave the church and became eager to hear more" (as cited in Paul, 1967, p. 56). His first experience of hearing a sermon in a church enlightened him. He did not want to leave the church. That was so intense that he felt that he had to know more about Christianity, which eventually led to his conversion. Moving to a recent example, I present a story of a high-caste Hindu woman.

Rekha, a homemaker from an orthodox Hindu family, is married to a Brahmin convert. She had to walk out of her home to marry a believer in Jesus. When she was a college student she could not find true love. Wealth and cultural traditions kept a distance between her parents and her.

Rekha: I do not know why I was so stubborn that I wanted to study in a Christian college . . . My father and his friends were shocked as to why I would want to study again in a Christian institution, as I had already studied in a Christian school . . . They were of the opinion that Christians are undertakers who deal with dead bodies and funeral rites [meaning to indicate that Christians are a low-caste people]. My parents were so orthodox that they thought like this. They were against me joining a Christian college because I was brought up in the same orthodox manner. My caste is very orthodox. Being a doctor, he [her father] never wanted me to become a commerce graduate.

During my college days, I had several questions like, "Who would show me true love in this world?" My parents were very orthodox and they never wanted their children to be attached to them. I was broken, and I was looking for someone who could love me truly.

One of my best friends, who studied with me, told me about the gospel of Jesus Christ . . . but criticized my religion. I argued with her for criticizing my religion. Of course, being a Hindu, I got very angry because I worshiped all gods and goddesses. However, they did not show me true love.

I questioned, "Who would show me true love in this world?" I knew very well having studied in a Christian school—I knew 50 percent about Christianity—that Christ came into this world and he is the only one who could show true love and forgive people for their sins . . . However, I told my friend, "I will never enter the chapel in the college. I am a Hindu. Why should I attend the chapel service? I have no connection with it." She told me, "If you want to taste the true love of God, you must at least search for it."

In July 2002 I went to the college chapel. I attended a fifteen-minute service. I just sat over there and closed my eyes and started meditating. They talked about true love, and that was what I had in my mind. I was really surprised to know that Christ forgave even his betrayer, Judas, and it was very comforting to me. In my life, neither my parents nor my relatives loved me truly. We had enough money and wealth; I did not need to search for God to get anything more. In our home, we were always talking about money, money—we were money-minded people. But I was searching for true love. Only at that time did I realize that it is Christ who can save people from all kinds of bondages, no matter what position we are in, whether Hindu, Christian or Muslim.

Jesus Christ is the one who loves truly, and anyone who seeks him will find true love. When I got it, I was very happy. Days and days went by and I was growing in him. I started reading the Bible that my friend gave me. Actually, I went with her to buy the Bible. I began to read the New Testament from the beginning and slowly transformation started taking place.

After two months, Jesus gave me a vision where a stone was placed before me. This stone melted and melted and became a cross. Members in the fellowship explained to me that when I searched for true love, my heart was like a stone initially. Whatever sickness, bitterness, and anger I had in my mind and heart melted and went away, showing me the true love of Christ. When I got this explanation, I was happy that all these things went away. I was filled with happiness in my life and all these things have gone away. That was the true salvation I experienced in my life. Till today, I am able to see daily salvation at work. I was very happy. I was experiencing true joy and true love. I was convinced that Jesus Christ is the only Savior of the world and no one can be compared to him. I am fully convinced that no man can be a god or goddess and I have become very zealous in my conviction.

I stopped doing *pujas* [prayers]. Suddenly I stopped worshiping idols—not a slow process. Once I had to sit for a *yagam* [a special ritual to cast away the evil]. I could not escape because there was no other way, but God allowed me and gave me the assurance that nothing would happen to me. They thought that I was possessed by evil spirit and something was bothering me in my life. God told me, "Nothing will happen. Even if you sit before the sacred fire, my blood is shed for you and you will not be harmed." Despite these struggles, I never stopped worshiping him. In fact, I started growing in him day by day, and it was a rapid growth, not a slow one, but a steady life with him. I thank God for that. Moreover, God gave me a conviction about baptism, so I got baptized in my church.

Q: Could you please explain, how did you experience the true love of Jesus at the chapel?

Rekha: The worship was only fifteen minutes long. They read a psalm of David telling how he went away from God and how he came back to

God. It was similar to what might happen in any youngster's life, but it pierced my heart. Although, my situations were different . . . Out of ignorance, I did many things, yet I could repent and receive the forgiveness. I was filled with true joy. My sins were forgiven. I got the inner joy. My subconscious was cleared [from the fear of being hurt owing to a curse on her family]. I can find a lot of difference in me now. My subconscious was always preoccupied with my family—about what had been done to our family, etc. After the fifteen-minute service, I experienced total transformation and a revival in my life. It revived my heart, mind, and soul.

Q: What was your religious life like earlier?

Rekha: I was a normal Hindu. I went to temples as my mom used to insist. But I did not have a true devotion as I do now. I knew these were all a temporary satisfaction. However, I did not leave all that. Only after I went to college, I heard the gospel.

Q: When did you actually make up your mind to follow Jesus?

Rekha: My family was facing a lot of problems. When I prayed to Jesus, he answered me immediately. He was the true living God in my life. According to my horoscope I had to face a lot of troubles. I told God about all those things and he answered me. My troubles stopped. Though my people were torturing me like anything, God was with me. That made a strong impact on me . . . I started believing that Jesus is the true and living God. Since then, I have not had any depression.

Q: Did you find any changes in your life?

Rekha: Looking at the changes, my prayers became different, my attitudes were changed, my activities became very different. By nature I am an introvert. I used to keep everything within myself. I was so reserved that I did not mingle with anyone. After coming to Christ I am different. I started mingling with many girls. I started attending prayer fellowship. And my spiritual life began to grow and is continuously growing.

Q: When did your parents come to know about your conversion?

Rekha: Since April 2005 I started telling them about my conversion [but not to her father initially]. They were strong and tried to divert me.

They themselves told me that they came to brainwash me. It was funny that they said like this. I was prepared for anything and knew that one day I would have to face them. I had been doing everything secretly.

I was caught one day after returning from the church. No one reached the point of beating me, but they wounded me with harsh words. I came out of the persecution. I could face it by God's strength, and he is my refuge. God's strength alone made me to overcome.

Q: How were you caught while returning from church?

Rekha: I could not go to church for about a year. How could I go to church? And I did not go. One of my lecturers, who was guiding me and my friends, encouraged me and advised me that I need to go to church. They said, "Other fellowships are good, but attending church is very important." I wanted to know more and more, and they also encouraged me. My father used to go to his clinic from 7:00 to 9:00 in the morning. Usually I would hide the Bible inside a cover and go by autorickshaw. I could never attend an entire service, but I would go there for some time and return before my dad would return. Somehow God would speak to me in the church.

That day, I took the Bible without any cover or a bag, thinking that I would be back before my dad returns. I went boldly that day. The sermon went on and on, but I was tempted to stay back till the end of the sermon. Then I returned home. When I got down from the autorickshaw, my dad also arrived. He just looked at me having a Bible in my hand. I was scared that he might pull the Bible from my hand and throw it and send me out. I had this fear within me. All these negative thoughts came to my mind, but there was a voice—I could hear it at the back of me saying, "Face it boldly." I went inside the house. My father did not speak to me. I prayed within myself, "Tie his mouth, Lord." He did not ask me where I went. But since then he never allowed me to go out. I had to be at home. However, it did not affect my continuation of studies.

Q: How did you manage to marry a Christian?

Rekha: My parents received a few marriage proposals for me, and they earnestly began to consider them. But I did not know what was in their mind. I faced a very difficult time and finally told them, "I will only marry a believer who is a Christian as I am." They said, "We have sacrificed everything for you. If you want Christ, you have to give away everything. You have to give away your rights." But I wanted only Christ. I did not want anything else. God gave me the conviction that there is nothing beyond his glory. God only showed me this. My God was really a stronghold for me. Nothing else could have enabled me to overcome such situations. My concern was not to hurt my parents; rather, I was trying to make them understand that I want to marry a Christian. My pastor brought a marriage proposal of a Brahmin convert, but my parents did not agree for my marriage. They said, "If you want to marry in this manner, go and marry, but we would not come and participate." The Lord told me, "If there is going to be some good, it will be from me. It is possible only through me." I did not take it as a sensitive issue that my parents would not be attending my marriage. I could take it boldly, and I needed to be bold as a good Christian. With God, we can do everything. Blessing comes only from him, not from parents or money or anything. We are married now although it was a challenge for many. Praise be to God.

Q: Did your parents come?

Rekha: His parents came, but my parents did not attend our wedding.

Q: Wasn't it painful for you to leave your family?

Rekha: Yes . . . mmm, but one . . . mmm . . . of course, mmm . . . fleshly [in terms of worldly] thinking, definitely you feel . . . mmm, it was very painful. Of course, every child would expect his or her parents to be present and bless the marriage . . . But I was a secret believer. I knew my parents would stick on to the stand they took. They would not budge, no matter what happens. For this reason, I had to accept such things. I felt sorry for my mother because I am very close to her. It was painful, but I had to take a firm stand on this issue.

Q: Are there any changes in their stand now?

Rekha: I continue to speak to my mother as usual. Still, my father has not changed. My sister and my brother-in-law, a Catholic, felt that I was mentally sick, saying, "Some people have changed you, knowing your situation." They could not agree that it was a change of heart. They said, "You are mentally sick and you need rest." I said, "It's my own conviction and my own step. This is the truth that we need to follow; others are temporary." Since then, they shut their mouths.

Q: What is the one thing that keeps you in Christ?

Rekha: Yeah . . . mmm . . . one thing . . . that holds my faith is the confidence that God will not leave me even if I fail. If I am in a fiery furnace, he is not going to leave me. If he allows me to face certain things, definitely he would give me the strength to face everything. That is how I am brought up in my Christian faith. I have passed through such situations.

Q: Did you inform your parents about taking baptism?

Rekha: No, I did not.

Q: Did you feel that you were doing something against your parents?

Rekha: Baptism has different forms in all religions. In the Brahminical tradition, it was wearing a sacred thread. I was not feeling guilty about taking baptism. I did not make it a big issue. The anti-conversion law was enforced then in Tamil Nadu, but I did not make it a big issue. When the Lord himself gave me true love . . . Only in my marriage, I took a clear stand.

Q: How would you describe God based on your experience?

Rekha: Taking all these things into consideration . . . God is rather more possessive of his own people. He does not want his people to fall from the truth that sets them free. I am proud to be his child, not for anything else. All these experiences I had to go through because I am from another community. God had allowed certain things, and he himself made me to come out of it.

Q: Who is Jesus to you?

Rekha: He is my father. That is the first thing. Then he is my guide. I was in a dilemma with regard to continuing my studies, but God himself guided me.

Transformative Religious Experience

A fifteen-minute chapel service changed the life of Rekha and ended her search for true love. She felt the message was meant for her. This was Rekha's divine–human encounter. Later when she was caught returning from church, she heard a voice at her back saying, "Face it boldly." The presence of the "Other" is evident in such communications. Rekha longed for true love outside her family. Her family gave her everything except love. She found true love in Jesus.

Loneliness and the longing for love made people look for an alternative religious option. Their present relationships did not provide true love, and they felt that there was no one to express such love. Subconsciously or consciously, converts searched for fulfilling relationships elsewhere. The longing to be loved and to love was not working out according to their ideal expectation in any of their human relationships. In the first chapter, Selvi, who had seen a vision of a crucifixion, also had a similar longing for love. She found true love in Jesus. Her craving for true love—a lasting love and an unconditional acceptance—were only found in the religious experience with the divine. Such longing was redirected to the divine in the new religious option.

We will next look at a conversion experience of Nambiar, a medical doctor from a high caste, Namboodri Brahmin. Nambiar was curious to know what made his brother, a doctor, became a Christian in England. So he began to read the Bible and found himself being drawn to Jesus. He described his conversion experience:

Nambiar: My eldest brother, who is no more now, got converted in 1958 while he was working in a hospital in the UK. After hearing this, at home my people were very much perturbed and sent one of my uncles and my brother-in-law to the UK to bring him back. They brought him back and I had been observing his life and lifestyle since then. Thirteen years after his conversion, he came to Delhi IIT [Indian Institute of Technology] to speak to a small group. Since my brother was to speak, I also went there to hear him. He spoke about the Bible, but I do not remember now what he spoke about.

Later I went to a bookshop and bought a New Testament. I began reading from Matthew; I started reading from the beginning. When I came to the Sermon on the Mount, I was very much attracted by the Beatitudes: blessed are the poor in spirit; blessed are those who mourn; blessed are the meek; blessed are the peacemakers; blessed are those persecuted; blessed are those who are hunger and thirst for righteousness.

As I read, I had a very transitory kind of vision of Lord Jesus Christ. It was very, very momentary. I think so it was a vision. I do not know. But I felt like that. That is how I began to like Jesus Christ. I was working in a hospital, and as I was on call duty, I had plenty of time to read this book. I went on reading although I did not understand the Bible. I went on reading it because I liked the content. After a year, I felt I must be baptized. Nobody told me to do so.

In [a North Indian state] I asked a CNI [Church of North India] pastor to baptize me. But he refused: "No, no, you have to ask the permission of a magistrate." So I was unhappy. Later I had to go to Delhi for some work. There I went to a bookshop and found a church next to the bookshop. I asked someone in the church, "I want to be baptized. Will you help me?" He also gave me the same answer, "No, no, I cannot baptize you. I do not know who you are. I have to get permission from a magistrate." So again I had to return disheartened.

Then on another occasion in Delhi as I was walking in . . . I found a bookshop. Next to it, I found a signboard saying, "Gospel Hall. All are welcome." Some meeting was going on inside. I went inside boldly. They accepted me and welcomed me with a smile. They asked me about what happened to me and about my background and why I was there. I said, "I wanted to be baptized." They said, "Anyway we will consider that. Meanwhile, come and join us in our meetings then we will see what we can do." As I had to stay in Delhi for about a month, I attended all the meetings there. Finally, they decided to . . . I think that they wrote to my elder brother who was in [a place in Northwest India], mentioning of my background. They did inquire. Anyway, they knew I was genuine and they baptized me. I began to fellowship with those people when I was in Delhi and returned to my work.

Although I had many Christian friends during my college days and in the medical college, none of them had told me about the Lord Jesus Christ. But interestingly one of my Hindu friends gave me a New Testament. I do not know why he gave me that. I read it, but could not continue as it was full of genealogy.

Q: You said nobody told you to take baptism, but you felt that you should take baptism. How was that?

Nambiar: I got that idea by reading the Bible only . . . Someone inside of me told me that I must be baptized. I do not know why . . . very strange because there was no one to teach or help me. Maybe it was some passage that I might have read on baptism; now I do not remember. I do not know—maybe the Holy Spirit. At that time I did not know about the Holy Spirit, and now I know the Holy Spirit.

Q: What were your feelings and thoughts when you considered taking baptism?

Nambiar: I did not have any fear of people or anything. All my brothers and sisters had grown up and were independent. We make our own decisions. I was about thirty-one years and I did not have any problem. I did not even tell my wife about me being baptized. I did not know whether I should tell her or not. [Laughs.] But she came to know that I was converted.

Q: When your elder brother got converted what was your family's reaction?

Nambiar: Oh . . . he was persecuted, and he was brought to our native place in [South India]. They tried to reconvert him, but they could not. He said, "My faith in Christianity is unshakable." Then they thought he was mentally ill or something else might have happened to him. They wondered how a Namboodri Brahmin could become a Christian! Therefore, they took him to a psychiatrist, and he was given electroconvulsive therapy. It is a painful thing, giving electric shock to the brain to change people's attitude, etc. But nothing succeeded. Then they left him have his way. They did not interfere in his life thereafter.

Q: Were you persecuted for your conversion?

Nambiar: Because my family and relatives could not succeed with my brother, they did not persecute me. They would have thought that I might have followed him. They did nothing. I did not tell them . . . somehow they came to know. Only my wife was unhappy. She did not tell me, but she was very angry and unhappy with my faith. Whenever Christian friends used to come home, she would not entertain them; she would go inside. This happened for fifteen years. Whenever I wanted to take my children for a walk, she would even suspect that I was taking them to church or somewhere . . . When some believers used to come and say something to her about Jesus, she would go into the kitchen without responding to them. She never gave me any trouble, but she was very unhappy and angry with me.

Q: When your eldest brother got converted, what was your reaction?

Nambiar: Mmm . . . I was not unhappy. But I was a little inquisitive to know why he got converted. I also thought that he must have become little—I do not know how to explain—I thought something might have happened to him. I did not know what it was because I did not know the meaning of conversion. I was watching him and listened to whatever he said. It took fifteen years for me to convert. We used to meet in various places. At some stage, when he said something I just listened, and I wondered what my family had done to him! Persecuting him was wrong. I felt sorry for him because I was afraid the electric shock would damage his brain. I did not know that it does not really damage the nerves.

Q: What made you read the Bible?

Nambiar: I was interested in reading. I wanted to know why he spoke so much good about the Bible. I wanted to inquire. I was inquisitive. When I took the book, I did not know that I would be converted.

Q: Did you find any difference in your life?

Nambiar: I was very happy. I preferred to work in a Christian hospital than in a government hospital. My ambitions, my motivations changed after conversion. I enjoy the fellowship with many believers. I was very happy. I was growing in the knowledge of the Lord. A lot of changes took place. I stopped smoking, taking alcohol, and watching movies. No one told me to stop. Spontaneously I stopped everything. Instead, I started reading Christian books and listening to Christian programs on the radio.

Many people helped me grow in my faith, by teaching and training me. I learned to pray and worship; that was new to me. All my shyness disappeared. Earlier I was an introvert; I did not talk much. But after conversion I slowly started speaking to my friends, neighbors, colleagues, doctors, patients, nurses, etc. My communication skills were improved. God has done this in my life. Having faith in Christ, I could face any difficulty. Earlier I did not know what to do in difficult situations, but now I pray and Jesus helps me in difficult situations in my family and professional life. That is a remarkable change in my life.

Q: You said you stopped some habits. Was it sudden or gradual?

Nambiar: Immediately... yeah... immediately.

Q: Who was the key person instrumental in your conversion?

Nambiar: My eldest brother was the key person and of course the Holy Spirit. My elder brother was like a father to me. In a Hindu family, we relate to him as if he were the father. Younger brothers look up to him. After my conversion, we become closer to each other as we belong to the same family of God in faith.

Q: In light of your experience, how do you describe God?

Nambiar: God is spirit. He has emotions and is a person. He is very compassionate, merciful, and loving. At the same time, he is almighty and forgiving. Jesus, of course, is the same as God. We can communicate to God through Jesus more easily than directly to God. Because Jesus Christ will take our prayers to the Father... that is my understanding.

And... another thing: sometimes, I wonder why God gave me the salvation experience. I still do not understand because there are more intelligent and smarter people, more influential or successful, rich, or powerful people and it would not be very difficult for them to believe. Because of his compassion, he has chosen an ordinary person like me. He knew that I was helpless. I was groping for growth and some kind of faith to cling on to lead my life—something to hold on to—and he provided that. Otherwise it was an aimless life, doing what others were doing. Now I do not do what others do. I want to do what God wants me to do. That is my impression about God. He understands. At the same time he is very frightening, in the sense that he does not like wrong things, bad things, sinful things, because he is holy. We stand in his presence with great awe. He knows our weakness and fallibility and our need for a strong person to handle our affairs. The Lord Jesus Christ has provided that to us and his comforting words are a great encouragement when we are passing through difficulties, hardships and sorrows, or confusion in taking decisions. We can go to him in prayer or read the Word of God and he will guide us. I was following the world; now I am following the Lord. Now I do not say that I am 100 percent committed, but I try for that.

Q: Will you go back to your previous religion?

Nambiar: No, never, never . . . I can never imagine such a thing. I will tell you why: even if my faith is wrong— hypothetically speaking, suppose there is no God, and suppose there is no Christ and other things—the teachings of Christ by themselves are very good. Following a person who practiced strictly what he said is a very good formula for living happily. I used to say that even if I am wrong—I mean wrong in the sense that there is no Christ, all my belief is false, and all these are only imagination, or mythology, though I do not believe so, but even if it is so—still it is worth becoming a Christian because Jesus has told only good things. So I will never go back to my old religion. I am interested in sharing the gospel with others. We have shared with most of our relatives.

That was Nambiar's story of conversion. His brother's conversion made him curious to know what is in the Bible. He began to read the Bible and eventually he became a Christian. He felt someone or something within him nudging him to take baptism. He was not sure what it was, and in light of the knowledge gained over the years he attributes that to the Holy Spirit. The presence of the "Other" is evident in his conversion experience.

Converts hear God's voice in diverse ways. I think it is appropriate to present the narrative of Praveena, Nambiar's wife, here. As we have heard from Nambiar, she was very upset that her husband had become a Christian. However, she did not oppose him, but rather she developed hatred towards Jesus, whom she had admired earlier. Later she became a Christian not because of her husband's words, but because she had an unusual experience. She narrated:

Praveena: It was in 1983, I had had a spondylitis attack. I was completely bedridden. I was with my mother at that time. I was a very staunch

Hindu and hated Christians. When my husband became a Christian, I even hated Jesus Christ. Previously I used to read the Bible. Somehow, I do not know, my people say, "We do not hate Jesus Christ. He is one of the gods." But I hated him when he [her husband] became a Christian. I sometimes read the Bible. He used to bring the Bible, but he had not told me that he had become a Christian. I liked John's Gospel very much, though I did not understand a word of it. But I would always read John's Gospel. I liked it and I got converted by reading John's Gospel while I was bedridden.

I used to pray to all my gods. I was not bothered about my sickness. I could not turn on my own to the left or right. I had to depend on my mother or sister for everything. I thought I would be like this for the rest of my life. But I never bothered about it. It never bothered me mentally; I was happy. My children were in the boarding school. The sickness had not driven me to read the Bible, but it was something else.

The Namboodris have a practice of chanting the names of all gods repeatedly for a hundred times or a thousand times. I also did that regularly. Since I could not go to the *puja* room, I used to chant the names of gods while lying on my bed. I used to chant and get peace. One day, as I was chanting the names, suddenly I felt something different. I did not know what it was, but there were some sort of feelings. A strange thought flashed over my mind . . . that they [the gods] were not there. It was a sort of an echo, "Not there! Not there! Not there! No! No!" So I stopped chanting. When I started chanting again, the same thought— "Not there! Not there!"—flashed over my mind. Then I would stop. I used to keep quiet for some time and then I would start again. This was repeated again and again.

I thought I was actually becoming mad because I never had such an experience all through the thirty-five or thirty-six years of my life. So I told my younger sister, who was looking after me, "I think I am on the brink of madness. I have never experienced this. Maybe I am going out of my mind because of the heavy dose of medicines." My sister also felt the same and told me, "Do not worry." But I insisted my sister tell my parents what had happened to me because if I go mad, I would not be able to tell my parents.

It continued for three or four days. So, one day I told . . . the gods, whom I had been worshiping all these years, especially the deity with whom I was specially attached to, "I am not going to chant your names any more or call on you anymore." And so I stopped. I stopped chanting their names. However, the practice had become a habit to me. So many times, I started chanting before going to sleep as I did earlier. Then I would stop. Three or four days it happened like that.

Then I remembered that my daughter had received a New Testament for winning a competition in her school. As I told you, I used to read the Bible earlier. When my husband had become a Christian, I never touched the Bible again for twelve or thirteen years. I hated it like anything, even to touch it.

My younger daughter asked me before she went back to school, "Where should I keep the New Testament?" I told her to put it in a suitcase and keep it under my cot. She knew that I would not touch it. But one fine day, I got up from the bed. Something made me get up that was physically impossible for me to do at all. Only with a support of my sister I could sit up, not even for a few seconds. But that day I got up . . . something prompted me to get up. I did not know at that time what it was. I got up and pulled the suitcase out from under the cot and took the New Testament that had been kept inside. Humanly speaking, I was not able to do anything because of the pain, but I took the New Testament.

I did not think about Jesus as God or anything like that. So I took that book and laid down on my bed and straight away started reading John's Gospel. I was under heavy medication and painkillers, but still I started reading it. I never understood a word—it was the King James Version. But when I came to the phrase, "Verily, verily I say unto you," that Jesus says before starting to speak . . . whenever I read that phrase, I felt like something was going to open up. I did not know what it was. I do not remember anything now, but this phrase, "Verily, verily I say unto you" is very vivid. I do not know through which verse I was converted. But I realized that I was a sinner and he [Jesus] left God and came to save me. Since then, I started praying to him. I do not remember what all I said [prayed].

Then I sat and wrote a letter to my husband the same day. He was not with me, as I was with my parents. He was in the village. I wrote a letter immediately to him that I had received the Lord. When I read it now, it seems full of confusion, but I had mentioned the name of Jesus often. I know that I received him that day.

After two or three months, I got better and went to my home. I had placed the photos of gods in the bedroom [a place of worship at home]. When I return, as I used to do, I would go there to pray, but I did not pray to them; I prayed to Jesus. Then one day my husband asked me, "Why do you want to go there and pray?" But I did not know why I went there; I did not know why I did that. Even now I do not know . . . maybe something sentimental . . . yeah . . . I do not know.

Within a few months I had another spondylitis attack, I was again bedridden and ultimately that led to complete conversion. I threw away all the photos and everything the second time. Now I consider my sickness a blessing. Even now, whenever I get slight pain, I thank him for the pain. Otherwise, he would not have gotten my attention. He had to strike me badly twice to get my attention. Otherwise, I would have been very stubborn. My personal nature is like that. He knows me as he has created me. He knows me. Unlike my husband, who converted immediately when he read the Beatitudes in Matthew, mine was difficult. But anyway he did not leave me like that. It was a wonderful experience.

Q: What were your feelings or thoughts when you realized that Jesus is God?

Praveena: The first thought that came to me was that I was a sinner. What sins? I do not remember. But I was not a . . . I used to be very proud, because we are from a very, very rich family . . . But I was very proud that I was born in such a family. I thought others did not get that opportunity. That itself is a sin, is not it? In God's sight all are equal, but I was very proud.

Q: What was your religious life like before conversion?

Praveena: I used to go to temples, break coconuts [a Hindu religious ritual], and write down the names of gods [another religious practice]. I was admitted in a hospital for ten days because of spondylitis. There also I was writing [the name of a Hindu guru] one hundred thousand times while I was on the bed lying down.

Q: How do you differentiate your religious life now?

Praveena: Before my conversion, I never had any conviction that I was doing something wrong. We just took it for granted that we would be forgiven—that's all. I never did anything wrong; I never had any guilty feeling . . . I never had any assurance also. Rather, we did not think about sin or salvation. I never thought, "When I die, where will I go?" They have all the rituals for the soul, and we were brought up in that way—to believe in that. However, there was no assurance that I would go to god. Nobody tells you about that. You just go there and worship and come back. Though they talk about rebirths, but actually no one believes in it, I suppose. We never had any idea of life after death. Everyone talks about it; I don't think anybody gives a serious thought to it.

Now I am very, very sure that there is only one birth. God created us to worship him and to have fellowship with him. He gives us the assurance of forgiveness of sins and the hope of life after death. My people are not able to understand when I tell them now. But they ask me, "Why did you leave Hinduism?" They question, "Why did you become a Christian?" But I tell them that I did not become a Christian. [The idea of] "Christian" itself was made by man. Jesus did not mention Christianity, but he said, "Believe in me," that's all. I believe in him.

Q: Weren't you worried about leaving your religion?

Praveena: No! I never bothered about leaving my religion or my faith. Nothing bothered me. I was not worried about it.

Q: What were your reactions when your husband became a Christian?

Praveena: I was very angry, very angry. In fact, I even told him, "I will take my children and go away . . ." [Laughs.] But for my parents, [I would have walked away from him]. If I were to leave, a bad name would come to my father's house. [In a South Indian culture, a married woman walking out of a marriage is considered a shame to the parents.] I am very, very sentimental about it. Even now, I am very, very attached to my mother and my father's house. I didn't want to bring dishonor to my father's house by breaking my marriage.

Q: Did you show your anger to him?

Praveena: No! I wouldn't shout. But I told him once and for all, "Never mention about Jesus Christ." He wouldn't; he is a very mild person, unlike me. I told him, "Please don't tell me about Jesus Christ." I think once or twice he tried. But I warned him in the beginning itself, "Please don't tell about Jesus to my children." His friends used to come home, and the moment they came they would start to talk about Jesus Christ, which I didn't like. They would start by telling, "Two thousand years ago Jesus Christ came." I knew all that. But I couldn't tell them because they were his friends. So I told him, "They can come and have whatever they want, dinner or . . . but please tell them not to mention Jesus Christ inside the house." I told him straight away.

Q: When did you first hear about Jesus?

Praveena: I studied in a convent school. My friends used to go to the chapel, but I was terrified to go there. There were photos and I was afraid to go there. I didn't like it. They have a prayer, "Our Heavenly Father . . ." in the assembly before the classes begin, and I wouldn't say that prayer too. I remember that. I studied in [a Muslim college] and somebody gave me all the four Gospels.

    I remember reading John's Gospel, but I never understood. I told my younger brother that among all the four books, I liked John's Gospel. He told me, "Please don't read that. If you read, you will get converted." [Laughs.] He is a very intelligent person. That was many years ago, during my college days. Eventually, I got converted by reading John's Gospel. [Laughs.]

Q: What was your reaction when you got the spondylitis attack?

Praveena: I was very happy. I was not bothered or concerned about the illness . . . The illness did not make me turn to the Lord; it was only because those so-called gods were not responding to me. The feeling that they were not there made me to follow Jesus. So I feel now, after conversion, that it was the Holy Spirit who separated me for three or four days completely for him to make me turn to him. I am grateful to God for giving me the spondylitis that I suffered for many years. But now I am all right. I suffered for three or four years, but I feel the Lord took away the sickness after his intention of converting me. [Laughs.] He took that away. Otherwise, how would he have gotten my attention? I wouldn't listen because I always rejected him.

I was feeling so bad. I was worried about my future and my children because my husband had become a Christian. We lived in a big bungalow. Once, I directly ordered Jesus Christ to get out of my house, "You get away from my house." Twice I ordered him. I remember that I shouted very loudly when nobody was there in the house. I ordered Jesus twice to get away from my house. But he didn't leave me! If I had told you like that, you would go immediately and you wouldn't return. Jesus Christ, being God, he didn't leave me!

I had a strange dream many years before my conversion. There was a big hall and there was a large balcony that was crowded. I was in the downstairs among the people, moving around. I sensed that somebody was looking at me from the balcony. It was crowded. Somebody was wearing a long dress [cloak]. I don't know why the picture came. There was a hood but I never saw his face . . . the face was just blank . . . nothing was there . . . only a hood and a long dress. I could see somebody standing there and staring at me. So I ran away from there. I ran into a long street that had many shops on both the sides and was crowded. I was moving very fast, however, I could sense that person was following me steadily. Whenever I turned, he also turned back, so that I could never see his face. I remember running away from him. That was the end of the dream.

Q: What was your reaction to the dream?

Praveena: I just wondered what it was!

Q: In light of your experience, how do you describe God?

Praveena: He is my Savior. He saved me. God came to take away my sins. He left all the glory and suffered for my sins on the cross. I had no idea about it. I don't know how to put it into words. His love is constant; he is always present. People are not always with us. We depend on people so much, but they are not there always. But he is always with us. I was shocked when I heard the death of my uncle in 1970, because I always looked up to him for each and everything. And in 1987 my father died; it shook me all the more. They have gone, but Jesus is the one who is always with me.

Q: Will you ever go back to your previous religion?

Praveena: [Laughs!] Ha . . . ha . . . Will I go back? Ha . . . ha . . . God willing, no! Ha . . . He is the protector of my faith. Only he is the author and finisher of my faith. So I pray every day that nothing should shake me. Anything can happen. I have heard of so many people backsliding. I used to get scared whenever I read such news. I used to get frightened that it might happen to me. You won't know what will happen in the future. So I ask him to protect my faith. He started this faith in me; he will finish this. I am only a human being. He knows I am weak. Only he knows where I stumble. I don't trust myself, but I trust him.

Q: What is the one significant thing that holds you in Christ?

Praveena: I don't know how to answer this! . . . Salvation . . . and I want to be with him.

Q: Who were the people instrumental in your conversion?

Praveena: Nobody! Not even my husband! My people think that I became Christian for my husband's sake. Even my mother said to me once, "You don't have to become a Christian just because he became a Christian. You can come back." My husband had almost given up hope on me [that she would convert]. Now he is very happy.

Despite her exposure to Christianity for a long time, Praveena never doubted her religion. She recollected in the interview that someone had given her the four Gospels during her college days. She was fond of reading John's Gospel. Nevertheless, when her husband converted, she started hating Christianity and Jesus. Praveena had a dream, but that did not lead to her conversion. Though she did not have any disenchantment with her religion, on her sickbed when she was chanting the names of gods, she felt within her that "they were not there." All of a sudden, she felt that her gods ceased to exist. It was not an acceptable thing for her, so she thought that she was losing her mental balance due to the medicine. It was easier for her to believe that she was becoming mad than to believe that her religion was false. This phenomenon triggered a struggle within Praveena. The result was that she stopped chanting the names of gods.

But a thought came to her to pick up the New Testament and to read at that moment. How could she suddenly think of reading the New Testament? This is unexplainable. On the other hand, she claimed that, humanly, it was impossible for her to get up and pull the suitcase from under the bed to take the New Testament. She was already shaken by the experience of suddenly feeling that all the gods she believed were not real. If she had asked her sister to take the New Testament, she might not have obliged, or Praveena would have felt that it might not be appropriate to let the family know at that stage that she was reading the New Testament. She had an urge to make the move to quench her quest. She claimed that God made her do what was impossible.

We have to make note of the fact that she did not understand anything when she read the New Testament on that day. But whenever the phrase "Verily, verily I say unto you" appeared, she felt something was going to happen. There was no room for rational analysis of the phrase or any claim of understanding what she read. However, she is certain that she had accepted the Lord Jesus Christ on that day and wrote to her husband immediately. Similar to other experiences discussed in this chapter, we find the presence of the "Other" within, communicating a message that led her to convert.

These kinds of experiences made the converts feel that they had received a communication from the divine. The message was always apt to the situation, in which they were searching for a solution. The search could be for the truth, for the true God, for true love, or for a solution to life's crises. While they were reading the Bible or listening to a sermon, a message appropriate to the situation came to their minds as a solution. Sometimes divine communication interrupted them when they did not expect it. They were also convinced that it was from the divine. This is a religious experience where the converts emphasize that they encounter Jesus. The presence and communication of the "Other" is the divine–human encounter that serves as the foundation for their newfound faith. There were no extraordinary elements in some of these conversion experiences; however, they were assured that they had found a solution to their crisis or answers to their ultimate questions.

The timely and suitable message and the conviction that the message was from the divine are the core elements of this experience. Luhrmann in her study of evangelical Christians analyzed this phenomenon. She explained the difference between thoughts and perceptions: thoughts are generated in the mind without external stimulus, and perceptions are stimulated by external sources. Let me illustrate: We know the difference between thinking about a meal that we relished last night (thoughts) and the smell of food cooking in the kitchen that makes us anticipate the upcoming next meal (perception). Luhrmann claims that this difference is blunted when evangelicals speak about God talking to them in their minds. This is made possible through prayer, in which they relate to God as a friend in their minds and hear him speak as if a person were talking. She also found that the participants of her study claimed that God speaks to them while reading the Bible. Luhrmann (2012, p. 41) observes, "These evangelical Christians, then, not only have to accept the basic idea that they can experience God directly; they must develop the interpretive tools to do so in a way that they can authentically experience what feels like inner thought as God-generated. They have to pick out the thoughts that count as God's and learn to trust that they really are God's, not their own, and they have to do so in a way that does not violate the realistic demands of the everyday world." She has proposed a new theory of mind, called *participatory theory of mind*, in which God can participate in the mind, and one can hear him speak in the mind. She points out that such communication from God is noetic; often the participants claimed, "I knew it was true and then I found out that it was" (p. 58). However, she points out that it is a complex process that requires expertise, discernment, practice, and persistence. The characteristics of God speaking to the members of Vineyard Fellowship are similar to the experiences of converts to Christianity; however, converts experienced God speaking to them without any training or practice. Converts to Christianity instantly recognized the voice of God in their minds, and only after did they begin to become familiarized with the voice of God through practice and discernment. Another type of conversion experience involves miracles, where an extraordinary turnaround of a situation happens. We will discuss this in the next chapter.

4 Miracles

> A miracle is a violation of the laws of nature.
>
> —David Hume (1902/2011, p. 50)

> It is the existence and activity of God that sustains the laws of nature rather than the other way around.
>
> —Amos Yong (2008, p. 973)

Do miracles happen? Some converts experience miracles in their lives during difficult times which lead to their conversion. When they face difficulties or hopeless situations divine intervention brings a dramatic turnaround. Miracles are events that evade any natural explanation, but come with the certainty that they are acts of God. The sense of certainty of God's intervention is the religious dimension that makes an event a miracle. Otherwise it could be considered a chance or coincidence. Converts' certainty in interpreting an event in their lives as an act of God leads them to follow Jesus. They consider the miracle as proof or evidence of the truth of Christianity. The event could be a miraculous escape, a solution to a crisis, a healing, an ability to do something that would normally be impossible, and so on. We will discuss here some narratives of miracles that led people to follow Jesus.

Jayasudha, a famous South Indian actor, had acted in about three hundred movies over more than three decades. She is a recipient of the Lifetime Achievement Award of the Andhra Pradesh Cinegoers' Association. She was born a Hindu and studied in a Christian school where she came to know about Jesus. In a news portal, she narrated her hair-raising experience of a miraculous escape. She and her husband went to Bangkok for their honeymoon in 1985. They were riding a water scooter, but only her husband had a life jacket. Since she did not know swimming, she asked her husband to drive slowly. However, when another scooter passed by at high speed, she was thrown out of the scooter and was drowning. She was fond of gods like Jesus, *Venkateshwara*, and *Hanuman*. While she was drowning, she cried out the name of Jesus. At once she saw the face of Jesus under the water, and the next moment she came up floating. She said, "I don't know how I came up or who brought me up. But I know one thing: I saw the face of Jesus Christ in front of me. It was nothing but a miracle that I survived. It took me nearly four months to recover from the shock. I couldn't close my eyes or sleep for several months. It was an amazing experience which I will never forget" (Jayasudha, 2000). After that she became a Christian, and she is now involved in philanthropic activities. Such dramatic experiences have led people to believe in Jesus.

Another woman (whom I will call Ezhil) consumed poison but miraculously survived. She narrated her story:

Ezhil: We are Hindus. Near our house there is a Brethren Assembly. My elder sister used to attend the church, but I never wanted to attend. One aunty [a neighbor] would call me to the church, but I would refuse to go with her. However, my sister would go to the church. I did go to church whenever my mother asked me to bring my sister from the church. But that aunty was concerned that I should be touched by the Lord. I was in the tenth standard. I had a superstition that during the examination time I would pray more to our gods. That aunty shared with me about Jesus, so I prayed to Jesus to help me in my studies. I was weak in English, but by God's grace I was able to pass; however, I discontinued my studies . . . Sometimes I was forced to accompany my sister to church. I was never interested in church activities.

During one Christmas season I had a quarrel with my sister because my parents bought a costly dress for her but not for me. My mother used vulgar words and scolded me. The whole night I cried. I was dismayed and decided to end my life. People use pesticide to kill the worms in coconut trees. The next day I went to a nearby village and in the groves I consumed those poisonous pills. I was expecting that I would die in a moment, and held on to a mango tree tightly but nothing happened! Then I came back to the field to work, but I could not work. I went back to the place where I took the poison and vomited.

At that time I made a small prayer. I prayed, "Lord, if I die now, I will go to hell, but if you save my life now, I will live for you for the rest of my life." I made this prayer then. But truly speaking, whoever consumes those pills would die within five minutes. Many had died like that. But Jesus had kept me alive for himself. After I prayed, I vomited so much and I was rolling down.

People who were working with me in the field carried me for three kilometers, and then reached my village by bicycle. I was admitted in a government hospital. At that time God spoke to me, "If you remain quiet for five minutes, I will give your life back." So I remained quiet. I also prayed, "Lord, I should not feel thirsty or hungry, because those who consume poison would feel thirsty and that would lead to death." I was in drips for three days. They were giving me only glucose—no food, nothing. [She recovered fully.]

Since Jesus saved my life, I started going to church regularly. My parents brought a proposal of a Hindu boy for my marriage. [In India, parents and elders in the family find a suitable life partner for their children, especially for girls.] I requested my brother, "Please find me a Christian boy. I do not want to marry a Hindu boy." But my brother told me, "If your God is a true God, let him change your family." I accepted the challenge because Jesus raised me from the dead [referring to not dying from the poison], and he can transform a Hindu husband too. So I did not oppose my marriage to a Hindu. But I prayed, "Lord, me and my family will serve you. Even if I am married into a Hindu family, I should worship you alone, no one else."

I married a Hindu and moved . . . I told my parents-in-law that I would not worship Hindu gods, and I would worship only Jesus. But they told me, "If you want, you can go to church, but we will not come to church." My husband also told me the same. Initially I did not go to church for about a month, but when I shared the love of God with him [her husband], he said, "You can go, but I will not come." However, he used to come and drop me [at the church]. Then I prayed to the Lord, "God, I wish we both should attend church together." I cried and prayed to the Lord, and Jesus answered my prayer.

After a year, we both started going to church. It was my prayer that I should not have a baby till the whole family come to Jesus. Because they were all Hindus, I thought that they might take my child to a temple and shave its hair and offer it to an idol.

My father-in-law used to go to a temple . . . once in a month to offer *pujas* [prayers] . . . They were in so much debt. I told them that we could stay together [as a joint family] and settle all the debts. We all can go to church together" [Indicating that their financial crisis would be resolved by attending church]. But my mother-in-law told me, "I have my circle of friends and I will not come out of it. But if you want, you can go." But I cried and prayed so much.

My mother-in-law had so much debt and she went away when I was in my mother's place. She had gone to a town to sell her kidney to settle the debts. When I returned, my father-in-law told me all this. I prayed to the Lord that she should not do like that. If she gives away her kidney and returns, I only have to take care of her. I prayed, "You are a true God; you can stop her selling her kidney." In the kidney bank, someone asked her, "Is this what God wanted you to do?" So she dropped that idea [of selling her kidney] and returned home. Since then, my mother-in-law started attending the church. And now all our debts are cleared. As a family, we are saved and happy. My sisters-in-law and father-in-law—everyone in the family—has accepted Christ.

Ezhil consumed poison and expected immediate death, but nothing happened. The fear of death gripped her, and she changed her mind and wanted to live again. Instead of praying to her gods, she prayed to Jesus asking him to save her life. It was a miracle, and her faith in Jesus saved her.

Let me introduce you to a young and wealthy businessman, Kumar. He described his struggle as a teenager suffering from rheumatism. In this narrative you will find more than one episode of divine intervention in different people's lives connected to Kumar.

Kumar: Though my mother comes from a Hindu family, she had faith in Jesus because she was healed from tuberculosis at a young age. She used to tell us about Jesus and taught us, "If you are afraid of anything tell, 'Victory in the blood of Jesus.'" So we had a high opinion about Jesus, but never followed him, because my father was a very devout Hindu and we were brought up in the Hindu tradition. We were deeply religious in the Hindu tradition like our father. We liked our father's religion as well as Jesus.

Though my mother was healed from tuberculosis when she was young, she was not very serious about her faith in Jesus. In 1987, my father's relative was sick and the doctors had given up hope. So they sought many gods. Then they invited one Christian to pray for him, and he was healed. During the prayer, my mother also prayed for her own infirmities and was healed. Her faith was rekindled after the prayer, and she became serious about her faith in Jesus. She began to grow in the Lord. We five brothers also started showing some interest in Jesus since then. My mother started attending a prayer cell and later she began to attend a church. We also began to grow in the Lord.

Whenever there was a problem in the business, my mother would pray to Jesus. Her prayers were answered and the problems were solved on many occasions. So my father allowed her to attend a prayer cell, though, initially, he was very much against her faith in Jesus. He allowed my mother to attend a prayer cell only after his relative was healed by prayer. Later, he would drop my mother at the church, but he wouldn't go inside the church.

Once there was a big crisis in the business [a printing press] and a heavy loss was incurred. We were under heavy debts. Only one machine was working, but then that also stopped working. My father could pay only the interest on the loans. Since this machine also stopped working, he couldn't even pay the interest on the loans. He was totally broke. He told my mother about the situation. She suggested going to an evangelist who was also a Hindu convert for prayer. But my father was hesitant, saying, "How could I go to a stranger and tell him about my problems?" However, my father spoke to him over the phone and the evangelist prayed that God would meet us in our crisis. That gave my father some comfort. He prayed in the morning and the same afternoon the problem got resolved.

So my father started believing in Jesus, but he didn't leave his religion. However, his interest in Jesus began to grow steadily. He allowed us to go to church and he also began to attend church. In one of the memorial services, he was convinced of eternal life and realized that this life is not the only one. Then he decided to take baptism. Three of us brothers also took baptism along with my father. Though I took baptism, there was no change in my life. I liked Jesus, but I was not interested in reading the Bible or praying or even going to church.

I play all games, but I wanted to be a cricket player. I didn't study properly in plus two [final school year] because I was all the time playing. So I didn't get a seat in any engineering college and joined an arts college. Then I fell sick. Doctors couldn't diagnose my sickness exactly, but I was treated for typhoid. I was cured, but I couldn't get up from the bed or walk because of severe pain in my leg. Doctors could not identify the problem. Finally, one doctor diagnosed that it was a rheumatic attack and had affected the bone marrow and the heart. The doctor advised that I had to be under lifelong medication and should not play any games or do any heavy work.

I was only seventeen then and was very disappointed that I could not play any games. I was thinking, "How can I face life!" I couldn't even walk freely. I could not be a normal person . . . My close friends began to avoid me. I felt nothing was lasting in life.

Then I began to read the Bible with a realization that I needed Jesus. When I read the miracles in the Gospels, I asked Jesus, "You did such great miracles, and if you are still alive, why not do a miracle in my life? My disease is not a big thing for you because you have healed a blind man, etc. This is nothing for you." This is how I used to talk to him within myself. Almost every day I was crying and thinking about my condition. I thought that probably I had committed many sins; that is why I was suffering.

At one of the meetings in the church, they were praying for the Holy Spirit. I also prayed and felt I received the Holy Spirit. So I said to myself, "Now I have the Holy Spirit and God has anointed me with his Spirit, so my sickness would have been healed by now." I had been taking the medicines regularly, and once in three weeks I had to take an injection. If I didn't take the injection, the next day I wouldn't be able to walk. Then I decided by faith to stop taking medicine. That particular month, I also decided not to have the injection. I felt that I should exercise my faith, as the Bible says that faith without deeds is dead. One month had gone, and two and then three months had gone, but nothing had happened. I could walk and be normal. Then I realized that the Lord had healed me.

Miracles

Six months later, the doctor came to our house for some other purpose, and my mother told him about my healing. He was surprised to see me normal and wondered— medically it was not possible! Now it has been thirteen years since I stopped taking any medicine for this. Recently I consulted a senior doctor and showed him all the medical reports, and he heard my story. He verified and said, "It was a medical miracle; no one could be healed of this disease completely. You got it at the age of seventeen and it should have relapsed at the age of twenty-six. But if you don't have any problems, it means you are healed. People have suffered like anything. It can only be controlled, but it cannot be completely cured." He advised me to have a checkup once in a while to see whether it relapses any time in the future. I did consult the doctors and they were surprised because when it has affected the heart it should have been more severe by now, but there are no symptoms at all.

When life was smooth, I had forgotten the Lord and got into some problems. Then I returned to the Lord. After 1994 only, I personally experienced the Lord, and my life got transformed. Ever since the Lord healed me, I began to live for him. I began to read the Bible sincerely and I began to tell others about Christ. I realized this is the time that I should do something for the Lord. I started a prayer cell for the youth and started sharing from the Bible. As I read the Bible and started sharing, I found it very useful to me. I could see many changes taking place in my life. Others also were blessed, and then only I understood the power of the Word of God. The Word has power to accomplish, so all my fears about speaking to others about the Lord have gone. I am confident that God will bless my life when I meditate on the word of God day and night.

Q: Are there any changes in your personal life?

Kumar: Yes, there are many. When I took baptism there wasn't any change in my life. But when I accepted the Lord, I could see lots of changes in my life. I believed along with my friends that whatever you get is your lot. They wanted to live by what they see and I did the same. But now I wanted to live for what I have not seen. What I have not seen is permanent and what I could see is temporary; I witnessed this in my life that everything was vanishing. The eternal perspective on life brought changes in my outlook of this life. Earlier the philosophy of my life was to enjoy. Life is meant for enjoyment and I committed many sins. However, I was trying to convince myself that they were not sins, but my conscience used to prick me. It started with small, small sins, but later it led to greater sins. I decided not to watch movies or read unwanted books or materials. It was difficult. I felt miserable whenever I fell into such things. I was not able to lead a good spiritual life. I was keeping my legs in two boats, one life for the Lord and one for the world. That is changed. So there was a big change in my life. Either I should go according to the Lord or according to my friends.

I was lucky that at the age of seventeen I came to the Lord, so I could understand all these things at a young age. I realized that all these things would affect my life later. What I consider sin now was not sin then. Now I want to do only what pleases the Lord. My circle of friends is changed, but I don't disrespect my old friends. Now I keep myself in the company of believers. God has blessed my business greatly and he has strengthened me physically and healed me.

Q: Based on your spiritual experiences, how do you describe God?

Kumar: I have been sincerely walking with the Lord for about twelve years. I cannot count all the blessings he has done in my life. He is always good. When we obey his Word there is nothing lacking in our life. Whatever happens in our life is good for us. God is good. When my father died, all of us brothers never questioned God nor said anything against God, because he is good. His wisdom is great and he has allowed it to happen. I wonder, he being such a great God, why he thinks about me! He is so good. He is great and good.

Q: Will you return to your religion of birth?

Kumar: That is not possible even if I am burned to death. Nothing can make me to do that. Even if my life is threatened, I cannot even entertain such a thought. When I close my eyes here, I will open my eyes in heaven. Then why should I be afraid of death? The fear of death is gone. No one can do anything to my belief. Physical harm can be done, but not to my belief. There is no room for this question at all! There is no room to talk about it. It is not simply for the good things he has done, but what he has stored for us is much greater. It is foolish to leave him. We need to think about the eternal life always. I am even afraid to mention the word "against him"; such a thought should not appear in my mind. I have received so many blessings and have learned about him so much, and he has given me so many opportunities to know him. How could I go back?

My feelings, thoughts, and whole being are bound with Jesus. Jesus is part of my life. I have experienced him. It flows in my life, so there is no doubt about it and no chance of going back. It is not an ideology that we could change. Some have gone back because they have not known the way they should have known Jesus. They probably came with some expectations and for material gain. It is a big loss to leave the Lord.

Q: Who is Jesus to you?

Kumar: Jesus is always with me. He plays different roles at different times. My father is dead, so he is my father. When I am alone, he is my friend. When I pray, he is the person whom I like the most and also whom I fear and tremble before. When I have done something wrong, he is strict in disciplining me. When I am broken, no one comforts me like him. He loves me always and he is a loving God. His love is constant whether he comforts or rebukes. Jesus is a loving God and he deals with me according to the situation.

Q: Who was instrumental in leading you to the Lord?

Kumar: One *akka* [referring to a woman who is older than him]. She never shared the gospel to me, but she was very loving. That made an impact on me. To live like Christ is more important than claiming to be a Christian. Such a life will make an impact on many. She is one such person. She rebukes, but she always loves. I began to accept whatever she says. Even now, I consult her and she prays for me. I am grateful to her.

Kumar began his narrative by saying his mother was healed of tuberculosis. Then he told a story of his relative being healed, and in the same prayer his mother received healing for some other infirmity. He also talked about the crisis in the business that was resolved by prayer. This caused his father to believe in Jesus. Finally, he came to his story of being healed of rheumatism, which led him to experience Jesus personally.

Converts consider such change of situations as proofs that Jesus is real and continues to work miracles.

We need to make note of another aspect in the process of conversion. Kumar took baptism, but he was neither interested in Jesus nor reading the Bible, etc. Only when he received the Holy Spirit did he experience Jesus personally and was healed. The real change in his life began only at this point. Change of religion by fulfilling the prescribed ritual does not necessarily involve divine–human encounter.

Another businessman (whom I will call Devaraj) narrated how a family crisis was resolved by a friend's prayer. He says that the crisis could have claimed his life or even the lives of his whole family, but his friend's prayer changed the situation. He is from a Hindu family and had a printing press with a monthly turnover of ten lakhs rupees [US$ 20,000] at the time of the interview in 2006. Devaraj narrated his conversion:

Devaraj: I come from a Hindu family. In 1981 I accepted Jesus. On that day there was a serious problem in my life. It was a very critical situation. It could not be solved either by man or by money. Earlier on, I had heard about Jesus Christ, but on that day God opened a way for me. I surrendered my life to him, and on the same day the problem was also solved. That was a big surprise for me. Since then, I have slowly come to the Lord.

Q: When was the first time you heard about Jesus?

Devaraj: I heard about Jesus from my childhood days. My grandmother was a follower of Jesus. She often told me about Christ. But I was following my father's ways in the Hindu tradition. My marriage was conducted in Hindu tradition. My wife studied in a Christian school and had some faith in Christ. However, in our family we were following Hindu tradition without any connection to Christian faith. Only when the problem came in 1981 did I fully accept the Lord Jesus.

Q: When did your wife accept Jesus?

Devaraj: She also accepted the Lord on the same day. We both accepted him.

Miracles

In Tamil culture, men normally do not share their problems with anyone, unless the person is a close confidant. Devaraj did not disclose the nature of the crisis in the interview. But I was curious to know what the problem was that led him to convert, so I asked him for details, but he did not want to share with me. I understood the sensitivity and the seriousness of the problem from the tone of his voice as he was talking about it. It had to do with his family and could have claimed either his life or both his and his wife's. This much I could sense from the conversation. We continued:

Q: How far did the crisis affect you?

Devaraj: It was a matter of life and death. If the problem had not been solved, probably it would have been a different situation. We would have been no more!

Q: Was the problem solved on the same day?

Devaraj: It was solved through my elder brother on that day. It was a very critical moment, but it was solved. However, the problem persisted, and in order to solve the problem totally, we began loving the Bible and started reading it and came closer to the Lord. After two years, the problem was totally solved.

Q: Why didn't you try your father's religion to solve the problem?

Devaraj: I had tried on various occasions for other things and was following that way only. I used to go to various temples. I was worshiping my father's gods earlier, but they failed. After my marriage, we didn't have a child for ten years. I was seeking blessings from all the gods, but nothing had happened. But on that day it was beyond anyone to solve the problem. Only after believing in Jesus Christ I found a way for my life.

Q: How did you come to the conviction that Jesus is God?

Devaraj: I have Christian friends who had told me that if I face any problem I could pray to Jesus and he would help me. That day when I faced this problem, I remembered my friend—God only brought his name to my mind. I accepted the Lord because of my friend.

Q: What were your feelings after accepting Jesus Christ?

Devaraj: I received unlimited peace. I could forgive those who were against me.

Q: How could you suddenly forgive?

Devaraj: No, it was not suddenly! But slowly as I was growing in the Lord, reading the Bible, as I moved with Christian friends, I was able to forgive them and start loving them.

Q: What were your family members' reactions to your conversion?

Devaraj: They couldn't accept my conversion. I was a very staunch Hindu. They were shocked and wondered how I could become a Christian! In order to stop me from following Jesus, they went to their deities, made some *pujas* [prayers]. Due to that, we faced a lot of problems. They did some witchcraft against us, and it affected us. But God had revealed many things ahead of the dangers through dreams or through the Word of God. The Lord gave us strength to overcome everything. The same year I accepted the Lord Jesus, I took baptism and I also got the anointment [of the Holy Spirit]. That sustained me in all these situations.

Q: Any examples of warning?

Devaraj: I can say many things. I had to go to make many business trips. For example, if I had to go to Bombay, the Spirit of the Lord would reveal a week before or the previous day through dreams what would happen, like missing a train, or missing my luggage or falling sick, etc. I took these things into consideration and changed my plans. Sometimes I went ahead in spite of the warnings and faced serious problems. Now I take these warnings seriously.

Q: Do you find any changes in your life?

Devaraj: Yes, there are lots of changes. My character is changed. I used to be very shy and introverted. Now I can talk in public and in the family or among friends. God gives me wisdom to deal with any matter, be it matters relating to family or business or any other. Moreover, I have great blessings in my business. Earlier my turnover was very little, but after accepting the Lord my turnover doubled every year. I could see that in my own eyes. By looking at my life, many have accepted the Lord.

Q: Is it the same business?

Devaraj: No! Now I am on my own. [He started his own printing press.] Earlier it was our family business. I faced lots of problems because I couldn't join my brothers in worshiping their gods. However, ever since I accepted the Lord, I prayed to God during 1981 to 2003 for the success of our business. Our family business had increased tremendously. It was the talk of the town. I gave the credit to the Lord, but my brothers would say it was because of their gods. [So he came out of his family business and started his own.]

Q: How does God help you in your business?

Devaraj: Through prayer I get good clients and orders. I could develop my business with God's help. I always pray for a client before I meet him and ask the Lord to give me wisdom to talk to him. I pray, "If the client is good, only then should he continue to have business with me. Otherwise, the client should leave on his own." Now I am getting good clients with big projects.

Q: There is a general opinion that one cannot be honest in running a business. Does accepting the Lord Jesus make any difference?

Devaraj: There were problems in our business after accepting the Lord. On some occasions while dealing with the government, some challenging situations had come. As I was in a joint-family business, I couldn't avoid those situations [indicating that he had to compromise on ethical issues]. That is why I was feeling bad. By 2004, I wanted to be free from the joint business. We are seven brothers. All others are Hindus. As a single person, I could not do anything, so I came out of our family business.

When I started my business independently in 2004, I made Jesus my senior partner. The Lord holds 51 percent and I hold 49 percent. Fifty-one percent of the profit goes to the Lord's work and various ministries. In two years' time, the Lord has been making things possible for me, as he is my partner in my business.

Q: How do you compare your religious life before and after accepting Jesus?

Devaraj: Earlier it was external... only momentary peace... not a lasting peace... and no blessings even. Only after accepting the Lord Jesus, many things have happened . . . and whatever I ask Jesus, he answers immediately—of course, some things takes time. He convicts us of our sins. In all these things I have peace always. When I share with others about my blessings, they accept and receive blessings also. This gives me joy.

Q: How do you describe God?

Devaraj: God is love. He cares. He rebukes when we commit sin. When we call on him, he immediately answers. He delivers us from our troubles and also gives us strength to bear our problems.

Q: Will you go back to your previous faith?

Devaraj: How could I go back? I cannot even think of it . . . I have come to a holy God and heavenly Father. Hereafter I am in his hands only. Like a lamb in his hands, life goes on.

Q: Who is Jesus to you personally?

Devaraj: Personally, Jesus is my refuge. He is the one who counsels me when I call on him in my trouble. He is my adviser and opens the way for me. He gives me the desire to deny the world, flesh, and pleasure. He is a very good friend. Like a mother he comforts me; like a father he carries me; like a brother he gives me advice. All in all, he is for me.

Q: What is the one significant thing that keeps you with Jesus?

Devaraj: As I said earlier, when all had forsaken me, money could not solve the serious crisis, friends couldn't solve it, relatives couldn't do anything, but on that day Jesus solved my problem. Like a father, he helped me on that day. That's why no one could separate me from his love.

Q: Who was instrumental in leading you to Christ?

Devaraj: It was my friend. He is from a well-known family in this town. Earlier his life was very bad and he lived a wicked life. But when he accepted the Lord his life was completely transformed. I knew how his life was three or four years prior to his conversion. After he became a child of God I know how his life got transformed. It was a total transformation. He became loving, prayerful and interceding for others. He was liberated from his wicked life. His life was a challenge to me. He used to tell me, "Believe in Jesus and he will give you peace."

When I faced this problem, immediately I thought of him. He prayed for me and also introduced other men of God to me. I cannot forget that day. On the same day one Christian lady came to our house in the afternoon. She felt that God had spoken to her that she should come to our house to pray for us. Though we faced the problem only in the evening, she came in the afternoon to pray, and she prayed with tears for us.

Devaraj knew about Christianity since his childhood through his grandmother, but he never believed. When his friend's life was dramatically transformed, he knew it was due to his conversion to Christianity. However, he never felt his own need to accept Jesus. It was only when he faced a serious crisis and when he felt helpless that he tried Christianity. The problem was resolved on the same day that led him to follow Jesus.

Converts attribute the cause of inexplicable change in their situation to the divine. It could be a matter of healing, a miraculous escape from danger, a solution to a crisis, or being successful and so on. There was no human explanation for the change of situation and was considered a miracle. They could not find a rational explanation, but acknowledged the role of the divine. The belief that it was an act of God, a miracle, is based neither on a rational exercise nor on a prior belief. This sense of certainty that it is an act of God made converts believe in Jesus, contrary to their previously held religious belief. This is the divine–human encounter in this type of religious experience. The event could have been taken as a chance or coincidence, but because of the divine–human encounter the person believes it is an act of God. This perception alters one's self-image and the direction of life. It results in following Jesus. Converts feel confident that the divine is interested in their life and that leads to conversion and transformation of life.

Alister Hardy (1979/1984, p. 139) in his study of religious experience talked about experimental faith and differentiated it from general experiential faith. Experimental faith is that one arrives at based on an experiment or test or trial. He added, "To become a real faith the word 'chance' in the definition must become converted into 'certainty' by the very experiment having succeeded." Luhrmann (2012) observes that evangelicals view certain events as miracles that might be viewed by skeptics as coincidences. Converts do not accept a new religion immediately when they hear about it. They try out the claims of Christianity, not necessarily with great faith, but with a mixed faith. However, when something inexplicable happens that comes with a sense of certainty that it is an act of Jesus, they take it as a miracle. They test the workability of Christianity in their lives and the miracles are considered evidences that Jesus is real. Then they convert to Christianity. We will discuss religious experience associated with prayer in the next chapter.

5   Prayers

> As men's prayers are a disease of the will, so are their creeds a disease of the intellect.
>
> —Ralph Waldo Emerson (2008)

> In prayer, spiritual energy, which otherwise would slumber, does become active, and spiritual work of some kind is effected really.
>
> —William James (1902/2004, p. 411)

Prayer can be a ritual for many. But for converts, prayer is an acid test and a channel of communication with the divine. When prayers are answered by Jesus, converts accept him. Exposure to Christianity shakes the belief of the converts in the religion of their birth. They begin to see the inconsistencies in the religion of their birth in light of their exposure to Christianity. However, at this stage they are not willing to accept Christianity. This struggle makes them call on a generic God—not using any name or symbol or identifying the divine with any particular religion. Such prayers are answered by Jesus. Some pray to Jesus for various situations in their lives, from the simple to the very threatening, and find their prayers answered by Jesus. Answered prayers are taken as proofs of the claims of Christianity and then people convert.

In this study, some prayed to a generic God, while others prayed to Jesus for various reasons. Teenagers prayed for their success in studies or for admission into the courses of their choice. Others prayed for healing or deliverance from witchcraft. However, they all found Jesus answering their

Transformative Religious Experience

prayers. In this chapter, we will discuss some of the religious experiences associated with prayer that led to conversion. Jemmu Bai, a man from one of the tribes in the Western India, was suffering from some kind of sickness that could not be healed. He prayed and a saw a vision.

Jemmu Bai: I was born in a family with ten magicians and had a family god of our own, which we faithfully and religiously served. I owned a big farm where groundnuts were grown and owned a flour grinding machine. I had several cattle and flocks too, but had no peace of mind and true blessing. The groundnut farm was infested with pests and ran into a loss. The grinding machine ceased to work and my flocks and cattle started dying one by one. I was very sick and none of the ten magicians in the family could help me in any way. I lost my peace. I sought the help of several doctors and magicians and spent 50,000 rupees [US$ 1,000]. I went up to Maharashtra and Madhya Pradesh to treat my sickness, but could not find peace or deliverance that I was so badly seeking for.

On June 4, 1998, Friday, I was lying on a bench and telling myself, "If there is a true God, please reveal yourself to me today, or else tomorrow I will kill myself by falling on the railway track." I said this and went off to sleep.

Suddenly, I saw a ladder coming from heaven. On one end stood a man who said, "I am the true God and my name is Jesus." He made me to climb the other end. The ladder went up and was lengthened till it reached a Christian home, four kilometers away ... where a meeting was going on, and there it stopped. The one who stood on the ladder came down and told me to enter the house. He said he would reveal himself to me there. Then he and the ladder disappeared.

Later Jemmu Bai located that particular Christian home and attended worship on a Sunday. There he learned more about Jesus, and he adopted Christianity. Nathan, a chartered accountant, reported his experience of struggling with the ultimate question, "Who is the true God?"

Nathan: After schooling, I joined a college for a commerce degree and one of my friends joined an engineering college. We were always together during our school days ... He had become a Christian and met all our friends and told them about Jesus. At that time I was in the hostel. It seemed that his life was completely transformed.

When I went home for a vacation, all my friends told me, "So-and-so has become a Christian and changed his name. He has taken all his friends to a church." When I heard this, I was so annoyed. I met some of them and asked, "Why did you go to church with him?" They said that their life was transformed after going there. A few had even changed their names.

One day I confronted him [the friend who had become a Christian] and asked him, "Why are you converting people?" But I could see a great change in him. He was totally different ... He stopped watching television, etc. I was the only person who would argue with him while all the other friends were quietly listening to him. I was pulling his leg by saying, "You've got only one god, but we have many gods."

However, during the summer vacation, all of us would go for a walk. He would share from the Bible, and ask for prayer requests. During this time, I asked other friends, "Why did you convert?" And they told me about the changes in their lives.

At that time, I struggled within myself about watching movies, reading sex books, masturbation, etc. I was interacting with these friends and I began to feel that I was doing something wrong, though these habits were not considered as great sins. Everyone knew me as a good boy, but I was not. I was good only outside. My conscience, however, started pricking me because I was a hypocrite. I began to see my real self and my thoughts were impure.

I asked my friend what changed him because he was also like me. He said, "Jesus Christ changed me." I asked, "What Jesus, Jesus? Tell me, how could your life be transformed?" Another friend told me, "If you believe and are faithful, then you will experience transformation in your life."

Nathan could not accept the fact that conversion to Christianity would transform somebody. On one hand, he was upset that his friends became Christians. On the other hand, he could not understand how his friends' lives were transformed dramatically. He began to feel miserable about his own life in light of his friends' transformed lives. Another incident made him think about the power of Jesus.

Nathan: My village church has an evangelist. She was freed from the attacks of evil and witchcraft. Once she was about to die, but she was delivered miraculously. It was a big question to me, how she could be delivered. She didn't have any hope. Her family members felt that if she died, the demons would not attack them anymore, so purposely they left her outside the house and closed the doors, thinking that she would die soon. That night she saw a vision of Jesus standing above the Earth. The next morning they came out to see her dead, but to everyone's surprise she was alive. She told them that she had seen Jesus. Later she went to a church and prayed and one by one the demons left her. She began to do ministry. These kinds of testimonies challenged me, and I began to feel that there was something in it.

However, I was not ready to accept Christianity. My father was a devotee of *Murugan* [a popular deity in Tamil Nadu] and I too. Daily after having a bath, I used to go to the temple and circle it three times. But I didn't know much about the theology and philosophy behind it. I was only following the practices I had learned. I thought there is one God and each one has his own religion. But I couldn't accept Jesus as the true God.

The fact that I was good outside, bad inside was troubling me. One day, as I was alone, I felt an urge to pray. But I didn't want to pray to Jesus as I was not sure who the real God was. So I prayed, "I don't know who you are. I have committed many wrongs. I am ready to accept the punishment for the wrongs I have done. I want to be good, but I am unable to. Help me." Immediately, after I had said this, there was a great joy that flooded my heart, and my heart was bubbling with joy. Since then, I began to sincerely seek to learn what is in this faith.

While I was in the hostel, I was given a New Testament. As the cover was attractive, I kept it with me, but I never had any intention of reading it. Then I searched for the New Testament and began to read. I also went and talked to the evangelist in the church. I began to seriously think about Christianity. I started reading the New Testament before going to sleep. I also started going to church secretly.

My parents thought that I was going with my friends elsewhere. I didn't think about my family at that time. One day a special speaker came to the church. I went to hear him and this news reached home that I had gone to church. My father scolded me for going to church, [saying] that our way was different and I should not do this. That was the first time I faced opposition from home.

I was wondering what to do! I thought, "If I accept the Lord Jesus Christ, I will go to heaven. But since my family says no to this, they would go to hell. Why should I be separated from my family?" I was telling my friends that my parents were against it, so I would not proceed further and I wanted to quit. My friends encouraged me, "Don't leave this because of one person. Your whole family could turn to the Lord." But I said, "I am not going to continue this. This will not be suitable for me."

As usual, that night also I read the Bible, and it was Acts 16:31: "Believe in the Lord Jesus, and you will be saved—you and your household." I felt the Lord was speaking to me. Prior to this, I never knew how the Lord speaks. This verse gave me some kind of assurance that if I am sincere and faithful, my family would also come to the Lord. Since I got this hope, I decided that I should not leave the Lord, but follow him secretly. My family thought that since they had warned me I would have stopped it.

In the second year, my roommate was a Christian and I used to hide the New Testament within other books and read secretly. After many days, while I was praying, he came to know that I was a Christian. He told the leaders of Evangelical Union in the hostel about me. Then I started attending the prayer cell, but would hide my Bible in a bag and go.

I was struggling with fantasies. I realized that it was due to reading the sex books, watching movies, and talking to friends about dirty things. So I began to avoid all those things. I lost my interests in all those things. In my college, there was a welcome party for the first-year students and we all went for a movie, but I was reluctant to go with them. Still I went and sat inside the movie hall, but I couldn't enjoy watching the movie and I felt miserable. I sat there with my head down and later, I walked out of the movie hall. That was the first time that I couldn't enjoy a movie and was the last time I went to a theater. I could feel a growing dislike towards watching movies.

One day I decided that I should inform my parents. I wrote a letter explaining my bad behavior as a boy and how my life was transformed. They had been to a *Murugan* temple to offer hair. On their return, when they received the letter they were very much annoyed. My father was a respected man in my village, and people seek his advice. He felt that hereafter nobody would respect him or listen to him. He was feeling very bad and wondered, "How could someone from a [higher] caste become a Christian!" [Christianity is always associated with the lowest caste.] My brother had committed suicide [for some reasons], so they were afraid to confront me, thinking that if they tried to control me I might also take that eventual step. So there was not much opposition from my home. In fact, my brother's suicide helped me this way.

The prayer cell and graduates [senior believers and volunteers in the student movement of Evangelical Union] helped me to grow steadily in the Lord. I had a burden for souls and began telling other students about Christ. My friends used to make fun of me, saying, "You always used to put the sacred ash on your head. How come you are converted?" I didn't bother their comments. There was a big problem in the hostel because another Hindu student was also attending the prayer. College authorities came to know about the prayer cell, and we were warned that we should not continue the prayer anymore. It was difficult to face all these things at that time. Since then, we were having prayer meetings secretly. This is how I grew in the Lord.

Q: What made you to hold on to Jesus in spite of the opposition?

Nathan: The Word of God only is my anchor. Whenever I read the Bible, it speaks to me according to my situation. I understood that it was not only me, but everyone has gone through this path. The opposition was not a big issue because I had the Word of God with me. The Lord himself said that the world would hate you. And he himself had gone through such situations. I came to know that family won't support anyone in his or her spiritual journey because the Lord himself faced this—his brothers didn't understand him. In the fellowship, we were taught all these things. The fellowship was very helpful.

Q: What were the changes happened in your life?

Nathan: Earlier God was not a big thing in my life. Whenever I go out, I think of God [for seeking his protection]. My devotion was only at that level. When I started reading the Bible, I began to think about

God. Earlier I sought God only for my needs. But now I think of him as my creator, feel the need of pleasing him, and am conscious of not doing anything that displeases him. I am able to see his blessings in my life. When I was thinking about my future, after my B. Com. [Bachelor of Commerce], I never thought of doing CA [Chartered Accountant]. I was anxious about what to do next. But I got a job in a Christian office, and later I passed two levels of CA exam. It was a big surprise that I cleared those exams. The present office is also a blessing from the Lord that I am able to directly move to this level. [He has his own auditing firm, which had been developed by his friend who moved out of the city, which then Nathan took over. This gave him the advantage of not having to start his own business from scratch.] It's a big miracle.

Regarding my marriage, my family thought that I would marry someone from another caste. However, my parents were happy because the girl was from the same caste. It was not in order to please them, but it worked out in that way. [Marriage is a serious issue for converts in India. The family might accept the conversion reluctantly, but marrying someone from another caste is a bone of contention between the family and the convert.] I could see God's guidance and blessings in my life.

Q: How do you describe God based on your spiritual experience?

Nathan: God wants to have a personal relationship with individuals. He lives in us. He is a personal God. I cannot say I know everything; I am still learning to know him.

Q: What is the one thing that holds you to Jesus?

Nathan: It is the transformed life. I have a clear conviction about sin and repentance. I got freedom from sins. Later, I understood what Christ has accomplished for me on the cross. Other things are insignificant.

Q: Who is Jesus to you personally?

Nathan: He is God. He is like a friend who is nearer to me. When we say "God," he seems far away, but he is closer to us than a friend.

We can see Nathan's annoyance at his friend influencing other friends to become Christians. He was very upset and agitated that his friend got converted to Christianity and got all their other friends to follow him. He did not agree that the transformation in his friend's life was due to conversion. He was not ready to accept Jesus. However, the sense of moral hypocrisy within him drove him to seek the same solution that his friends talked about. However, he did not want to pray to Jesus but prayed to a generic God, "I do not know who you are." He claimed that he was filled with joy immediately and had a desire to read the New Testament. Though he did not address his prayer to Jesus, he felt that the answer was from Jesus and that the joy that he received was an indication of the forgiveness of his sins. Such conviction that Jesus answered his prayer was taken as a proof. This is the divine–human encounter in his conversion. Though there was nothing to indicate that Jesus answered his prayer, he had the certainty that his prayer was answered by Jesus. The divine is revealed in this manner in the divine–human encounter.

Let me illustrate with a prayer of Balan, an engineer by profession, who hails from a Brahmin family. He was exposed to Christianity during his school days since he had studied in a Christian school. He had a Bible with him that he got at the school. All of a sudden he was interested in reading the Bible while he was in college and began to question his religious beliefs and practices. He described his experience of prayer:

Balan: I began to think within myself, "Should I try to ask God who he is rather than just believing what I have been taught all these years?" Slowly I started praying to a generic God, not with any name and not with any figure. This went on for months. Maybe due to my past experience, or some other reason I didn't know, I started praying to Jesus. It was a very different kind of experience . . . It was a very different kind of experience for me. Somehow it was . . . the religious experience I had over the years was very different, but the experience of praying to Jesus was very personal.

I asked Balan to explain further about the change in praying to Jesus. He was struggling to describe how he moved from praying to a generic God to Jesus:

Balan: I cannot really explain it. I was praying to God. I was just praying and realized that idol worship was wrong. Until then, I was holding on to what my parents had taught me for about twenty years. But somehow at that time I felt that it was wrong and maybe there was something beyond idols. I thought, if so, I needed to know about that God. Somehow the more I wanted to pray to God, I began praying to Jesus. It was almost . . . unconsciously . . . the more I tried to seek God, somehow it was Christ that I was looking up to. Maybe because I had the Bible with me, it pointed to Jesus. I don't really . . . I cannot clearly say why I switched over and looked up to Jesus. But somehow I felt that I should be praying to God and it so happened that it was Jesus; he was the first person who came to my mind. Whatever I prayed, no matter whether small or big, my prayers always got answered. I experienced some kind of feeling when I prayed to Jesus. I never had such experience in my previous religion.

Q: Is it possible to recollect what kind of feelings you had?

Balan: Yeah . . . I had mixed feelings. It was the most joyful experience, yet somehow I was struggling with my personal life. I used to observe the rituals to please my gods. But internally, I knew that my entire nature was sinful; I was doing a lot of things. My thoughts and deeds in college life, especially, were not good and were not pleasing in God's sight.

But when I accepted Jesus the consciousness of sin was strong. Though moving with friends and watching something bad were not big sins earlier, now I am sensitive to such habits. I was always scared—not that I am afraid of God, but always I am conscious that God is with me. He is always watching me. I was not forced in any way. But I felt that I need to respond to this God who loves me. At the same time, he is also holy. Somehow, my own sinfulness was coming back to me and that was . . . what pointed me to Jesus.

Q: Are you saying that consciousness of sin came after coming to Jesus?

Balan: Correct.

Transformative Religious Experience

Q: What is the gain in believing in Christ and feeling guilty about all that you enjoyed in your life?

Balan: Earlier, spiritual life and worldly life were two separate entities. If you don't smoke, don't drink, or hang out with bad guys then you are good . . . I did not have any of these bad habits.

Once, everyone else in the class had the question paper that was leaked, but I did not get it. It was very tempting; maybe if I did not have Christ I would have gone ahead [doing what others did]. Now it is not about scoring good marks or being successful, but pleasing God is the driving force in my life. Now the whole concept of success is redefined. For me, being right is the most important thing. Maybe if I were an unbeliever, I would have taken up the paper and scored good grades and that was the sensible thing to do. But now it is not getting good marks, but there is something else. Pleasing God is the most important thing in my life. I think that is the major difference.

Q: What were your thoughts on leaving your family, culture, and religion?

Balan: Yes! At least for the first two years, it was a great struggle for me, and it was a great struggle. I knew that accepting Christ would mean a lot of trouble for me. I was concerned about my family accepting me and me marrying a Christian. Being a Christian means following a different culture in India. So I was really scared for the first two years. Initially when I accepted Christ, I did not reveal that to anyone except to a few close friends. Nobody knew that I believed in Jesus. In fact, at home when they called me for *pujas* [prayers], I used to go and stand there, but in my heart I prayed, "Lord I am worshiping you, not the idols." That's how life was. I was very scared. Somehow I knew that I was supposed to please God. However, I was worried about my family—how they would feel. Certainly I would not hurt them and make them feel bad. But I knew that if I am pleasing God he would take care of everything. Even if I had to go through some trials or some kind of problems at home, he was always there with me. So, slowly, over a period of two years I overcame the hurdles and was formally baptized and converted to Christianity.

Q: What made you hang on to Jesus despite all the troubles?

Balan: No one encouraged me. It was just the relationship between me and Christ that enabled me to hold on to Jesus. I was not even going to church. No one knew that I became a Christian. Somehow the experience I had ... I didn't want to lose. At one point, I was thinking, "Let it be secret all through my life. Maybe I will stay on like this and even marry a girl of my parents' choice and live as a secret Christian. I would still be God's child." But somehow the whole idea got changed. I knew that I could not have both, half of this and half of that. I needed to take a decision and be on one side. Having the experience of Christ in my life, I knew the right thing to do, even if it meant going against my traditions, values, and rituals that I was holding on to.

Q: Did you inform your parents?

Balan: No, I did not inform them. Even today they do not know that I am baptized and converted. But I was caught on a few occasions. They noticed the changes in me. Earlier, I was spending most of my time with my friends, going for movies, and spending a lot of money. Being the youngest in the family, I was pampered. I never used to respect anyone, and I complained about everything. It was a different life. But when I accepted Christ they saw the changes in me. They also caught me while praying and reading the Bible. They told me, "Don't do all these things; you can do it after we die. Don't leave your religion; you can pray to any god you want." I never came across a situation in which I had to tell them that I was baptized. I didn't feel the need to inform them. They knew that I pray to Jesus and noticed the changes in me. I don't participate in any of the *pujas* or festivals; however, they never questioned me. Initially there were some troubles. They used to argue with me that I was not right.

In fact, my respect and love for my family grew more after accepting Christ. I did not displease them or dishonor them in any other way. They also knew that I was not lavish anymore, not going around with my friends, having fun like all the others. I was also doing ministry by visiting an old-age home. They noticed that something was different in me. They saw that my attitude towards everyone in the family changed. After some time they let me have my way. I foresee my marriage as the next hurdle.

That was Balan's experience of praying to a generic God and then feeling that he was drawn to Jesus. However, he could not explain how the

Transformative Religious Experience

transition happened. It was not a conscious choice he made, but something made him pray to Jesus, and he felt his prayers were always answered. He differentiated the experience of praying to Jesus from his former experience of praying. He found praying to Jesus a different kind of experience that he could not explain.

In the narratives presented above, we saw that Jemmu Bai tried his religion for healing but never was healed. So he prayed to God, wanting to know who the real God is who could heal him. He got an answer in the form of a vision, in which the person introduced himself as Jesus, the true God. Nathan had prejudices against Christianity in spite of seeing the transformed lives of his friends. However, at one point he decided to pray to a generic God. He claimed that he got an instant answer to his prayer and was filled with joy and happiness. Balan prayed to generic God for a few months and later he slowly started praying to Jesus. He was not sure of how the shift occurred. Sania, whose vision we discussed in the first chapter, got an answer immediately when she prayed to a generic God to reveal who he was. She saw a vision of Jesus. Komala prayed to generic God, wanting to know who the true God is, and saw Jesus in a dream. Sadhu Sunder Singh, a Sikh convert, is another person from history who prayed to a generic God and got a vision of Jesus.

To find answers to their ultimate questions, converts approached the divine. When their deeply held beliefs were shaken, they called on the divine without using any name or symbols. This was the first step in moving away from the religion of their birth and one step closer to accepting Jesus. Their prayers addressed to a generic God were answered by Jesus. Converts were surprised rather shocked to have their prayers answered by Jesus because it was contrary to their expectation. However, when they received the answer they accepted Jesus as the true God. This triggered a quest to know more about Christianity and eventually led them to follow Jesus.

On the other hand, converts prayed to Jesus to test whether he would answer their prayers. Let me illustrate with some experiences of answered prayers. A student told the person who presented Christianity to him that if he passes the higher secondary school exams he would believe in Jesus. To his surprise, he passed and he believed in Jesus. Another student was suffering from tuberculosis. His teacher prayed for him and he was healed, and he also stood first in school. These things made him believe that Jesus answers prayers. A woman named Ezhil consumed poison, but then decided she did not want to die, so she prayed to Jesus to save her life and she escaped. Since her prayer was answered, she decided to follow Jesus. Kemiben, a tribal woman who was suffering from chronic stomach pain, attempted to hang herself, but her mother intervened and saved her. Her mother took her to a church for prayer. The missionary prayed for her and she was healed instantly. Another woman prayed for a solution to a crisis. She said, "We as a family went through a critical situation. It was a painful experience. We cried and prayed to Jesus. The crisis came like a storm, but it went away as if it were nothing. We could feel God's presence. Only God had solved it. Otherwise, we would have been no more." Converts prayed or requested others to pray for them. When these prayers were answered they began to believe in Jesus.

Sushila, a poor woman, narrated her story of suffering due to her sickness and how she was delivered by Jesus:

Sushila: I am from a Hindu family and did not know anything about Jesus. We are not educated, and we did not know anything about the Bible. But my husband is an educated man and a Catholic. We were happily married till our third child was born. We had our own shop, and I was taking care of it.

Often I used to suffer with severe headaches. I was on self-medication because I thought it was an ordinary headache. I would take Anacin tablets and did not care much about my health. I would be working in the shop for the whole day. After heavy work I would get a severe headache and I would feel dizzy. I used to feel itching on one side of my head; on other side I used to feel some kind of burning sensation. Sometimes the headache was unbearable; I would roll on the floor. Whenever I consulted a doctor, always he would say, "Nothing to worry! You should eat nicely and take proper rest." My family took me to several doctors and all of them said the same thing: that I should eat nicely and take proper rest. But I could not eat properly. If I forced myself, then I would vomit. I was in such a bad shape.

Some suggested that if I go to Hindu temples and offer my hair I would be healed. I did that too. Once when I returned home from the temple, I found all the three children were down with fever. At that time my third child was only three or four months old. I was holding her in my hands, while I myself was in a dying condition.

Finally, my family took me to a doctor in [another town]. It happened sixteen years ago. They hurriedly took me to him. He said, "She will live only for ten days. There is no hope for her." He said that I had a tumor in my brain and it had to be operated. They could not take any scans as there was no such facility. So he suggested us to take a scan in [another city]. He could give the details only after getting the scan report. But he told my husband, "You are an educated man. Do not let your young wife suffer like this. No one can cure cancer. She might live only for ten days. But things will happen according to her fate. Take her home." He also gave me some medicines worth 400 rupees [US$ 8]. We bought the medicines. I was trying to walk but couldn't. I was gripped with a fear of death. I was in deep sorrow, thinking that I would die in ten days.

You would not know how I felt! Even my mother one day asked me, "Haven't you died yet! Are you still alive! We sold all the property for treating you, why should you live anymore?" Everyone despised me. I sat alone with my three children and cried. I did not have anyone to console me. I was so sad and down in my spirit that I was going to die. I felt no one was there for me.

One Christian man used to visit our house. He asked me, "What happened? You used to be healthy, and now what happened?" I told him, "I was suffering from severe headaches and the doctor told me that I would live only for ten days. My husband went away leaving me to die, and even my father and mother also have abandoned me. I don't have anyone. I am left alone to die." I was broken and cried a lot. He told me, "Jesus would never leave you . . . You pray to Jesus and he will definitely save you." I didn't even ask him how to pray.

About 7:00 at night I closed the door. I did not know how to pray, but I had seen some Catholics kneeling down while praying. I could not even kneel down because I was very weak. I said, "Jesus, save me. Hereafter, I will not watch television and tell lies. I will be truthful and will not commit any wrong." The biggest sin I did was that I used to watch movies in television—nothing else. So I said, "I will not do those things anymore. Jesus, at any cost, you must save me because I do not have anyone. My husband left me and my parents too have abandoned me. That brother [the one who told her about Jesus] told me that you would not leave me. So you must save me." I don't know how I prayed, but with tears [I prayed] and then I slept.

As I was sleeping, I saw a bright light coming towards me. We had a big tree in front of our house. As if there were ten tube lights lit together, it was so bright; it was very bright. I saw a cross in the light. I never saw a cross like that and I felt someone was talking to me from the cross. The light splashed and went back. Then I got up with a fear. But I could find some kind of relief in my body. I felt some kind of spirit left my body, but I didn't know. It was a spirit only. Then I became all right. I felt better then.

I wanted to see my husband because it was three days since he had left. So I prayed, "God, you please bring him back to me." As I was thinking of him, he came in and said, "I went to [another city] for three days, but I couldn't stay without you." After many months, only on that day he asked me, "Did you eat?" I was very happy that he asked me. I felt that it was Jesus who made this possible and my husband was back.

The following day was a Sunday, and I wanted to go to church. I did not know where a church was. I took my three children and went by walk. I was not able to walk; I do not know how I walked. While entering the church, two of my children started crying and telling me to go home. I felt some kind of spirit was preventing me entering the church. The pastor was filled with the Holy Spirit and praying, and I could feel some kind of evil spirit leaving me. Then I could freely enter the church. That was the day the Lord delivered me. It has been sixteen years since then. By the grace of the Lord, I was saved in 1989. Till today the Lord has given me life, a house, and a blessed family. The Lord has been leading us graciously. I was dead once, but now I am alive. I tell my testimony wherever I go. Without Jesus, I cannot live. Jesus only gave me life. I don't know how to tell . . . [She cries.] I was dead once, but he has given me my life back and kept me alive.

Sushila claims that her small prayer saved her life and that she received healing. Prayers for divine help were made by the converts or by others on behalf of them. Whether it was their own prayer or a prayer on their behalf, their prayers were answered by Jesus. They began to believe that Jesus answers prayers, and that he would do so in the future as well.

Answered prayer is a predominant religious experience associated with conversion. Moreover, many converts claimed answered prayer as a

Transformative Religious Experience

subsequent religious experience after conversion. Both men and women found this type of religious experience pivotal for them in changing their religious belief. The sense of one's prayer being answered by Jesus gave them the impetus to trust in Jesus. Some tried their own religion to solve a crisis and got disillusioned when there was no response to their prayers. When they tried Jesus, they were surprised that it worked. This increased their faith in the new religious option. Such an experience gave them the certainty of having known the God who answers their prayers. It gave them the assurance that Jesus would always help them.

I would now like to draw your attention to another convert, Aravind, who prayed to Jesus with great expectation of healing. There was no healing, however, he still converted to Christianity, claiming that his inner being was healed. He is a professor in a college and from a Hindu family.

Aravind: I had a peculiar belief that all religions are the same. Near my home in the village there is a Catholic church. Though, I was a devoted Hindu, I would go there and worship. I was trying to lead a righteous life. When I was in the ninth standard, some Christian friends had distributed Christian literatures. One was about a correspondence course that was offered from Bangalore, and at the end of the course they would give attractive certificates.

So I started reading the literature with two motives. One was to get the attractive certificates and the other was to find a job in a Christian institution, assuming those certificates would fetch me such a job. I started reading the course material that was sent from Bangalore. I gained some theoretical knowledge of Christianity and Christ. It was purely a theoretical input. The literature didn't say anything about personal experience, etc.

Then, towards the end of the ninth standard, I was down with jaundice and related complications. I was gripped by the fear of death. I was very scared thinking of dying at the age of fourteen or fifteen. I was very young and the fear of death gripped me like anything. I became helpless. Something happened within me. Whatever I read about Jesus Christ from the Gospel portion flashed in my memory. Then I decided, "If I pray to the Lord Jesus, probably he will heal me—really cure me and remove the fear of death." I didn't know how to pray and nobody was at home or in the village [to teach him how to pray].

I mumbled a few words. I don't know what kind of prayer it was. I don't remember the date either. So I mumbled a few words in prayer and expected a dramatic healing to take place. I was really disappointed at that time because nothing had happened. My disease was not healed, nor was I freed from the fear of death.

But I experienced some changes in my attitude. Later I started reading the Scriptures and understood that when someone invites Jesus he would experience a great change. Then in the course of time, I, by simple faith, stopped taking medicine and my jaundice was gradually healed . . . Then I realized, first I had experienced inner transformation and then physical healing. Of course, if God had allowed healing first before the inner transformation, probably I wouldn't have surrendered at the feet of the Lord Jesus Christ. So inner transformation happened earlier, followed by physical healing.

Then I became an ardent follower of Jesus Christ and started reading the New Testament given to me by one of my Christian friends in my village. Unfortunately, there were only a few Christian homes and families. In a remote village there was a small church. I needed fellowship and I did not have a chance to grow in the Lord. I faced opposition for practicing my newfound faith. I was not able to grow in the Lord. I had many doubts. "How Jesus could be the only true and living God? We have many gods and deities." I was oscillating with doubts, but I never stopped praying or reading the Bible.

In 1977, when I joined a college . . . I was interested in attending the Bible study by the Evangelical Union in my college. They gave me fellowship and nurtured me in the faith. And then I was growing steadily.

Q: What were your feelings when your prayer was not answered?

Aravind: I was praying with lot of expectation, thinking, "God is going to deliver me from the disease as well as from the fear of death." With a sense of anticipation and anxiety I prayed.

I was actually disappointed because I had read in the Scriptures and in the lessons that Jesus healed many people, delivered many from demonic attacks, is living today, and [that] if we believe in him he would do the same. So I felt those claims were not true in my life. That was a contradiction—a contradiction between what I read and what had happened to me.

Transformative Religious Experience

Q: If so, what made you to pray continually?

Aravind: Though I was not healed, my life was transformed. There was a dramatic change. I experienced a transformation in my attitudes and bad habits. It was a turnaround, a complete change of life. My attitude was changed and my friends could notice the changes in me. I became a new man. I started enjoying my new relationship with the Lord. I felt as if I were born in a different kingdom. The transformation that I experienced made my faith in the Lord unshakable. Probably if I had not experienced these changes, I would have lost my faith.

Q: What do you mean by inner transformation?

Aravind: Okay, I was a teenager studying ninth standard. I was trying to lead a righteous life and godly life. But in my inner most being I had a battle. I was trying to lead a godly life, but the forces within me were trying to pull me down. So it became impossible for me to lead a godly life. I was occupied with bad thoughts and evil thoughts. I thought, "If I go on [like this] my life will be a mess in the company of bad friends." My friends were trying to do everything that was bad. So I felt that I was going in a wrong way . . . When I made a decision to follow Lord Jesus, I experienced transformation.

Q: Did the changes happen immediately after prayer?

Aravind: It was gradual. I won't say that it was sudden. It was over a period of time—gradual. It may have been over a week, but not sudden.

Q: Who is Jesus to you?

Aravind: He is more of a personal friend. Even my wife cannot understand me, but he can understand me. He can accept me as I am. He is God.

Similar to Aravind, Manjuben, a tribal woman, came to missionaries hoping for a physical healing, but she was never healed. However, she held on to her new faith in spite of not having any remarkable recovery from her sickness. She held on to Jesus because of inner healing. We saw that Aravind didn't receive physical healing when he prayed, but his life began to be transformed. We find that both their prayers were not answered by Jesus as they expected, however, they claimed that they had experienced something within them—inner transformation and inner healing. The divine-human encounter that triggered the transformation made them believe in Jesus.

Converts used prayer as an acid test to verify the claims of Christianity before accepting it. Some addressed their prayers to generic God without using any name or symbol. Their prayers drew them to Jesus. Some prayed to Jesus to see whether he would answer their prayers, and they got answers that enabled them to put their faith in Jesus. For some, their prayers were not answered as expected, but they experienced transformation in their lives. Such experiences convinced them that they had experienced the real God. Converts also reported a number of subsequent religious experiences associated with prayer that sustained them in their newfound faith. We will discuss them in the chapter 9, which deals with hostilities.

Hardy (1979/1984) found that prayer generates new power in people. James (1902/2004, p. 411) found that purpose is realized and a new spiritual energy is released. He said, "Through prayer the purpose, often far from obvious, comes home to them, and if it be 'trial,' strength to endure the trial is given. Thus at all stages of the prayerful life we find the persuasion that in the process of communion energy from on high flows in to meet demand, and becomes operative within the phenomenal world." Through prayer, converts find new meaning and purpose in their lives and a new strength to lead a life pleasing to God. This new spiritual energy helps the convert to be successful, overcome sin, and face persecutions. In the next chapter, we will discuss mild religious experiences.

6 Mild Experiences

> The theist ... may believe that his experiences are cognitive experiences, but, unless he can formulate his "knowledge" in propositions that are empirically verifiable, we may be sure that he is deceiving himself.
>
> —ALFRED J. AYER (1952, P. 120)

> Philosophy lives in words, but truth and fact well up into our lives in ways that exceed verbal formulation.
>
> —WILLIAM JAMES (1902/2004, P. 393)

IN MILD EXPERIENCES, we find the absence of sensory elements. Converts do not experience any spectacular happenings. The act of personalizing the claims of Christianity is the core of the mild experience. Gaining religious knowledge does not lead to conversion. In a moment, converts realize that they are sinners, and only Jesus can save them. This moment is the divine–human encounter in the mild experience. Nieto (1997, pp. 105–6), differentiated religious experience from mystical experience: "It comes upon the personal life as a flash and goes away in a flash, leaving its luminosity as a permanent compelling force within the individual's life. One could describe it as a transient experience with enduring permanence, to use the paradoxical language of the mystical experience. This experience is not necessarily ecstatic, although mild forms of ecstasy are not alien to it." The mild experiences presented here fall within this category of religious experience, a spark of spiritual insight with awareness of the divine presence.

Converts are rationally convinced that the new religious option is true, but it is only personalized in a given moment. Converts seek to quench their spiritual thirst outside their religion, and this leads them to have a mild experience. When converts struggle with their sin, they weigh the new religious option rationally. The new option is weighed rationally and the suitability of Christianity to their need is considered carefully before adopting it, however, the act of acceptance or the act of personalizing the claims of Christianity is not just a change of religious ideology; it is something more than that. In all such instances, while considering the new religious option a spark of realization comes to mind that he or she is a sinner who needs a savior and that Jesus is true.

Converts are exposed to the new religious option in different contexts: in a religious meeting, while reading the Bible, in a personal conversation with a Christian, and so on. The gospel is presented as the truth, as logically consistent, and as the only solution to a crisis. Converts begin to weigh the option before accepting it. They may be rationally convinced either before or after the divine–human encounter, however, the encounter is the anchor that enables them to hold on to the newfound faith. Similar to other types of experience, the divine–human encounter is central in bringing the turning point.

I would like to present the narrative of Karan, who is a professor in an engineering college. Though he was born in a Hindu family, he claimed that he never believed in Hinduism and that he was an atheist. His parents, however, converted to Christianity, and from then on he began to hate them as well as Christianity.

Karan: I had been opposing my parents for converting to Christianity and I always thought that they were wrong. It was shameful among the relatives to see my parents converted from the religion they had been born into. Sometimes I had told my mother, "I was a born Hindu and I will die a Hindu." That's how I was opposing them.

I didn't like them praying, going to church, and conducting prayer meetings in our house, etc. But it went on for many years. All this went on during my engineering studies. I thought that I shouldn't go home after completing my studies. Sometimes I thought, "I should earn enough money and teach them a lesson that we don't need this god—this god particular, and for that matter any god." But they went on praying [for me]. I used to tell them, "You don't pray for me. I don't like you kneeling down and crying for me."

I was into many sins by the time I completed my engineering studies: playing cards, roaming around with friends, browsing bad websites—into all kinds of things in college and even after that I continued. Then I got a job, but not a good one [the job did not match his level of education]. I found it difficult. I could not get along with the people there. Within a month and a half I quit the job. Then I was jobless for some time. Then again I took another job, but I worked only for four or five months. I picked up a quarrel with my boss and fought with him. I had to leave the job.

At that time a thought came to me: "I should go back. I can go home and stay and I can prepare for a better job." In those days, public sector jobs [companies run by the Government of India] were good. I thought that I could sit at home to prepare for the entrance examinations and get a better job. But I never wanted to go home because my parents were conducting meetings and Bible studies at home.

When I looked around at the world, I felt that nobody loved me, including my parents. I always thought they were wrong. In my eyes I was good, but they were not good. I started counting one by one, and I would say, "They are not good, not good, and not good." Finally, I decided not to go home, but I could not stay in that place because I lost my job. Then I said to myself, "I will go far away from home."

I applied for a job and left to [a neighboring state] and I was teaching in an engineering college. There they paid me only 1,100 rupees [US$ 22] per month; and out of that they deducted 200 rupees as a precautionary deposit in case of me leaving the job. My certificates were also held by them. I worked there for some time. Again I underwent loneliness and depression. Though I used to watch movies often and go around with friends, I was lonely. I always felt, "Why am I here?" I also felt, "Why did my parents follow Christianity? I could have gone to them, if they had simply followed the Hindu *dharma* [way]."

As time passed, the bounds of depression were increasing . . . I used to go to late-night movie showings. After watching the movies I wondered, "Why have I become such a miserable person?"

In a sense, I was a good student; I performed well throughout my studies. I got scholarships from sixth class onward that took care of all my educational expenses and always managed well. Not that I was a topper or anything, but always I stood above average. At least at that time I thought that I was an excellent guy. But that *excellent guy* didn't get any good job and was filled with depression. This *excellent guy* could not gain many things in life. My colleagues and the faculty were treating the *excellent guy* badly. So I was not satisfied with my job.

Many times I sought the meaning of life—"What is this life?" Sometimes I felt, "Why not let me end my life? I am not much of use." These thoughts were taunting me as I walked, as I traveled, as I watched movies. Outwardly, I was okay, but inside . . .

I had some kind of idea that, "If Jesus is God why doesn't he help me out of this mess?" In fact, during my college days I would say, "If Jesus is God, he should help me pass my exam." It always happened that I would pass, but I would tell myself that it was a coincident. So it went on like that while studying. So the testing of God was going on, in a sense. "If Jesus is God, why not let him help me? Why not let him bring me out of this pathetic situation? I am suffering here and God doesn't care and does nothing." I would argue like this with God, you know. Whenever I was in trouble, I would question, "Why isn't God merciful to me?" I cursed God because he was not helping me.

I was so depressed. At that time I received a letter from my father saying, "Why are you staying far away from us? Why are you going away from us like this? We love you. You come here. We will give you whatever salary you are getting now. We will not obstruct your life style; whatever you want to do, you can do. But we want you to stay with us, so that we will be happy. We love you. Come back and prepare for something that is better for your life." So I had decided to go back.

Somehow I got my certificates back from the institution and informed a few of my friends about my plan to go home. I reached home in a bad shape. I told my parents I had come because of their letter and they were very happy. They provided me a separate room and gave enough money for my needs. I started preparing for GATE [the Graduate Aptitude Test in Engineering, an entrance exam for higher education in premier institutions] and M Tech.

I also started reading the Bible. Earlier I would read the Bible to argue with my parents, but this time I wanted to know what it really says. As I read, I realized that I was not a good person. As I read, God reminded me of my sins, like telling lies, keeping an affair [having an unacceptable relationship with a girl], stealing ... mmm ... all kinds of sins. I realized I was not a good person; I was not a good man at all. If others did not love me, it didn't matter, because I didn't love them either. And then many times I cried, "Why have I become like this? Why have I brought myself to this condition?"

I could see the changes in my heart as I read [the Bible]. I was convinced as the days passed by, and within two months I found that except for Jesus no one could be God. As I read further, I was convinced that it [the Bible] is God's Word. I was convicted that I was a sinner like everybody else and worthy of punishment, and only God could forgive me. I don't remember the date or time, but I distinctly remember that one night I knelt and cried, "Lord, forgive my sins," and I confessed all my sins. "I want you to forgive me. I want you to take over my life. I want you to make me a useful person and I want to live a meaningful life." That was the prayer I made.

I knew that my sins were forgiven at once. The joy that I received at that time still lingers in my life. That gives me great joy even now. When I think of my failures, I recollect that moment and say, "Lord Jesus, forgive me once again." So the next day I told [my parents] that I received Christ. Then the following day I appeared for an exam and I didn't do well. I told my father, "Dad, you don't worry about the result. I don't mind whether I get through or not, but I have received Christ. I would like to be baptized." My father and my mother had already planned for that. In February 1990 I was baptized. Since then I have found no reason to disbelieve. God has kept me in the faith.

Q: Could you please explain your feelings at that time?

Karan: In a sense, I felt that I couldn't get rid of my sins and I was helpless. I was worthy of God's wrath and punishment. I thought, "If God punishes me, he is just in doing so." I realized that the only way to escape from punishment for my sins was through Christ. I wanted to be a child of God.

Q: How was your life transformed?

Karan: Yeah! When I went back . . . my friends told me that a wild tiger became a cat. Without telling them anything, they just commented, "Now you've become like a cat." Earlier, they were afraid of me. If they woke me up from my sleep, I would get up and give them a slap. They were afraid of me. If they needed to wake me up, they would stand near the door and call me, "It's time to wake up. Get up." My former roommates said that I've changed tremendously. Then I shared with them what had happened to me.

I knew that I didn't love my parents. I always went after their money, and I took their money. I deceived them. I cheated them. But when I got converted I had a genuine love for my mom and dad. I could appreciate them for what they had been doing for me. I was thankful. In fact, I had never been thankful to anyone. After becoming a Christian, I am always thankful. The sense of being thankful is part of my being now. I used to be revengeful, but that is changed. After coming to Christ, I have changed. Suddenly, I have learned to forgive others.

I was addicted to playing cards—even while traveling in the train I used to play cards for money with others—and that habit disappeared suddenly. After coming to Christ I never touched it. And then watching movies: I used to watch many movies, but now I have completely stopped watching movies. I do not get any desire to watch a movie. Since then I haven't visited a movie theatre. Earlier on, I had even watched three movies in a day. I can see a big change now. [Pauses.] Now I can see the softness in my heart, because earlier I was a hard-hearted person.

Before conversion I was ignorant and aimless. I never had any consideration for others, for God, or for anything else. There was no planning—absolutely nothing. I won't say that I made a 180-degree change after conversion, but there are a lot of changes. Now I have found meaning in my life and have goals for my life. I may not have very big goals, but still, I want to do what God wants me to do. Now I seek to do only what is acceptable to God, to Scripture, to society, and the church. I don't do whatever comes to my mind and that's the major change. I do fail, but of course there are many successes.

Q: When did you first hear about Jesus Christ? Was it through your parents or from someone else?

Karan: Hmmm . . . No, my schoolmate who was a singer introduced me to Jesus. Also through my aunty who used to tell us Bible stories. She was the first convert in our family. I was a very small boy then. During plus two [precollege course], one of my Catholic friends talked to me about Christ. Till my tenth class I was the topper in my class, but after coming to the city for precollege my life became very bad. I became addicted to movies and was unable to study and I was depressed. During that time my friend told me about Jesus. I even bought a cross and wore it. All my friends were surprised to see me wearing a cross, but after sometime I removed it. That was my first contact with Jesus Christ.

Later when I was doing my engineering course, I started opposing Christianity. In fact, I never believed in Hindu gods, but my father would beat me and make me sit for *pujas* [prayers]. Probably I was an atheist during my younger days. But I read extensively on Hindu mythology. I used to compare and ask various questions from Ramayana and Mahabharatha.

Q: How do you describe Jesus?

Karan: Mostly I see him as a friend who is really very kind to me. He loves me and cares for me. Sometimes I wonder, "God who made the heavens and earth is so humble and so lowly!" When we were not even worthy to be servants, Jesus said, "I call you my friends and brothers." I like that. Jesus is part of my life . . . I meet him every day. I consult Jesus for many things. It could be troubles, a dilemma, or confusion, and in everything I consult him. Without him, a day does not pass by . . . I take his help for everything. Jesus, for me, is extremely kind and merciful. But he is also Almighty.

Q: Will you go back to atheism?

Karan: I don't think it's possible because I have read these things once again and looked at them with the knowledge God has given me. Because of this I trust in God all the more. God has filled me with his Holy Spirit and he is a very good testimony. And I don't see any way of getting away from the Spirit of God who lives in me, and that is a good evidence that I am saved. By having such solid evidence, how could I go back?

Q: Such solid evidence in the sense . . . Can you explain further?

Karan: I also studied these things logically, scientifically, and whatever way you look at it, the Bible is tremendously powerful. It's God's Word. He tells you that you are a child of God.

Q: When did you get this assurance?

Karan: Yeah, I got it on that night and it continues.

Q: What holds you now to Jesus?

Karan: Many things hold me to Jesus. But the most important thing that holds me to Jesus is that every morning he tells me, "Yes! You are a child of God. You've been forgiven; you've been washed by the blood of Christ. And you have the right to be a Christian" . . . Frankly speaking, this is what holds me. I've logically analyzed Christianity, philosophy, apologetics, and many things. I've studied some of the strongest arguments of atheists, etc., and at some point I was shaken, but this inner voice keeps me from doubting. I feel this is what holds me.

Karan was exposed to Christianity from his childhood. Later he read the Bible in order to argue with his parents. He even prayed to Jesus at times for his exams and got answers but explained them away as coincidences. Therefore, we need to take into consideration that converts do not convert the moment they are exposed to a new religion. It is a process. Karan went through difficult times in his life and struggled with existential issues like, "What is life?" He even contemplated committing suicide. At one point, he had a quest to read the Bible and was convicted that he was not right, and he needed Jesus to escape from punishment for his sins. This is the moment of the divine–human encounter that results in transformation. Before this encounter he was rationally convinced that God does not exist, but after this encounter he became rationally convinced that Christianity is true. He finds the indwelling of the Holy Spirit as the solid evidence against his earlier belief in atheism and then draws support from other arguments to validate his belief in God and Christianity.

I will now introduce you to Mohan, a convert from the Brahmin caste in Hinduism. Now he is a popular preacher in South India and he is instrumental in leading many Brahmins to Jesus. As a teenager, he was deeply into his spiritual journey and explored all that was possible in his religion to experience the Supreme God, but was not successful. Then he found his quest quenched while reading the New Testament.

Q: How did you accept Jesus?

Mohan: It was a blessed thing that I came to Christ. Jesus said, "Seek and you will find." I was seeking God through yearly visits to [a temple in South India where people make a pilgrimage visit every year during winter, which involves forty days of preparation]. I used to fast weekly thrice; I tried to control my five senses to remove the fears in my heart. I spent more time on spiritual activities than for my studies. I was involved in RSS [*Rashtrya Swayamsevak Sangh*, which simply means National Voluntary Organization, a Hindu fundamentalist organization]. I was actually involved in the *Hindu Munnani* [Hindu Front, an outfit of RSS in Tamil Nadu]. I also tried to reach God through meditation. I was a *pujari* [priest] in a temple in the evenings. [He was only a teenager at that time.] I had a lot of questions like, "Which God will take away my sins?" Every morning, I used to worship the sun as I was taught. One day, I had the question, "If God created the sun, and it is so bright that we cannot see it with our eyes, then how much brighter the God who created the sun would be! Who is that God?" I wanted to see that God; I wanted to speak to him and wanted to be with him. I wanted these three things in my life. I had this longing and sought God.

I was looking for an answer to my question. *Ohm Maha Deva* means the Great God. My question was, "How can this Great God could be confined to man-made idols, arts, and pictures?" It was not possible . . . But I believed in one God, yet I had these questions—"Who is he? Who is he that is all-powerful?" I was longing to see him, to speak to him, and to be with him. I had an urge to search for the true God. God means the one who comes down; he is *Iraivan*, meaning *Irangi Varubavan*. [He was explaining the Tamil word for God, *Iraivan*, which means one who comes down from above, to communicate the contrast that God comes down, but people are trying to reach him above]. People try to do so many things to reach God, but God has chosen me. Salvation is purely by his grace. Jesus said, "You have not revealed this to wise men but children." By God's grace I was saved.

Q: In what situation did you accept Christ?

Mohan: I had lots of questions within me. I had hunger in my soul. I was in search of peace. Outside, I was like any other child, but in my heart I was searching for peace. God chooses the one who has devotion to him. In India there is no dearth of temples. People have devotion, and devotion should lead the people to *Mukti*, or salvation, where they become holy. I don't know how many have reached that.

One of my Christian friends noticed my devotion and commitment in worshiping and fulfilling all the religious requirements. He told me, "What you are searching for can be found in the New Testament." He gave me a New Testament as a gift. He told me, "Please read this; you will find the true God and peace in this." He did not compel me, but gave me the New Testament as a gift. He encouraged me to read.

Q: Did you read the New Testament?

Mohan: I was a *pujari* [priest]; on the other hand, I considered having the Bible as a great gift in my life. I skipped meals, [and] my sleep, and was always reading the New Testament. I was secretly reading the Bible day and night. No one knew about it. Even I tore a few pages from the New Testament and read it secretly [he thought carrying a full New Testament would be risky], because we Brahmins are very much devoted Hindus. From 1988 to 1992 I read the Bible four times. I read with deep thirst and with an expectation. Only Jesus and I knew that I was a child of God; no one else knew about it.

Q: When did you actually get convinced that Jesus was the Supreme God for whom you were searching?

Mohan: The day I received the Bible, Jesus came into my heart. The words of Jesus opened my heart to his love: simple words like "the wages of sin is death," and his forgiveness. In our religion, all the incarnations were meant to destroy. But Jesus is the incarnation who came to forgive. The day I got the Bible, I confessed my sins to Jesus. My friend had asked me to pray to Jesus, "Lord Jesus, come into my heart and take away my sins. Please accept me as your son." He asked me to believe this and then read the Bible. At once Jesus came into my heart. It cannot be described by words. I was filled with joy, and there is no other word to describe that joy. As in the Psalms, "Taste and see that the Lord is good," it cannot be described in words. Only when someone opens his heart can he experience this feeling. The same day I got the Bible, I accepted Jesus.

Q: What were your feelings at that time?

Mohan: As the Bible says, "Those who are burdened, come to me, and I will give you rest;" I felt as if a burden had been lifted and I was relieved of the burden. I didn't have hope for the future. When I was a *pujari*, I didn't have any assurance about life after death. I had external purity, but only after accepting Jesus did I get inner purity. My soul/heart was washed by the blood of Jesus. I had great happiness and joy, such joy that cannot be compared. Even if I get an opportunity to speak to the president or prime minister or become a billionaire, it would not give me such a great joy. It was truly a great experience. Out of his mercy I had this experience, and I praise God for this.

Q: What were your feelings and thoughts about leaving your religion and traditions?

Mohan: As I told you, I left my religion because of my search of the Supreme God. I believed that my forefathers would have experienced the true God and that's why they had written or developed this tradition and they might have seen the true light. But the day I read the Bible, I realized that God does not live in man-made objects or even in temples built by men. By the grace of the Almighty God, I am happy that I am liberated from this tradition. I never felt that I was losing something, nor did I think that I was doing something wrong. Some may think wrongly that I, being a Brahmin, betrayed my tradition. Jesus is the one who never committed a sin, but was punished for our sins. I am lucky and blessed to have him as my personal God. Not everyone may accept him; even those born as Christians may not have this favor because God said, "I will show mercy on those whom I have chosen." The old practices, traditions, caste, and religions are man-made; they cannot take a person to the glorious God. As the Bible says, "All things become new and the old has gone." Darkness is removed and the light has come into my life. Old things have gone, so I wasn't afraid of anything. I never had any hesitation to leave the old practices.

Q: After coming to Christ, how was your life different?

Mohan: I should not talk about my life . . . People talk about my transformed life. But for your question, first of all, I got peace that cannot be described in words; secondly, I have the assurance for life after death. Even if I die today, even if the Lord comes now, I will be with him in his kingdom. Even if I die tonight, I will reach the Father in heaven, *Parameshwaran* ["God who is above"]; I have this unshakable assurance. The assurance of life after death is strong and the hope of eternity is unshakable.

The most important thing is that my nature is transformed. Gifts [of the Holy Spirit] are okay, but the fruits [of the Holy Spirit] are very important. People have seen Christ through gifts and signs for many years and centuries. Fruits are very important and Christ-likeness is very important. I have not hesitated to say this; by God's grace I am able to show [Christ-likeness] even at times of difficulties.

At this juncture, Mohan narrated an incident to show how his Christ-likeness was evident to others when his friends came to kill him. We will take up that part of the story in the chapter dealing with hostilities. I continue the later part of our conversation here.

Q: You were deeply involved in your religion. How do you compare your spiritual life in Hinduism and Christianity?

Mohan: Earlier I was living for myself, but now with Jesus I have started loving others. My selfishness, bitterness, and pride all were cleansed. I did not care about others, but now I am a blessing to all, irrespective of their backgrounds. When I was saying mantras, I did not understand the meanings. Now I have the confidence that when I pray to Jesus he answers my prayer; earlier it was simply a petition. I never had any hope of eternal life.

Q: What is the most significant factor that keeps you with Jesus?

Mohan: It is God's grace. In spite of the sufferings, it is by God's grace that I live for him.

When I asked him, "Will you go back to Hinduism?," he was so annoyed and got angry with me, saying, "How could you ask such a question after listening to everything that I have said!" I had to pacify him, saying that I ask this question to all the participants of my study, and that for the research it is a significant question to know why people hold on to the newfound faith. Then he answered, "I don't like this question. After experiencing the love and grace of Jesus, I cannot look back. There is no one greater than Jesus who could come, who is holy and loving."

Mohan was a faithful and ardent follower of his religion. His quest for reaching the Supreme God caused him to explore his religion beyond his age, however, he did not find what he was searching for. Then he began to question his own religious beliefs and practices. He wondered how the Supreme God could be confined to man-made objects and buildings. In the process a kind of disenchantment set in about the religion of his birth. When his friend gave him the New Testament, out of his spiritual thirst he accepted it and considered it a privilege to have a copy of it. He simply made a prayer as his friend suggested and started reading the New Testament. He claimed that the very day when he read the New Testament he found what he was searching for. The conviction that Jesus was the Supreme God for whom he had been searching dawned on him without any spectacular elements. This moment is the divine–human encounter in the conversion process. Similar to other converts, he was also passionate in reading the New Testament after this religious experience.

Contrary to Mohan, who read the New Testament in search of finding the Supreme God, Vinitha, an architect by profession from a Hindu family, resisted the attempts of a Christian woman trying to persuade her to accept Jesus.

Vinitha: While I was doing my degree course in Kerala, I had to go to Delhi for six months of training. There I stayed in a hostel. On one occasion, one of the roommates asked another girl why she became a Christian. So I was also listening to her as she narrated her conversion experience; rather, I was overhearing it. I noticed her way of living, her way of accepting other people; her love for others seemed very genuine and sincere. That attracted me to her. Even though we stayed together for a very short time, she introduced Christ to me. Even though I knew about Christianity earlier, she told me the good news. I had been to church sometimes, but through her only I came to know about the good news. She only told me that Christ died for my sins, but he lives.

She took me to a students' fellowship where I met people who were similar to her in behaviors and loving others. I could see something common in them. Another time, she took me to a church and to a believer's house. I kept on listening about the love of Jesus, how Jesus died for me, etc., but I never believed, and I was not willing to accept it.

I held the view that it is her belief, and that I believe in all three religions—Hinduism, Islam, and Christianity—and that they are all different ways of reaching God. People call God by different names. My father had taught me this. I thought that it was her belief, so I didn't give any serious thought to it. But I did like her for what she was and how she related to me. I really started enjoying the fellowship with other believers. I liked them so much, but I didn't accept their claims.

Once she took me to a family in . . . After having a good meal the aunty [the lady of the house] called me and started sharing the good news once again. I said, "Aunty I have heard all this many times and I don't want to hear it again." But she insisted that I hear it once again. She explained the whole thing once again to me saying, "Jesus died for my sins" and "Jesus is the only way," etc. I listened reluctantly. After hearing everything, I just asked her, "Why did you insist that I should listen when I said I have heard them already?" Then she told me, "After leaving this earth, when I meet Jesus, he will ask me about the girl who came to my house and why hadn't I shared the gospel with her? Now I have done my part, and you have to take a decision." Then I was bit . . . oh, she was putting me in a cage and that I had to really take a decision; either I accept or leave it.

Then I was wondering, "If it is really true, then I must be missing something." I said within myself, "Okay, if Jesus is really true, Jesus, you tell me, but I cannot believe just . . . I don't feel anything special. You have to tell me. If you are true God, prove it to me." Then the three of us—the aunty, my friend, and I—were kneeling down and started praying.

Suddenly, I felt a kind of peace engulf me. I was crying for no reason. I did not have any particular reason to cry at that moment. I was crying because of joy. I did not know what it was really. That was my salvation experience. I didn't take a decision or anything like that.

>> They gave me a New Testament, and I was going through it. They taught me the Bible . . . They were teaching me the Bible verses to help me understand that Jesus is the only true God. They were quoting all those verses, and slowly I too started believing.

Q: How was your life different since then?

Vinitha: I was not a happy person . . . I never knew what love was. I never loved my parents. They took care of me, but I thought they did everything to me because it was their duty . . . So the word *love* was meaningful only after my conversion. I had no hope prior to my conversion. I was not scared, but I was trying to pull myself into something, say something, yet I never knew that I was looking for God. I wanted to be free because . . . I felt always somebody or something was controlling me. I never liked even my parents. But it was all changed after the prayer.

Q: Only after this experience that you felt you are free . . . ? Can you explain?

Vinitha: Yes, of course. The old person is changed. When you genuinely have a relationship with the Lord, you feel light, and you feel the love of God. I don't know how to explain. But I felt a kind of a burden was removed from my mind. There were changes within me also and the way I look at things became different.

Q: Did you find any remarkable changes immediately?

Vinitha: It was not soon after my conversion that I changed; however, there was a change. When opposition came from my family, I determined to move in this way and I clung to it. So I didn't feel that I was jumping from there to Christianity . . . I was firm that I shouldn't tell lies. Even if it hurt others, I wouldn't tell a lie, and in fact I tried to be honest. The changes occurred gradually . . . I used to be very stubborn, but after conversion I was trying to understand others and ready to forgive.

Q: What were your thoughts or feelings about leaving your religion?

Vinitha: I didn't think about leaving my religion. The aunty was inviting me to pray; I didn't have anything against Christianity, so I didn't mind praying with her. I kept asking, "Okay, I need something as a proof from God and something to prove it." I didn't expect any immediate experience. So there was no time to think about me leaving my religion.

Q: How did your family react to your conversion?

Vinitha: When I reached home, my father talked to me about religion, his beliefs, and conversion, etc. He tried to bring me back. He thought as the time passed by I would lose interest. I was attending the fellowship regularly in my college. When my father came to know about it, he was against it and was angry with me. He resisted. Whenever my father was angry, my mother supported me. Though she did not believe anything, she did not want me to go away from home. She was trying to hold the family together.

Q: How do you differentiate your spiritual experience?

Vinitha: Earlier God was an unknown person . . . The idea of a personal God was absent. We were taught to pray [at the temple], but it was not intentional. Whenever I appeared for an exam or when I needed something or if I felt sad, then I would pray. I did not find any meaning in it. When we went to some pilgrim center we would pray for good things, for goodness to happen in our lives. That's all.

Q: Perhaps you did not know much about your religion?

Vinitha: Yeah, my father was telling me the same thing. He was trying to bring me back to Hinduism by saying, "You haven't seen Vedas or you haven't read through anything. That's why you left" . . . It was not the religion that I loved so I became a Christian; it was the person Jesus, who is very personal to me. This is something true in my life. I have never experienced anything like this.

Q: In light of your experience, how do you describe Jesus?

Vinitha: I cannot describe him. He is faithful to me. He is faithful to me even though I am not faithful to him. He loves me. He is the only person who can understand me and accept me.

Q: What is the one thing that holds you to Jesus?

Vinitha: I tried to find out many times and wondered why I am clinging to this God! I was so discouraged at times; even after coming to

Christ, I was discouraged and disappointed. But still I held on to this God. I wondered why! I haven't experienced anything else more true than this God.

Vinitha was reluctant to listen to the woman who insisted that she hear the good news, as she had listened to the same story many times from her friend earlier. It was not the doctrine that Jesus accomplished salvation on the cross for sinners that persuaded Vinitha accept Christianity. While praying, she wanted a proof from God; she did not decide to accept Christianity or to leave her religion at that point. It was the experience of peace and joy while praying, and the fact that she was crying for no reason, that caused her to believe in Jesus; she took this as a proof from God. Later, through the teachings she received, she was convinced that Jesus is the true God. The experience of joy and peace and crying for no reason was the divine–human encounter for Vinitha. Later in the interview, she mentioned that it was the personal experience of this God that makes her hold on to her newfound faith.

Let me introduce you to Vinay, an assistant professor of commerce. He hails from a Brahmin family. He talked about a fear that gripped him after attending a Sunday school in his friend's house.

Vinay: To begin with, I studied in a Christian school. We had moral science and Scripture classes, in which teachers used to tell Scripture stories. We had prayer every day in the school assembly. During my eighth and ninth classless, Scripture classes became livelier than earlier. That was the stage in which I began to practice my Hindu rituals and say all the *slogas* [mantras] as my grandma taught me.

Once, when the teacher in a Scripture class said that God created the world, one of the students contended that it was the Hindu god who created the world according to Hindu scriptures, not the Christian God. The teacher simply smiled and asked him to go on. I seconded his opinion and emphasized that the world was created by our gods, Brahma and others. This incident is very vivid in my memory.

But the biggest turning point came in my life during my ninth class. One of my close friends who was a devout Hindu became a Christian. He was known as an *Ayyappa Bhakta* [a devotee of a

Mild Experiences

South Indian deity], who fervently visit all the temples and do all the rituals. He was addressed by other students in the school as *Samy* [Sadhu] for his devotion. It was the biggest shock for many of us that he became a Christian. He had stopped worshiping all the idols and started worshiping Christ. His life was basically a challenge and something new to me. He faithfully invited me to attend a Sunday school in his house. I dodged him, but dropped into the class to satisfy him. Then, somehow, I felt that I should continue to attend. Something . . . some kind of fear gripped me about this God who loved me and did everything for me. Secondly, I wanted to act in the skits for the Christmas program. I realized that I needed to be regular to take part in the skit, so I started attending.

I guess the real transformation took place in 1994 during my tenth class. I needed some extra support to face my board exam. [Students in India undergo tremendous stress before the tenth class exam as it is conducted by the State Board.] Then some of other friends also joined for the Sunday school. I began to take the faith seriously; I started taking Jesus really. There was a real change in me. I stopped worshiping idols and stopped saying the *slogas*. I started praying to Jesus and reading the Bible every day, attending fellowship twice a week, and attending church on Sundays. Since then, it has been a long journey.

Elders who nurtured me told me about baptism, that I need to publicly affirm Jesus . . . In August 1995 I took baptism and felt a great burden was released; I could publicly affirm that I was a Christian. Now it is almost a decade in my journey of faith. God has been good to me despite my limitations, depressions, and my low ebb. I just cannot doubt God's goodness; no matter what happens to me or my family, God is good to me.

Q: What was the fear that gripped you?

Vinay: I framed it as fear; it could be the fear of God. I understood this later when I read the Bible. Only late in 1995, as I was reading the Bible, I came to know this verse, "The fear of the Lord is the beginning of knowledge" (Prov 1:7). That could be the fear of God. But at that time I could not make out what it was. Every Sunday morning something would wake me up by 6:00 or 6:15 in the morning; otherwise, usually I get up late. I go to church at 7:00 in the morning. I could not find any other explanation than the fear of God that made me to attend church. When I read this verse, it struck me that it is the fear of the Lord that directed me those days. Something within me was nudging me to attend church. I was enjoying my newfound experience; I love singing, praying, etc.

Q: You said that you needed some extra support to face the board exam. What kind of support you were looking for?

Vinay: I was basically looking for support from the Supreme Being, help from above. I knew I was on the right track. I thought it was not a bad idea to seek God's help in my studies while I concentrated on my studies. God honored me, and not only me, all our friends in the fellowship. I got the support from God.

Q: How did your result turn out?

Vinay: When I told my brother that I got 82 percent, he said, "Okay, tell me what is the real mark." That was my family members' expectation of me. He could not believe that I scored 82 percent. God helped me.

Q: Were there any changes in your life?

Vinay: I cannot say that I became a saint or become like Jesus Christ. But I began to apologize for my short temper. People were surprised at me for doing that. That was a sign of my transformation; it was an obvious transformation. If I had not known the Lord, I would not have apologized to anyone. People have noticed this and reminded me when I lose my temper. One day when I was yelling at my father, my mom came and asked me, "Is this what you read in the Bible?" Sometime, when I watch movies, they point out to me saying, "You normally do not watch movies!" I have become a better son to my mom and dad; I became responsible and trustworthy; my uncle and others trust me so much, especially in handling cash. I could see some definite changes in me. Everyone in the family knows that if some work is given to me it will be completed. I attribute all these changes to God. My faith in Christ and the Bible teaches me that I should be responsible to my family.

Q: What were your feelings immediately after taking baptism?

Vinay: I had a big sigh of relief after taking baptism. I was only fifteen at that time. I did not even take a spare cloth when I went for baptism. I borrowed my friend's dress for baptism, then I put on my dress.

Q: What was your religious life like before conversion?

Vinjay: My mom and my grandmother told me Hindu stories. Through them I gained all my knowledge of Hinduism. I gained little from my reading. I had an earnest desire to be a good Brahmin. My grandma told me that I need to dedicate myself to God and be pure in body and soul. I used to take baths, wear *dhothi* [South Indian traditional dress for men, a four-meter-long white cloth tied around the waist], and sit in front of gods and goddesses and say the *slogas*. I did all these things to please my grandma out of my love for her. I wanted to earn a name of being a good Brahmin, a good Hindu, but never had any deeper experience. I used to sing in the *pujas* [prayers], as I am a good singer. But I did not find any personal satisfaction or in-depth knowledge; I enjoyed nothing. It only gave me a sense of feeling that it was my religion and I was a Brahmin and I was on the top of the hierarchy [in the caste structure]. I was a proud Brahmin, a proud Hindu.

Q: How could you think of leaving your religion as a Brahmin?

Vinay: That did not have any impact on me and it was very shallow. I did not find it significant. I was only told that I was a Brahmin and superior to everyone. The Hindu epics on television were great moments in the family to watch. My grandma used to explain them. But I did not have any personal experience; it was only a shallow. But I thought about what others would say about me, a Brahmin leaving my religion; this fear was there. But reading the Bible and praying became a personal experience and something used to grip me. It was a personal experience that was missing in my religion. Earlier there was a fear, but the knowledge was shallow and I never had any personal experience; I was only told about my religion.

My newfound faith was secret at home. I used to read the Bible and pray in my room. I had a tough time in practicing my newfound faith at home. Though my family was not very orthodox, as a young boy it was tough for me to practice my faith; it was not easy. My parents did not have time for religious activities; only during festivals I faced problems. Sometimes I resisted and yielded at times to please them. I really . . . I do not know how I came out of such situations. I think God had helped me somehow; I do not know how. At times, when I did not have any other option, I bowed down before idols. It was tough. I guess God helped me.

Last year or so, I publicly acknowledged in front of my parents and relatives that I was a Christian. Earlier I never told my family that I became a Christian, however, they knew that I became a Christian, but they never asked me about it. They knew that Sunday morning I would leave the house by 7:00 or 8:00 a.m. and return by noon or so, with a carry bag; they knew very well that I went to church, but they never confronted me. However, it was tough to practice my newfound faith. Ours is a closely knit family. Hurting my parents is unthinkable for me.

Q: How did your family and relatives react to your conversion?

Vinay: My dad lives in a different planet, with the devil's doctrine, "You don't bother me; I don't bother you." My mom is a sensitive mother. She told me, "Do not stand in the street corner and shout, 'Hallelujah and Praise the Lord,' and do not distribute tracts. And if you want to pray, read your Bible, listen to music—whatever you want to do—do it within the four walls, nothing outside of it." My brother was concerned about my studies. I was a good student; I did not have any bad habits, so he was happy with me. My mom and brother have some soft corner for my faith. My mother asked me to pray for some of the things. Once my brother wanted a change of job, and he wanted me to pray for him. They have understood that this was not a passing phase. Even my relatives have accepted me as Christian. I did not face any adverse reaction.

Q: When was the first time your family came to know that you were a Christian?

Vinay: During the festivals, initially I rebelled against worshiping idols. I was scolded, yelled at, etc. They forced me to worship the idols. Then they thought it was a passing cloud. The first two, three years it was like that.

Q: How do you describe God, based on your spiritual experience?

Vinay: The first thing comes to my mind is that God is a person. I have always felt that he cares for me, loves me, and he is there for me. He is the creator of the universe; there is awe, I cannot take him for granted. I always have a fear because he is awesome. Yet he is very good. God is someone who is real and close to my heart. He would not harm me.

Q: Have you ever had a second thought about your commitment to Christ?

Vinay: I guess not; I never ever thought that I could become a Hindu again. Having said that, probably, as a young person, getting married to a Christian girl would be a big challenge for me. I am anxious about it. I thought at times, "If I were a Hindu, I could marry a girl of my choice who is a Hindu." However, I don't find any reason to go back. I am having peace, satisfaction, and motivation from God. Above all, I have love from above. I am happy here. I think that is what matters.

Vinay was worried about marriage. He did not want to marry a Hindu girl because of his faith, but his parents and relatives would not accept a Christian girl. This was bothering him at the time of the interview because in Indian culture parents normally insist on their choice of a girl or boy for their children to marry. Vinay prayed that God would show him a Brahmin girl who is a Christian. His faith was honored. Later, Vinay was able to find a convert from the Brahmin caste, and the marriage was conducted in Brahminical tradition minus some of the *slogas* that Vinay found unacceptable. In the evening, another ceremony was conducted in the Christian tradition. Both the parents were happy about this arrangement.

In the mild experience, the new information about Christianity is weighed by the converts. When such reasoning is done, one accepts the new religious option. However, it is not simply the new information about Christianity that results in conversion. The act of acceptance is not just a change of religious ideology; there is something more to it. In a moment, converts realize that they are sinners and that only the Lord Jesus can save them. This moment is the divine–human encounter. Until then, converts never thought of themselves as sinners or felt the need of a savior.

It is not the information, but the encounter with the divine that makes one convert to Christianity. No one becomes a Christian the moment they hear about Jesus. While the cognitive faculty is preoccupied with reasoning out the claims of Christianity, the act of personalization of the claims of Christianity is processed at a different level. The cognitive processing of comparing beliefs and practices is done from the personal experience of the divine–human encounter. Since the encounter, converts view the claims of Christianity and beliefs and practices of their religion from this vantage point.

Mohan wanted to reach the Supreme God. When he read the New Testament, he realized that he had found what he was searching for all along. It was not that he read extensively to understand all that Jesus accomplished and was finally convinced of the claims. Rather, the moment he made a prayer and read the New Testament, his quest to reach the Supreme God was quenched. Karan had read the Bible on many occasions but was not convinced. However, in a moment, he felt that he was sinful and that he needed Jesus. Vinitha was not willing to accept the claims of Christianity, but during the prayer she was filled with joy and peace. In such cases, the converts had an encounter with the divine and that became the pivotal point in their conversion process.

In this type of religious experience converts do not perceive the divine through visions or dreams, but the presence of divine is felt without any sensory channels. However, converts are aware of the presence of the divine, identify the divine with Jesus, and perceive him as a real person. Nieto talked about transcendental awareness that comes in a flash. Rudolf Otto (1923/1958, p. 11) called this the "numinous," which is felt "as objective and outside of the self." He explained the difference between believing in a reality and experiencing it: "Religion is convinced not only that the holy and sacred reality is attested by the inward voice of conscience and the religious consciousness, the 'still, small voice' of the Spirit in the heart, by feeling, presentiment, and longing, but also that it may be directly encountered in particular occurrences and events, self-revealed in persons and displayed in actions, in a word, that beside the inner revelation from the Spirit there is an outward revelation of the divine nature" (p. 143). The self-revelation of the divine in mild experiences leads one to convert to Christianity and believe in Jesus. We will deal more with the divine–human encounter in the next chapter.

7 The Mystical Turning Point

> If a mystic admits that the object of his vision is something which cannot be described, then he must also admit that he is bound to talk nonsense when he describes it.
>
> —Alfred J. Ayer (1952, p. 118)

> We have progressed far enough to dismiss once and for all the misleading belief that only waking ego consciousness can provide us with real knowledge.
>
> —Kelly Bulkeley (2005, p. 173)

Deeply held convictions against Christianity prevent people in India from converting to Christianity. Though we have the historical tradition of St. Thomas bringing Christianity to India in the first century, people believe that Christianity was brought by the British. Another reason for people to shy away from Christianity is that it is associated with the Dalits, the outcastes in the Hindu caste structure. However, the hesitation to consider Christianity is not a permanent state. The turning point in the conversion process makes the convert change over from one faith to another. How does this turning point occur? How does one who is deeply committed to one's religion become a follower of another religion? How does a person who is against a religion suddenly find that same religion close to the heart? How does all the rhetoric against Christianity vanish in a moment so that one comes to embrace this faith? How does an atheist suddenly become religious and passionately follow a religion other than his or her religion of birth? Paloutzian (2005, p. 331) observed the lack of a model to explain such alterations: "In contrast to someone arriving at a point of belief through the process of socialization and other developmental mechanisms, the convert can identify a time before which the religion was not accepted and after which it was accepted. This is unique kind of change that has yet to be explained by a powerful model." This chapter attempts to explain this phenomenon by arguing that such alteration is plausible owing to the divine–human encounter in experiences of conversion to Christianity.

If we recollect the narratives presented in the previous chapters, we find that the change from one faith to another is not by rational choice but due to the divine–human encounter. The rational choice of adopting Christianity is made after the encounter. Sometimes the shift occurred when converts tried Christianity and felt that it worked in their lives; some prayed to Jesus and felt that their prayers were answered. Some claimed to have been rationally convinced about the Christian faith and experienced a flash of spiritual insight of realization or personalization of the message. Some felt that Christianity resolved their crisis or existential concerns in their lives. However, suddenly or gradually, converts claimed that a realization or a spark of spiritual insight dawned on them that Jesus is true and real. It happened beyond the normal waking state of consciousness. This moment—the divine–human encounter—is mystical and is the pivotal point in the conversion experience to Christianity. In other words, it can be termed the "born again" experience or the personal experience of Jesus. Whether in a vision or dream, sudden or gradual, spectacular or mild, irrespective of the type of religious experience, the divine–human encounter triggers transformation and makes a person change over from their religion to follow Jesus. The divine–human encounter is positive and pleasant. Converts feel that they are chosen by God and that God came in search of them.

Let me illustrate this with the conversion experience of Bakht Singh, a convert from Sikhism who started a Christian movement known as Jehovah Shammah, an indigenous form of Christianity. Once, while he was studying in England, he was traveling to the USA in a ship with his European friends. He was curious to attend the Christian worship in the first-class saloon and went in. When everyone knelt after the sermon, he was not comfortable to kneel. However, he did not want to disturb others who were kneeling by walking out, so he stayed and knelt down. He described, in his testimony, an unusual experience: "My whole body was

The Mystical Turning Point

trembling. I could feel divine power entering into me and lifting me. The first change that I noticed in me was that a great joy was flooding my soul. The second change was that I was repeating the name of Jesus, I began to say: 'Oh Lord Jesus, blessed be Thy Name, blessed be Thy Name.' The name of Jesus became very sweet to me. Before I used to despise the very name, and during discussions and conversations, I had made fun of it" (Singh, n.d., p. 4). He was biased against Europeans and Christianity. As a Sikh, he was very proud of his religious heritage while ridiculing Christianity. However, all that vanished at that moment. Earlier, he despised the name of Jesus, but the same name became sweet at his religious experience. This changeover was not by rational understanding of Christianity or by volition. The conscious choice was possible later, only as the effect of the religious experience that involved a bodily sensation and unintentionally repeating the name of Jesus.

To illustrate another dimension of a turning point with the absence of sensory experience, let me introduce Ganga, a girl from a Brahmin family. She was going through a personal crisis; she visited several temples and churches, seeking God's intervention to resolve her crisis. She said, "One night, after reciting my [Hindu] prayers, I went to bed. In the night, I did not know what had happened. Next day morning, I got up and decided, 'I will not worship Hindu gods hereafter.' That same night, Jesus accepted me and I was saved. The next morning, I told my mother everything and disposed of all the photographs of Hindu gods, and I committed myself fully to my *Appa*" ["Dad" in Tamil, referring to Jesus]. I asked her how she came to the decision on that night.

Ganga: Actually that night I slept. I did not know what had happened in the night, but in the morning, when I awoke, I was totally different. Suddenly, I lost all the belief that I had [in Hinduism]. I was thinking, "Why should I do all this [religious requirements of Hinduism]?" I disposed of all the photographs of gods. Till then, I did many things, I went to [a particular temple in Tamil Nadu] and many other temples, but I did not have peace of mind and there was no peace even at home. We sold all the gold jewelry, till the last piece, and spent all the money on visiting temples and offerings. Such was our fervor, but we were broke.

Now, I feel that my *Appa* [Jesus] would have felt sorry for me [for doing all those things]. God chooses those who have real devotion to him. I had real devotion but a misplaced devotion. I had been going from one temple to another. Actually, on that night I cried a lot, wondering, "Who is the real God? Who will solve my problems?" I thought so much about it and slept.

But when I woke up in the morning, my mind was very clear. I decided, "Hereafter, everything for me is Jesus only . . ." That day itself, I decided to follow Jesus and that day my dad [Jesus] saved me.

Here again we find that it was not a change of religious ideology due to an intellectual exercise. Though she was frustrated with her religion, the shift was not by volition. She could not explain how the shift occurred, but in the morning she was very clear that Jesus was the real God. And only then did she make a conscious decision to follow Jesus.

Another girl, Nithya, a medical student, said that the turning point—when and how it had happened—could not be explained. She said, "One day, suddenly a change came into my mind that Christ is the only God . . . I did not have any initiation or miracles." In her interview, she talked about her confusion of not knowing who the real God is. I asked her to clarify how that confusion got cleared. She laughed and said:

Nithya: If you can switch this [microphone] off, I can tell you one thing! If I can tell you in worldly terms, I cannot tell you exactly [laughs] . . . No one knows when someone would fall in love. I fell in love with Jesus; it was like my love towards my Lord. I do not know when it really happened! What I can say is that I love Jesus. People used to pinpoint "that day," "that time," but not with me. I used to wonder, "Lord, when did you come into my life?" I did not know. But one thing I know: he has come into my life. I do not know when the love came to me! Before that, so many confusions, and even I thought of committing suicide.

Nithya compared her turning point with falling in love with someone. The inability to pinpoint and the struggle to describe her turning point was evident. She claimed that falling in love with someone cannot

The Mystical Turning Point

be rationally explained; similarly, the divine–human encounter cannot be explained rationally but can be understood only by experience.

Kamal claimed that after attending church for a few months he realized that Jesus is a real person. He reported, "After I started attending a church, my life started changing. I did not feel the need to go to temples. I started realizing that Christ was God, who could be always with me and a real person who could hold my life. After that, I stopped going to the temples." Kamal speaks about his experience of Jesus being a real person in his life and is always with him. Converts' experience of the presence of God leads them to change over to Christianity. They also point out that such experience has no parallel in their religion of birth.

In the first chapter we discussed the experiences of vision. Sania had a vision of Jesus and immediately knelt and cried for being so poor and dark in front of the divine, though she is fair in complexion. Selvi had a vision of crucifixion and wet her pillow with tears as she was convicted of her sins. Sekar, who was addicted to alcohol, experienced automatism; though he was sleeping in his bedroom, he was brought out to the street in his vision, then he realized that he was outside his house and that the doors were left open that were closed when he went to bed. He saw a bright light that he identified immediately with Jesus. These stories indicate that the center of the religious experience is beyond the normal waking consciousness.

Komala's dream convinced her that Jesus is the true God. The dream came as an answer to her prayer for a revelation of who the real God is. She reported her turning point: "I asked, 'Who is God? What is his name?' I resolved that if I did not get an answer that night, I would not believe in any god. That day, I did not even think of Jesus and I had not even talked about him with others. The dream was not accidental; it was from God. So I believed very strongly that I received an answer to my question from heaven and from God." She strongly believes that the dream in which Jesus appeared was an answer to her prayer, which brought a turning point in her life and led her to became a Christian. Other stories of dream experiences also reveal that the dreamers encountered the divine in their dreams and identified the divine with Jesus. These dream experiences reveal that the divine–human encounter occurs beyond the normal waking consciousness.

Converts experience God speaking to them. The nature of divine communication varies from hearing a voice, having a sense of God speaking to them while reading the Bible, a sense of realization while hearing a sermon, a sense of personalization of the message of the gospel, a sense of the presence of the "Other" who spoke to them within, and so on. Inban, who teaches in a technical university, felt as if someone knew everything about his private life. He explained that the habits that gave him pleasure suddenly became bitter to him. He also talked about the conviction that dawned on him that his religious worship was wrong. These breaks were not the product of intellectual exercises but the result of the personal experience of Jesus. Similarly, other experiences of divine communication, presented in chapter 3, show that it is more of a revelation from God than a rational awakening.

The narratives in chapter 4 demonstrate that converts experience miracles in their lives that result in a turning point. Jayasudha, a South Indian actor, had an encounter with Jesus while she was drowning in a sea and she escaped miraculously, which led her to follow Jesus. Kumar took baptism and became a Christian but was not interested in Jesus or in reading the Bible. Only later when he had a miraculous healing did he really encountered the divine. Though Kumar converted from his prior religion to Christianity by taking baptism, the real turning point occurred only at the divine–human encounter. For Devaraj, the crisis that threatened the lives of his family members was resolved by a prayer of a Christian friend. This encounter with the divine resulted in Devaraj's turning point. The miraculous experiences of these converts indicate that the turnarounds in their lives are beyond rational explanation, as they are not bound by logical account. Nevertheless, the converts had certainty that these experiences were acts of God. This understanding was given to them at the divine–human encounter.

Prayer experiences lead some people to change from one religion to another. Converts consider prayer experiences as proofs for them to accept the claims of Jesus. Some prayed to God without addressing him by any name due to their confusion about who the true God is. To their surprise, their prayers were answered by Jesus and a conviction dawned on them that Jesus is real and is the true God. Others prayed for healing. Some were healed; others were not, but claimed that their inner being was healed. Teenagers mostly prayed for success in their studies and future. Jemmu Bai, a tribal man, made a small prayer that he wanted to know who the real God is. He decided if there was no answer to his prayer by night, he would commit suicide, but that night he had a vision in which a person appeared and said, "I am the true God and my name is Jesus." Some had prayer experiences like this where they got clear answers that were contrary to their expectations, which resulted in their conviction that

The Mystical Turning Point

Jesus answered their prayers, and their lives were touched by him. The process of arriving at this conviction was not a rational exercise, but due to the divine–human encounter in answer to their prayers.

Some people were led to convert through mild experiences, such as a flash of spiritual insight, an act of realization or personalization of the Christian message, or a feeling of the presence of God. Some converts felt that the Christian faith answered their ultimate questions. However, we find the personalization of the message of Jesus a mystery. It is a mystery how some felt sinful in a given moment when they never felt sinful earlier. Suddenly, in a particular moment, they felt that what had been sweet all those years turned bitter; it was not just a change of perception due to an intellectual exercise. How does this turnaround occur? How can one suddenly feel the need for a savior and realize that Jesus is the true savior? How can one suddenly find that the religion of one's birth is not true, but that Jesus is the true God? How do negative attitudes towards Christianity vanish suddenly? It is a mystery. I asked converts to explain their turning point, and they said that they could not understand how it had happened to them. It was not a conscious decision, but suddenly a realization came to their conscious mind. The conscious choice was made only after the realization or personalization of the message. So how did this shift occur? They could not explain and they struggled to put the turning point into words.

Balan expressed his inability to pinpoint how the shift occurred in his life from worshiping Hindu gods to praying to a generic God and then to Jesus:

Balan: I was holding on to what my parents had taught me [Hindu beliefs and practices] for about twenty years. But then, I felt that idol worship was wrong and maybe there was something beyond idols and I wanted to know about that God. Somehow, the more I wanted to pray to God, it was so happened that I was praying to Jesus, and this was almost unconscious. The more I tried to seek God, somehow it was Christ that I was looking for. Maybe because I had the Bible with me it pointed to Jesus. I do not really know . . . I cannot clearly say why I switched over and looked to Jesus. But somehow I felt I should be praying to God and it so happened that Jesus . . . was the first person, first thing that came to my mind.

Balan felt it happened unconsciously, as he had not made a conscious choice to pray to Jesus. Mala, a medical doctor, shared how her turning point from worshiping idols to worshiping Jesus came through a mild experience:

Mala: One day, as I was reading the Bible, I was stuck by the verse, "I am your God . . . do not follow other gods" . . . I felt that I should read it again. I read it again, then I realized that I had not yet removed the statues from my room. Immediately, I disposed of the idols that I had. Again I came and read and the same verse came up to me; then I found one guru's photograph in my room and I removed that also. Again I started reading the Bible and the same verse was repeated to me; then I found my drawings of gods with me and I disposed of them also. For the first time I got the conviction that Jesus is the only God; till then I knew that Jesus was God, but suddenly I realized. God did not appear before me, but revealed this in my mind.

Mala was comfortable practicing her religion alongside reading the Bible for a period of time. However, one day she got the conviction that "Jesus is the only God." We find that it was not an intellectual or rational understanding, but a conviction that dawned on her while reading the Bible. She claimed that God revealed this in her mind. Mala read the Bible and was convinced of the claims of Christianity and began to experience the presence of God in her life. Along similar lines, Praveena, who suffered from spondylitis, had a strange experience. While chanting the names of Hindu gods, she felt in her mind that they did not exist anymore. She thought that she was becoming mad due to the medicines she was taking. But she also felt an urge to pick up the New Testament to read, which eventually led her to follow Jesus. The flash of thought repeatedly came to her mind that her gods were "Not there! Not there!" It was not a logical conclusion based on reasoning, but a forceful thought that was popping up from beyond the normal waking consciousness indicating that her gods were not real. The urge to read the New Testament led her to follow Jesus, though she did not understand what she read then.

The personalization of the message of the gospel could not be explained by the converts. Not everyone who reads the Bible gets converted. Converts at some point had a realization dawn on them that Jesus is God and he alone can forgive their sins. How did they receive the message personally? How and what made the converts believe that it is true? Aruna, a professor in an engineering college, said, "I did not know how that thought came to me that Jesus died for my sins." Though many times she heard from her friend that Jesus died for her sins, she never felt the need to personalize it. But when she saw a movie on Jesus, she personalized its message that Jesus died for her sins, and she cried a lot. She was not sure how that conviction came suddenly.

Some were prejudiced against Christianity up till their turning point, which shows that it occurred before they made a conscious decision. While the conscious mind was preoccupied with the struggle to leave the religion of one's birth and to accept Christianity, the mystical states of mind were at work to address the struggle and brought the turning point. Then the new frame of belief was brought to the normal waking consciousness and was accepted as the truth without any question. Once the turning point occurred, they held on to it firmly as the truth. All their preconceived ideas and negative attitudes towards Christianity vanished. No longer was their conscious mind agitated over leaving the religion of their birth; though in some cases the struggle continued for days, they did not give up what they received at the divine–human encounter. Converts were strongly convinced that they had experienced the truth; they felt they had a personal encounter with God that they had never experienced in their former religion. It made a deep impact on their lives. It gave them a certainty that their newfound knowledge of God was true and was drawn from a very personal experience. They began to see themselves and the world differently through the lens of this experience.

Converts make a commitment prayer to mark the shift. They commit their lives to Jesus, surrender themselves to him, and confess their sins. This prayer could be very simple, such as the one-line prayer reported by a student, "Amen, Alleluia, save me." On the other hand, Karan made a lengthy prayer: "Lord, forgive my sins . . . I want you to forgive me. I want you to take over my life. I want you to make me a useful person and I want to live a meaningful life." When he made this prayer he immediately felt that his sins were forgiven and was filled with joy. Some converts prayed while having their religious experience. Selvi mentioned that someone within her was praying for her in her vision of the crucifixion. Some of them did not know how to pray, but prayed as they felt and expressed their feelings and thoughts. Others were taught how to make a commitment prayer to mark the beginning of their spiritual journey with Jesus.

During the divine–human encounter, converts confess their sins and receive a sense of being forgiven at once by the divine. This experience is often when they first become aware that they are sinful. Acts that they considered normal earlier are suddenly considered sinful. Habits and behaviors that were sweet to them earlier suddenly turn bitter at the divine–human encounter. Some were addicted to alcohol and other habits, but suddenly felt their urge vanish. Some even began considering certain attitudes and actions sinful that were considered acceptable to everyone. Some felt before the encounter that they were sinful and needed to repent, and they confessed their sins to accept Jesus. Confession of sin in prayer is one of the marks of self-surrender and accepting Jesus.

Converts' feeling of being sinful, dirty, and ashamed during their religious experience was very strong and intense. Yet despite these feelings, they felt that Jesus accepted them and forgave them at once. This gave them positive emotions like joy, happiness, and peace that lasted for a long time. Their encounter with Jesus in the conversion experience was unparalleled and beyond their comprehension. The joy of being connected to God, which had been missing in their lives earlier, was found in the conversion experience. The divine–human encounter is the essence of the conversion experience.

Some used the language of love to describe the intimacy they developed with Jesus. Nithya described the core of her conversion experience as falling in love with Jesus. She argued that no one can say when a person will fall in love. But she claimed that she was very sure that she had received his love. Conversion is similar to "love at first sight" in that it is beyond rational explanation. The divine–human encounter evades rational explanation.

The turning point experienced at conversion is multifaceted; it involves the conviction that Jesus is true, the awareness that one's religion of birth is false, the realization and personalization of the message of the gospel, the consciousness of sin, and the assurance of being forgiven. The turning point also occurs beyond the normal waking consciousness; it is not due to a conscious choice or an intellectual exercise. James (1902/2004, p. 218) pointed out that faith has not only an intellectual dimension but also an intuitive one. When referring to Luther's faith, he said, "This other part is something not intellectual but immediate and intuitive, the assurance, namely, that I, this individual I, just as I stand, without one plea, etc., am saved now and forever." In a sudden moment converts experience an intuitive awareness that they are sinners and they feel that their sins are forgiven at once. This is a result of the divine–human encounter in the conversion process that makes one change over from one's religion of birth to follow Jesus.

The Mystical Turning Point

Both in the sensory experiences and even in gradual conversions or mild experiences, the moment of realization or the personalization of the message of Jesus is the religious experience in conversion. People do not realize they are sinners every time they hear the gospel. Even if they had heard the message of the gospel earlier, it is only in the particular moment of religious experience that the message is personalized so that they are convicted of their sins and feel the need to accept Jesus Christ as their savior. Not everyone who reads the Bible is convinced that their former pattern of worship is wrong. Only in a given moment of religious experience do people realize that their former worship is incorrect and embrace Jesus as the true God, rejecting the gods who had been close to their hearts till that moment. This realization is the result of the religious experience of the divine–human encounter, which occurs beyond the normal waking consciousness. The change is not an ideological shift due to a rational exercise but is the result of the divine–human encounter.

James (1902/2004, p. 444) argued for the existence of other forms of consciousness besides normal waking consciousness or rational consciousness. He claimed, "The world of our present consciousness is only one out of many worlds of consciousness that exist, and that those other worlds must contain experiences which have a meaning for our life also." Recent research affirms James' claim of the existence of other forms of consciousness. Bulkeley (2005, pp. 175–76) says, "a large body of evidence has accumulated regarding the tremendous amount of brain-mind functioning that occurs outside the bounds of ordinary waking consciousness. Experiences of wonder, mystical awe, and religious revelation clearly have multiple points of contact with these nonconscious brain-mind systems, and James' hypothesis remains a fruitful way of accounting for the interaction of psychological and religious factors in such experiences." The divine–human encounter in the conversion process confirms this because the encounter occurs beyond the normal waking consciousness.

James (1902/2004, p. 328) argued, "Personal religious experience has its root and centre in mystical states of consciousness." As we have seen earlier, Bulkeley (1999, 2003) argued that both psychology and religious studies agree that dreams originate beyond the waking consciousness. Bulkeley (1999, p. 16) further argued, "*Dreams can bring a dreamer closer to the sacred*" (italics original). Conversion dreams show that the dreamers encounter the divine and experience conversion. Batson, Schoenrade, and Ventis (1993) also point out that a new vision—cognitive restructuring—that results in personal transformation arises from the transcendental realm.

James (1902/2004), Batson et al. (1993), and Bulkeley (1999, 2003) point out the existence of a realm of awareness beyond the normal waking conscious mind. They also spell out the possibility of interaction between the mystical states of consciousness and the divine. James (1902/2004) analyzed conversion experiences and claimed that psychology cannot reject the presence of a power beyond the conscious mind and the existence of a psychological condition for interaction between the divine and human in the subconscious region. He argued, "Just as our primary wide-awake consciousness throws open our senses to the touch of things material, so it is logically conceivable that *if there be* higher spiritual agencies that can directly touch us, the psychological condition of their doing so *might be* our possession of a subconscious region which alone should yield access to them. The hubbub of the waking life might close a door which in the dreamy Subliminal might remain ajar or open" (p. 215; italics original). No matter what type of conversion experience a person goes through—sudden or gradual, sensory or mild—the divine–human encounter occurs at the mystical states of consciousness. This divine–human encounter is the turning point in the process of conversion to Christianity.

I have found that the mystical turning point in conversion to Christianity is *revelatory, conversational, and intimate*, in addition to having the features James identified: *ineffable, noetic, transient*, and *passive*. The divine–human encounter is revelatory because previous religious belief is not a mediating factor, but is replaced with the identification of the divine with Jesus. Converts do not experience a union with the divine, but a conversation takes place at the divine–human encounter and this encounter establishes intimacy between the convert and the divine. Converts are unable to describe the turning point. What the converts could narrate about their conversion experience was limited by what the conscious mind perceived about the encounter. Religious experience in conversion is ineffable. The divine–human encounter is incomparable to any other experience and cannot be explained. Converts have the certainty of experiencing the truth or the true God. This is the noetic quality of The divine–human encounter. Converts gain knowledge of God based on their experience. The divine–human encounter is transient and the converts are passive during the religious experience. The divine–human encounter could last for hours, such as in some experiences involving visions or dreams, or it may last for only a fraction of a second, such as in the realization or

The Mystical Turning Point

personalization of the message of Jesus. Converts are passive in the religious experience. I will discuss these features in the following order: *revelatory, conversational, noetic, ineffabie, transient, passive,* and *intimate*.

Revelatory is a key feature of the mystical turning point in conversion to Christianity. Converts claim to have received authentic knowledge of God and identified the divine with Jesus in the divine–human encounter. Scholars hold the view that religious experience is mediated by previously held religious beliefs. Katz (1978, pp. 26–27) asserted, "the forms of consciousness which the mystic brings to experience set structured and limiting parameters on what the experience will be, i.e. on what will be experienced, and rule out in advance what is 'inexperienceable' in the particular given, concrete, context. Thus, for example, the nature of the Christian mystic's pre-mystical consciousness informs the mystical consciousness such that he experiences the mystic reality in terms of Jesus, the Trinity, or a personal God, etc., rather than in terms of the non-personal, non-everything, to be precise, Buddhist doctrine of nirvana." This might be true of mystics, who are trained to have mystical experiences or who practice mysticism in their tradition, but not with converts who move from their religious traditions to Christianity. Converts in my study were shocked and perplexed in experiencing Jesus at the divine–human encounter, as it was contrary to their religious belief. Though converts come from different religious traditions, all of them identify the divine in the religious experience with Jesus, and they are certain that the figure who encounters them is Jesus. The revelatory feature of the divine–human encounter in conversion to Christianity destabilizes the claim that Hindus or Muslims cannot not have a vision of Jesus. Contrary to the claim of Katz, the unshakable confidence Sania had that the divine in her vision was Jesus demonstrates the revelatory quality of the divine–human encounter.

Sania: For the first time in my life, never had I seen such a thing. I saw with my eyes closed; I saw the whole room and everything. Near my table, I saw one person was standing—a huge, tall person—but I could not see the face. His face was bright, very bright . . . mmm, very bright. The garment itself was very bright. I do not know what he was wearing; it was like a *kurtha* [a long top men wear in India], a very bright thing. But I knew it was a person. But I could not see the face. I knew *instantly* that it was Jesus. Now he did not say, "I am Jesus"—nothing! I knew in my heart immediately that it was Jesus. I did not have any doubt. I never had any doubt. I did not even question myself. I cannot explain . . . that feeling! I just knew it was Jesus.

I even further probed her certainty that it was Jesus, as she could not see the face of the person who appeared in the vision. However, Sania pointed out that it was unexplainable, but was very confident that it was Jesus. After the vision lapsed, she struggled with the question, "Why did Jesus appear to me?" for a week, as she was a devout Muslim. Contrary to her previously held belief, the knowledge she gained through the religious experience was that Jesus is the true God and her religion of birth is wrong. Though she struggled initially to accept what was given to her at the divine–human encounter, she held on to it and was ready to pay any price. In a later chapter we will discuss the ordeal she went through for holding on to her newfound faith.

This is not only Sania's experience; other converts spoke with similar confidence about their experience of Jesus that altered the direction of their lives. Some converts were against Christianity, but all the rhetoric vanished at the divine–human encounter when they experienced Jesus. These converts became very zealous for the name that they despised earlier. Sadhu Sunder Singh, a Christian mystic from the Punjab in Western India, had torn the pages of New Testament given to him in his school. Later he struggled with the question, "Who is the true God." One night, he made a prayer within himself that if by morning he did not come to know who the true God is, he would commit suicide by falling in front of a running train. He had a vision of Jesus on that night and became a zealous preacher of the gospel he despised earlier. Bakht Singh is another example who claimed that the name that he despised earlier became sweet at his religious experience. In other types of religious experience, converts, despite the absence of a figure or other forms of sensory experience, identified that it was Jesus who communicated, who did miracles, who answered their prayers, who was present with them, and who met their needs. This strong conviction is the sign of the revelatory nature of the divine–human encounter in conversion to Christianity.

Sekar saw a bright light and instantly cried out, "Jesus save me!" How did he identify the bright light with Jesus? Komala could identify the figure in her dream as because he resembled the picture of Jesus she had seen earlier. It never occurred to her that it could have been someone else; she was very certain that it was Jesus, the true God. Vinodha in her dream

The Mystical Turning Point

heard someone calling her as daughter and was convinced that it was Jesus, but she could not explain how she could be certain of her claim. Similarly, Sarala in her dream identified the person in a car as Jesus while the crowd saying that it was *Arul Raj* [King of mercy in Tamil], but she could not give an explanation for why she was certain that it was Jesus. Inban felt that someone within him was speaking to him about his private life, and he was certain that it was Jesus who spoke to him in the Bible study. Nambiar was reading the New Testament for a year and felt someone within him telling him to take baptism. Nambiar's wife, Praveena, while chanting the names of Hindu gods had the thought flash into her mind that they were not real, and this was repeated every time she tried to chant the names of her gods. She felt an urge to read the New Testament and started to believe that Jesus is true. None of these converts could explain how they got the conviction it was Jesus who spoke to them in their minds. Ezhil prayed to Jesus after consuming poison and escaped from death. She believes that it was Jesus who saved her life. Sushila saw a bright light splashing on her and experienced healing that made her to hold on to Jesus. A miracle always comes with the knowledge and certainty that the act was God's.

Jemmu Bai wanted to know who the true God is and wanted God to heal him. He had a vision and saw Jesus introducing himself as the true God. Nathan was hesitant to pray to Jesus, but prayed without addressing any name for deliverance from his sinful life. After the prayer, he felt that Jesus gave him joy and peace. Balan prayed to God without using any name, but slowly he started praying to Jesus and felt it was a different kind of experience. None of them could explain how they were convinced that their prayers were answered by Jesus. However, the confidence they expressed was unshakable.

Mohan wanted to encounter the Supreme God in his spiritual search. When he read the New Testament and prayed he instantly felt that Jesus was the Supreme God that he was in search of. Vinitha was not ready to believe in Jesus and was skeptical; she reluctantly joined for prayer only because of her friends, but she experienced peace during the prayer and was convinced that Jesus is true.

In all these experiences we find the self-revelation of Jesus. Wiebe (1997, pp. 219–20), based on his study of Christic visions, found that the participants in his study made similar claims, identifying the figure in their visions with Jesus and expressing confidence in this. He observed:

> Though one might argue that general beliefs that are part of the culture can adequately explain the identification, they are unlikely

to explain the confidence percipients feel. One cannot legitimately assert that percipients *know* who appears to them, for knowledge claims involve being able to supply a justification for a belief, and justifications are notoriously lacking when it comes to Christic apparitions. I consider the general problem of identifying an experience as Christic—whether it is visual, auditory, a sense of presence, a conversion experience, or whatever—to be incapable of satisfactory resolution. Something evidently convinces percipients that the experience is Christic, but the claim does not appear to admit of justification in a public sense. (italics original)

Converts to Christianity find their religious experience itself the source of confidence in identifying the person they encounter with Jesus. They are certain of the knowledge gained through the religious experience. Cultural knowledge or prior religious belief cannot be the basis of their confidence and certainty; however, it could be a source of identification because converts talk about their prior knowledge about Jesus gained through movies and other sources. The revelatory nature of the religious experience makes them certain of what they perceive in their religious experience. The knowledge they gain is not through sensory perception but by revelation given through their mystical states of consciousness.

In the New Testament, St. Paul's vision of Jesus has a similar feature. Paul's vision was not conditioned by his Jewish beliefs. His Jewish belief about Jesus was that he was a mere man claiming to be God, and that his followers were seriously wrong in claiming that Jesus is the Messiah, so he was on his way to destroy this emerging sect in Judaism. In his vision, Paul asked, "Who are you, Lord?" and Jesus answered, "I am Jesus, whom you are persecuting." Jesus did not say that he was the Son of God or Messiah, yet this sufficed for Paul to change his belief about Jesus. After his vision he believed that Jesus is the Messiah whom the Jews were expecting and is also the Son of God; he even sacrificed his life for this newfound belief. We do not find any theological discourse here to convince Paul that Jesus is the Son of God. However, the self-revelation of Jesus brought a radical shift in Paul's religious belief. The self-revelation of the divine is beyond the comprehension of the rational consciousness; however, the given knowledge in the divine–human encounter is accepted as the truth without any hesitation by the rational consciousness after the encounter. The self-revelatory feature is fundamental to Christian conversion experience. Converts' previous religious belief is replaced by the new knowledge of who Jesus is. This knowledge is given through the mystical states of

The Mystical Turning Point

consciousness at the divine–human encounter. Though a convert's waking consciousness is preoccupied with negative ideas about Jesus, as in the case of St. Paul, the new knowledge of Jesus received at the divine–human encounter alters their entire cognitive structure to see the divine, self, and the world in a new light. This cognitive restructuring is the core of the turning point that begins with the self-revelation of the divine at the divine–human encounter and involves replacement of previously held religious belief with a belief in Jesus.

Conversation between the divine and human is another feature of the divine–human encounter in conversion to Christianity. The union of the self with the Absolute is absent in all religious experience associated with conversion to Christianity from various religious traditions. In a mystical experience of union, the individuality of a person is dissolved in union with the divine, but in the divine–human encounter central to conversion to Christianity, a fundamental element is conversation between the divine and human. This conversation at the divine–human encounter is informal; the divine sets the tone of informality in the discourse by calling the person by name or addressing him or her as daughter or son.

Sekar and Sania heard their names being called in their visions. Sania prayed, in response to the voice asking her to pray, "I do not know who this is asking me to pray. If there is a God, then I want to see that God. I have done all that my parents have told me to do, but I have never felt or seen you. If there is a God . . . if it is true that I am not mad, then I need to see who it is that is calling me." In answer to her prayer, the divine appeared immediately. She felt dark and poor in his presence, and she expressed her dependence on him, saying, "I do not know who you are, but Jesus, I need you. I know I need you in my life because I am very poor; I cannot handle it. I am very poor on my own. I cannot do anything; I need you." The divine and the person experiencing the vision are two different selves communicating. We also see that converts feel total dependency on the divine.

Selvi, in her vision of crucifixion, heard Jesus calling her "daughter." Komala, in her dream, heard Jesus telling her to read the Sermon on the Mount. Vinodha had a dream in which Jesus said to her, "Daughter, come to me." Inban felt that someone who knew his crooked life was talking to him. Nambiar felt that somebody inside of him told him to take baptism. Jemmu Bai prayed for healing and wanted to know who the true God is, and the person in his vision said, "I am the true God and my name is Jesus." Ezhil, when she was struggling to save her life after taking poison, heard Jesus telling her in her mind, "If you remain quiet for five minutes, I will give your life back." While reading the Bible, Nathan felt Jesus spoke to him when he thought of giving up the newfound faith due to opposition from his parents. He felt that God spoke to him through the verse, "Believe in the Lord Jesus, and you will be saved—you and your household" (Acts 16:31). He said, "Earlier, I never knew how the Lord speaks." Converts experienced such conversations with the divine at the divine–human encounter and this is continued in their subsequent encounters.

In conversion to Christianity, the divine and the convert are two different selves conversing, and this initiates a long-lasting relationship. The divine addresses the convert by name. This is similar to St. Paul's vision where Jesus called him, "Saul, Saul." Peace (1999) calls this conversation "dialogue" and points out that the vision was not a "generalized encounter," but was individual and particular. This is contrary to the claim of James (1902/2004, pp. 362–63) that union of the divine and the self occurs in mystical experience: "In mystic states we both become one with the Absolute and we become aware of our oneness. This is the everlasting and triumphant mystical tradition, hardly altered by differences of clime and creed." Not every case presented by James in *Varieties* has this feature of union with the Absolute. Scholars contest James' claim of common core of mystical experience, i.e., union with the divine, in all traditions. Nieto, in his book *Religious Experience and Mysticism* (1997), differentiates religious experience from mystical experience. He observes that union occurs only in mystical experience but not in religious experience. He points out that dialogue is not plausible in mystical experience, but possible only in religious experience. Conversation is possible only in an encounter between two selves. He argues, "The religious experience so structured by space and time sees the world and the self as two separate entities and so perceives Divine Reality as independent from both the world and the self. Thus, the experience of *union* fundamental to all forms of mystical experience is alien to religious experience" (p. 110). He calls religious experience an "awareness of transcendence." He further claims that dialogue between the self and the divine is central to Judeo-Christian religious experience. Converts to Christianity talk about an intimate relationship with the divine rather than union. I call it divine–human encounter because only in an encounter can the self and the divine meet and communicate. Various narratives of conversion to Christianity demonstrate that conversation between the divine and the self is a fundamental element in the religious experience leading to conversion.

The Mystical Turning Point

The *noetic* quality is evident in all types of conversion experience. Religious experience is not only rich in emotional feelings but is also encumbered with knowledge. James (1902/2004, p. 329) described, "They are states of insight into depths of truth unplumbed by the discursive intellect. They are illuminations, revelations, full of significance and importance, all inarticulate though they remain; and as a rule they carry with them a curious sense of authority for after-time." Some are skeptical of this claim and of the opinion that in mystical experience cognitive functioning is bypassed. However, recent cognitive research supports James' position. Bulkeley (2005, p. 173), based on a survey of cognitive neuroscience research, observed, "Mystical states are plausible sources of authentic knowledge." Converts talked about their new knowledge of experiencing the truth, knowing Jesus as the true God, certainty of knowing God, and discovering purpose and meaning of life through the divine–human encounter. The experiential knowledge of the divine gave them a deep conviction that Jesus is true. Here we find the intellectual dimension of faith is modified based on the encounter with the divine, and the intuitive dimension of personalizing the gained knowledge is simultaneous at the divine–human encounter.

Converts describe the divine–human encounter as an experience of the truth. They claim that through their religious experience they have known the truth and understood the truth and experienced Jesus as the true God. No matter what type of conversion experience they had, they were certain of experiencing the true God; this was a result of the religious experience. Let me give you some examples here. A student said, "I was longing to have relationship with the true God. I wanted to see the true God. Someone told me that Christ was the true God. So I asked Christ, 'If you are true God, then I want to see you.' I saw him." He also said, "I have come to the light. I was ignorant, but now I have known the truth." Such were the experiences converts reported about their experience of the divine. Arun, a businessman with a monthly turnover of 15 million rupees [US$ 300,000], said, "I have known the truth. I did not get converted for any benefits; I did not know the truth earlier." A woman in her sixties said, "Jesus proved it to me that he is the true God by delivering me from the evil attacks." Komala claimed, "I was desperate in knowing the true God and he appeared to me." Rekha was convinced about the truth: "Though my people were giving me a bad time, God was with me. That convinced me strongly that he [Jesus] was the true living God." Samsudeen was a devoted Muslim, but disenchanted with his religion. He claimed, "I did everything [religious requirements], but I could not get anything, but only after tasting the Lord, I realized that Jesus was the true God." Sania claimed that her vision of Jesus and the subsequent experiences made her say, "God is real." Surya reasoned out that his life was transformed so he was sure of the truth. He testified, "All sinful and bad habits have gone from my life. Only Jesus changed my life; he is the true God who has changed my life." Their experience of truth varies from sensory to mild, however, they are certain of experiencing the true God.

Besides the knowledge of the divine, the divine–human encounter gave some converts clarity of thought and enhanced their understanding of life and ultimate concerns. They also said that some kind of darkness was removed from their mind and light flooded it. Subsequently, their decision to follow Jesus was a clear choice and there was no confusion in changing their faith. They claimed that their doubts about Christianity were cleared, and they were convinced about its logical consistency. They felt that all their questions with regard to life and ultimate concerns they had prior to the encounter were answered. They believe that the answers came through the religious experience.

The revelatory nature of the divine–human encounter reveals Jesus as the divine and the noetic feature of the divine–human encounter grants converts the certainty of their knowledge through the personal experience. The certainty came to them not on hearing an intellectual or logical discourse on Christianity but through their religious experience. The rational consciousness no longer questioned what is experienced at the divine–human encounter. Many had negative ideas and attitudes towards Christianity, but when the new knowledge was given through the divine–human encounter, it was accepted as the truth.

Converts discover new meaning and purpose in their lives through the religious experience. Some had an existential crisis and wondered why they were living. They raised questions related to the meaning of life. Ultimate questions were answered in the conversion experience. Balan, an engineer, claimed, "God is the purpose of my life." A teacher in her twenties said, "Now I know the purpose why I am born and there is an eternal life. The Lord died for me and I need to follow him. God has a plan for me and I should live for him." Their new identity, based on belonging to Jesus, gave them a new purpose in life. Sania and Surya claimed that finding the purpose of life made a great change in them. The very idea that God has a purpose and that God is the purpose of their lives gave them a new worldview and new direction in their lives. It brought transformation in their attitudes and behaviors. Inban found that the hope of life after death gave meaning to this life. The hope of eternal life gave them meaning that this life is not an end in itself, but there is something to look forward. The hope of eternal life brought a new meaning in their daily life. This resulted in a change of attitude towards life. They began to see life and everything from this point of view. Their perspective on life and their motives in doing certain things changed in conversion. Now they can accept life's realities with a hope that they can make up for it in the life after death.

Though they would have gained some knowledge over a period of time after the divine–human encounter, primarily these convictions set in at the religious experience itself. They bring in profound changes in the lives of converts. Bulkeley (2005, p. 173) asserted, "We have progressed far enough to dismiss once and for all the misleading belief that only waking ego consciousness can provide us with real knowledge." The divine–humane encounter, though occurring beyond normal rational or waking consciousness, brings authentic knowledge in the mystical states of consciousness. James (1902/2004, pp. 366–67) pointed out the authentic nature of knowledge gained in religious experience: "Our own more 'rational' beliefs are based on evidence exactly similar in nature to that which mystics quote for theirs. Our senses, namely, have assured us of certain states of fact; but mystical experiences are as direct perceptions of fact for those who have them as any sensations ever were for us . . . even though the five senses be in abeyance in them, they are absolutely sensational in their epistemological quality . . . they are face to face presentations of what seems immediately to exist." The plausibility of gaining knowledge aside from rational consciousness is an accepted fact in psychology and cognitive science and is true in religious experience.

Ineffability is palpable in the conversion narratives. Converts found it very difficult to describe the divine–human encounter in words. James (1902/2004, p. 329) observed, "It defies expression, that no adequate report of its contents can be given in words. It follows from this that its quality must be directly experienced; it cannot be imparted or transferred to others." Similarly, converts tried different terms to describe the mystical turning point: "cannot be expressed, unable to express, a different kind of experience, a wonderful experience, a great experience, a real experience, a personal experience, a slow process and a gradual process." A college student said, "This experience cannot be expressed and is unparalleled to any other experience." Kavia, a professor, said, "It is a personal experience. I do not know how to describe it in words." Converts felt that what they had experienced was something personal and different from the ordinary, which could not be expressed in words.

The divine–human encounter is *transient*. In the sensory experiences, like visions, it lasted from a few minutes to hours. Sekar's vision lasted only for a few minutes, whereas Selvi had a vision of the crucifixion for about three hours, and Sania's vision lasted for more than an hour. Similarly, dreams lasted for a few minutes. In other types of experiences, the divine–human encounter was only a moment in which converts realized that God spoke to them, answered their prayers, and intervened. The individual has no control over retaining the encounter. James noted that even for many mystics, who cultivated practices to induce mystical experiences, religious experience is a passing event. Converts were not trained to induce religious experience; they were ordinary people, some not even thinking of religion or God. However, when the divine–human encounter occurred, it was a passing event. This element takes us to the next feature of passivity.

Passivity is not only a feature in the classical paradigm of conversion, but is also present in all types of conversion experience. Classical studies on conversion regarded converts as passive; however, sociological studies on conversion projected converts being active in the conversion process. Many converts actively pursue the new religious option to resolve their crisis and test the workability in their lives; however, they are passive at the moment of divine–human encounter. James (1902/2004, p. 330) observed, "The mystic feels as if his own will were in abeyance, and indeed sometimes as if he were grasped and held by a superior power." In the visions reported in the first chapter, we find that the subjects were under the power of the divine. Selvi cried, Sekar walked out of the house, and Sania knelt and cried. These behaviors indicate that they were under the influence of an external power—the divine. For others, the conviction that Jesus was true, that their sins were forgiven, and that they were saved was given as a gift, as they were passive at that moment and experienced a loss of volition. Some were agitated to accept Christianity before the divine–human encounter but became ardent followers of Jesus since the divine–human encounter.

Evangelicals claim that the born-again experience is a rational exercise sans emotion. Contrarily, a person becomes a Christian through religious experience—the divine–human encounter that comes with rich emotion. The fact that converts suddenly realize their sins and experience a sense of being forgiven is not a rational exercise. Jesus told Nicodemus

The Mystical Turning Point

that he must be born again and used an analogy of wind, "The wind blows wherever it pleases. You hear its sound, but you cannot tell where it comes from or where it is going. So it is with everyone born of the Spirit" (John 3:8). The origin or the destination of the wind cannot be observed with our senses. However, anyone could feel the effects of wind when it blows, and the effects can be empirically studied. The experience of being born again cannot be captured with the senses, but the effects of the same are visible for anyone to see. Jesus was talking about an experience by the Spirit that is beyond the grasp of rational exercise, but Nicodemus mistook it and questioned Jesus about the irrational aspect of his suggestion. Spiritual birth is facilitated by the Spirit of God.

Christian conversion cannot be equated with an ideological shift, like a Democrat shifting allegiance to the Republican. It is much more than that. The intellectual dimension of the faith is only one aspect, as pointed out by James, however, the intuitive dimension where a sense of being saved, a sense of being forgiven and accepted by God, is *given* to a person at the divine–human encounter. As we have seen in the previous chapters, there are different forms of divine–human encounter, from sensory experiences of visions and dreams to mild experiences of profound realization of the message of the gospel or a spark of spiritual insight, but the intuitive dimension is common to all. Converts are passive in the divine–human encounter in which the revelatory knowledge of God is given.

Intimacy between the divine and converts begins at the religious experience. Converts experience the perfect love of God and feel closer to the divine at the encounter, and they make every effort to sustain the intimate relationship thereafter. Converts are fascinated by the love of the divine. Those who never received real love from their parents or from their friends were longing to experience true love and found true love in Jesus. Selvi, who had a vision of crucifixion, talked about her experience of divine love: "His [Jesus] unlimited love is incomprehensible. I was drawn to him only because of his love." Converts considered Jesus sacrificing his life for people to be the demonstration of true love. The sense of being unconditionally accepted by Jesus is a crucial factor in experiencing the divine love. Rekha, while she was in college, felt she did not get genuine love from her parents. She was actively searching for true love. She found that in Jesus. Ranjan said, "I felt happy that I have someone who understands me and loves me. I was longing for that, so I was happy." This experience of divine love gives converts a sense of intimacy with divine.

Janaki visualized herself in the position of the beloved, with Jesus as the lover, as described in the *Song of Songs*. She was captivated by the divine love. Earlier we saw Nithya describing her conversion experience as falling in love with Jesus and talked about her intimate relationship with him: "I am staying alone in this flat. People ask me, are you staying alone? I tell them, "No, I am with my Christ." I even say that I am with my boyfriend. [She laughs.] He is my good friend. I feel there is no better friend than him. I was seeking for people's love—he didn't love me or they didn't love me, etc.—but now I have Jesus's love." Jumbulingam, a young man, was forced to live in exile due to unexpected circumstances. Later he turned out to be a *dacoit* (an outlaw) and separated from his wife and children. He could not experience love from anyone. When Amy Carmichael, the founder of Dohnavur Fellowship, shared the gospel, Jumbulingam found the divine love and unconditional acceptance despite his social standing as a *dacoit*. This made him fascinated with the love of the divine. Converts like Jumbulingam could not find any fulfilled human relationship, but perceived the divine love as true and perfect at the divine–human encounter.

Sania was pampered with love in her home. Still, she was also captivated by the divine love. She was forced to leave the house due to her conversion. She compared her love for her dad and Jesus: "I love Jesus so much to give up for my dad, to give up Jesus for my dad . . . I love my dad also, but I love Jesus more." Sania was torn between her love for dad and the love of Jesus. She was willing to give up her dad rather than Jesus. Later she did that and walked out of the house to hold on to the love of Jesus.

The participants of my study were not nuns and monks spending all their time meditating on Jesus. They were ordinary folks, living amid daily chores and struggles. However, they were captivated by the love of Jesus. The divine–human encounter in conversion experience initiated an intimate relationship with the divine. They claimed that they could not find this kind of intimate relationship in any human relationship or even with the divine in the religion of their birth. Rambo (1993, p. 160) observed a similar feature in conversion experience: "God is no longer an abstract concept but a living reality . . . there is a sense of intimacy and connection that was not there before." Such intimate relationship is plausible only in an encounter, not in union. Converts cultivate habits and practices to maintain the intimacy with Jesus for the rest of their lives.

This aspect of intimate relationship with Jesus reflects the findings of Luhrmann (2012). She points out, "No humans have truly unconditional relationships after the complete dependency of infancy, after the

The Mystical Turning Point

expectations of right behavior become part of our relationships with even the most loving adult. It is hard to feel loved even in an ordinary way by an invisible being. Yet feeling loved unconditionally is clearly set out as the true experience of God at a church like the Vineyard" (p. 102). Similarly, the feeling of being loved unconditionally by the divine is a vital factor for converts and they are fascinated by this experience of divine love. Converts experience with the divine what is not possible in human relationships. Invariably, converts point out that one thing that holds them to Jesus is his unconditional love and acceptance.

Luhrmann claims that Vineyard members are being taught how to talk to God and listen to him when he talks back. She has presented various experiences of the members showing that this is real for them despite their doubts. They are trained to perceive Jesus as an imaginary and invisible friend. She points out that the church helps them listen to God by training them to differentiate their own thoughts in their minds and God's voice. She says, "The pastor teaches that when you are intimate and personal with a supernatural being, God speaks to you. Not all the time and usually not audibly, but in as real and as practical a way as if you were sitting down to coffee with a puzzle you had to solve" (Luhrmann, 2012, p. 6).

Unlike the Vineyard members, converts begin to experience intimacy with the divine instantly at the divine–human encounter, not out of skillful training. When the converts encountered Jesus, they were not Christians trained to recognize the presence of Jesus. The divine–human encounter was a surprise gift from God and they instantly identified the divine with Jesus. We discussed this above. The experience of the unconditional love of Jesus was not due to teachings by a pastor. The divine–human encounter was a personal experience. In fact, many were not ready for it and never expected anything like it. However, the divine–human encounter made them feel that Jesus is always with them, that they can talk to him, and that he guides them by talking to them. For converts the voice of God is sometimes audible many times not audible, but only recognizable in their minds. Converts do not train their minds to recognize an imaginary friend, but instantly recognize the presence of the divine and the voice at the divine–human encounter. Nobody in my study said that they were trained to imagine God's presence or to imagine hearing God's voice. They only talked about the presence of the divine within them that enables them to talk to God as if they were talking to a friend. However, some talked about a process of learning to recognize the voice of God while referring to subsequent interactions with the divine because sometimes they found it difficult and confusing to differentiate God's voice from their own thoughts. However, in my study and that of Luhrmann (2012) the intimate relationship people have with Jesus is common. We will see the transforming effects of the divine–human encounter in the following chapter.

8 Transforming Effects

> The active agent in "sacred mushrooms" can induce mystical/spiritual experiences descriptively identical to spontaneous ones people have reported for centuries.
>
> —Johns Hopkins Medicine (Press Release, 2006)

> The positive findings of the [above] study cannot help but raise concern in some that it will lead to increased experimenting with these substances by youth in the kind of uncontrolled and unmonitored fashion that produced casualties over the past three decades.
>
> —Herbert D. Kleber (2006)

THE DIVINE–HUMAN ENCOUNTER EXPERIENCED at conversion triggers personal transformation. All dimensions of converts' lives are touched by the religious experience. William James (1902/2004, p. 175) described transformation this way: "Our ordinary alterations of character, as we pass from one of our aims to another, are not commonly called transformations, because each of them is so rapidly succeeded by another in the reverse direction; but whenever one aim grows so stable as to expel definitely its previous rivals from the individual's life, we tend to speak of the phenomenon, and perhaps to wonder at it, as a 'transformation.'" In conversion to Christianity, previously held religious beliefs are replaced by belief in Jesus at the divine–human encounter. We saw in the previous chapter that this shift was brought to waking conscious by the divine–human encounter. Though conversion is a process, a radical or a sudden shift in the center occurs suddenly in the divine–human encounter. In conversion to Christianity, the shift in the center could be from being nonreligious to becoming a Christian, or from holding to one's religion of birth to following Jesus. What was interesting to them earlier was no longer appealing to converts because of the sensitivity to sin gained at the divine–human encounter. James (1902/2004, p. 177) called the center of a person the "habitual centre of his personal energy," "the group of ideas to which he devotes himself, and from which he works." In conversion to Christianity from different religious traditions, this center is suddenly occupied by Jesus, replacing one's religious beliefs, and views against Christianity. People become followers of Jesus who never thought that they would become Christians. Their aims, attitudes, and behaviors are redirected to please the divine—Jesus. James (1902/2004, p. 214) describes the effects of conversion: "What is attained is often an altogether new level of spiritual vitality, a relatively heroic level, in which impossible things have become possible, and new energies and endurances are shown. The personality is changed, the man *is* born anew" (italics original). In conversion to Christianity, the "new level of spiritual vitality" involves a change of religious belief from one's prior religion to believing in Jesus.

The transforming effects of conversion reach the spiritual, psychological, behavioral, physical, social, and economical dimensions of life.

Spiritual effects are related to God, sin, life after death, and ministry. Converts' understanding of God is modified in conversion and they begin to see God not as a distant factor, but as a close companion and an intimate friend. They develop a new understanding of sin. They begin to look at life from an eternal perspective and they obtain greater power to handle life situations.

Converts feel the divine presence always. While dealing with the mystical turning point, we saw how an intimate relationship with the divine is developed. They talk to Jesus about anything and feel his presence at all times. Jesus became a constant companion in the lives of converts. Inban said, "I could feel his power. I could feel his encouragement. I could feel his strength. I could feel his intimate fellowship. I could feel the presence of God." Mala, a doctor, claimed, "I can feel his presence always. He is with me and I enjoy him comforting me. I can experience God as a person who is always with me." Jesus became a constant companion who comforts, guides, and never leaves them. Ishwar, a medical doctor, said that he was saved providentially in two accidents by Jesus. Samsudeen, a convert from Islam, recalled, "When I was about to be attacked [for his conversion], God hid me from their sight." These kinds of event made the converts feel that Jesus is with them always.

Converts' lives become God-centered. Nathan, a charted accountant, said, "Earlier the idea of God was not a big thing in my life. Only whenever I went out, I sought God's protection. My devotion was only at that level. Only after I started reading the Bible, I began to think about God [seriously]. Earlier, I sought God only for my needs. But now I think about God because he created me and I need to please him. I should not do things that will displease him." Kamal, an engineer, was fascinated by the love of Jesus and expressed his intention to sustain the intimacy with Jesus for the rest of his life:

Kamal: Jesus is the indispensable person in my life. I cannot live without him; without him there is no hope in life and no eternity. The most important thing is that I cannot live without him—not for material [blessings]. He loves me so much. I cannot go back [to Hinduism]. I am his child. He will not leave me at any time. God as a friend does not reject me at any time, leave me in any situation, and is with me always by holding my hand. I do not see God as others see. He is there for me; I see him as the only person who can understand me, who can love me, and who can be with me. Nobody can understand me except God; only he can understand me, as I am a complex person. God is the only person who will not leave me. He loves me so much. I am trying to love him back. He is faithful to me all these days. He has not rejected me. I am trying to be faithful to him and trying to show my love to him. The love that Jesus showed on the cross could not be paid back by me even in eternity.

These kinds of experiences indicate that converts' lives began to revolve around the divine since the divine–human encounter.

Converts relate to Jesus as an intimate friend. They describe him as a close friend who is always with them and is everything to them. One person said, "He is the lover of my soul"; another said, "He is my love." Some said they feel that they are incomplete without him. This language contains the tone of love and intimacy between the divine and individuals.

Converts find that Jesus loves them so much and does not expect anything in return. The idea of love without strings attached is a forceful factor in their perception of God.

Besides considering Jesus as an intimate friend, converts perceive God as a father, mother, and brother. Some perceive God as teacher, adviser, counselor, guide, master, advocate, role model, and shepherd. They describe Jesus as the true God, living God, loving God, Savior, Lord, a family deity, prayer-answerer, refuge, helper, and physician, one who transforms life, and one who gives meaning in life. In all these descriptions, an intimate relationship with Jesus is evident. This intimacy is sustained through prayer.

The interaction between the divine and converts which began at the divine–human encounter continues in their daily lives through prayer. Converts claim that their prayers are answered by Jesus. Deensha, from a Muslim family, said, "If there is any problem, I can ask the Lord. I ask him with a determination. When I pray, immediately, I get a relief and I am satisfied. He also guides me." At the time of his conversion, Devaraj was part of his family printing business which has a well-earned brand name. When he got converted, he could not continue in his family business as he felt that the business dealings were not straightforward. He walked out of the business and started his own. People thought that it was suicidal in business for him. But he claimed that he took Jesus as his senior business partner and consulted him in every decision he made. He said, "By prayer, good customers and orders started coming and I could develop my business. Before meeting a client, I pray for him and ask the Lord to give me wisdom to talk to him. I pray, 'If the client is good, only then, he should continue [business] dealings with us. Otherwise he should leave on his own.' This is how very good clients started coming on our way." He was very confident that the success in his business is due to Jesus. Contrary to the expectation of people in his town that his business would collapse, he was successful in a short time and the business grew to a great extent. The entire town looked at his business growth with awe. He gave the credit to Jesus.

Kamal, prayed to Jesus as a school student: "I asked God that I should come first in my school. Till then I did not do well [in my studies], but I began to work hard and gained confidence. By God's grace, I was the school topper in class X [the final year of high school, in which the examination is conducted by the State Board]. People were surprised that I stood first." The confidence that their prayers are answered by the divine

Transforming Effects

made the converts feel that Jesus loves them. Their prayers are addressed to Jesus, who listens to them and acts on their requests. A sort of unlimited resource is found in Jesus; whether it is for studies, day-to-day struggles, business dealings, or sickness, they can approach Jesus. This enabled them to have complete trust in Jesus. Sarala, who lost her husband, said, "Everything is in the Lord's hand. The one who is gone is gone. So, hereafter, for me everything is God. With that assurance, I became bold [to face life]." When her husband died suddenly, she did not have any support to take care of her two young daughters. At conversion, she came to feel that she could lean on Jesus. She began to trust Jesus for everything.

Converts continue to have religious experiences of visions and dreams and hearing the voice of God, which bring them closer to the divine over time. They hear the voice of Jesus telling them what will happen or what to do in a given situation. Some converts see visions and have auditory experiences frequently. Some see dreams often that guide them. Some have precognition and considered it a special power given by God to know of dangers in advance.

Subsequent religious experiences of Jesus reinforce converts' faith in him. Komala described her vision of Jesus on Easter:

Komala: I am very sure that Jesus is listening to my words and prayers; he is listening to our conversations. I could feel his presence in early-morning prayers. He is with us and answers us. If I tell him to wake me at 3:00 in the morning for prayer, he would wake me. He has assured us that he is in us and with us. Even if you do not have anything or anybody, he is with us. Often I think of a song: "Whoever may leave, but Jesus will never leave me." I love the songs sung by [a Christian music artist]. While doing my work I will sing those songs, and they are like tonic to me. I always feel him in me. Always he dwells in my house, as it is written, "This is my resting place for ever and ever; here I will sit enthroned, for I have desired it." (Psalm 132:14)

Three years back, on Easter morning, one of my relatives and I had planned to attend the 5:00 a.m. service in the church. I was waiting for her and was reading the Bible. There was a new iron pot over there [pointing to a corner of the room]. I could see the reflections on it as it was shining. I was reading John chapter 20. I was reading the verse, "Early on the first day of the week, while it was dark, some of the women went to the tomb." I was visualizing the whole incident: At 5:00 in the morning, it was very dark. How it would have been on those days! They would not have had slippers and the way to the tomb would have been very dreadful, but still they made it. How much they would have loved him to do that!

As I was thinking, I saw Jesus in a vision. I was sitting on this bed and reading. I saw him dressed in white and coming, walking towards me. I saw his reflection down to his waist region. I was trying to see his face, but suddenly he disappeared. He is here; he lives in this house. So his blessings are always with us. Because he is here, we have peace in this house. We sit together as a family and pray for solutions to all our problems. By his grace, we can solve all the problems.

Converts hear Jesus speak to them, sometimes audibly and they feel the presence of Jesus constantly. Janaki, a secret Christian for about thirty years, reported, "God would constantly speak to me. He was leading me always. Because I was praying, I could understand his voice. Sometimes I would hear him calling me by name. I thought my husband was calling me and came out to see!" I asked her, do you hear him calling you by name? She said, "Yes, clearly, he would call me by my name. Sometimes I thought that my husband was calling me. So I went running to him, but he would be sleeping. Then I realized that the Lord had called me. He revealed many things in advance except the death of my son-in-law. In the nights, he would call me and reveal things to me, so I could pray about those things." Such experiences made her pray meaningfully. She did not have any social support from a church or a fellowship because her husband never allowed her to practice her faith publicly; despite this, she held on to Jesus. These kinds of religious experience sustained her in her newfound faith. Another woman, Chitra, said, "I hear his voice by 3:00 or 4:00 in the morning. He wakes me up. I get up and kneel down to pray." She narrated an incident in which she had an argument with her husband, who was not a Christian. He went to work after the quarrel. She recalled, "I was alone in the house and I heard a voice loudly asking me, 'Which way would you like to go?' I was terrified and realized immediately that I should not have spoken to my husband like that. He [Jesus] never spoke to me like that. I realized that I made a mistake and was terrified and went out of the house. I felt that the Lord did not like the way I spoke to my husband. When my husband came back, I told him that 'The Lord did not like the way I spoke to you' and what had happened after he had left the house." She was not able to openly practice her newfound faith but had restricted freedom. This is not the only incident after her conversion. She claims that the Holy Spirit guided her and taught her what to do in everything and how to go about in her faith journey.

Another woman could not go to church as her mother-in-law was against her attending church. She was discouraged. She had a vision: "One night I was sleeping alone and was very sick. The Lord appeared to me and patted me and said, 'Eat well.' Then he disappeared. Since then, I told my mother-in-law that I would go to church and would not come to the temple anymore."

Sania claimed that she was introduced to various beliefs and practices of Christianity through visions: "He [Jesus] was speaking to me directly from that day [the day she had a vision of Jesus] because I did not know the Bible. Every time, I used to pray in my own style. I would go into my room and close my eyes and talk to him as I did that day. I would just talk. I would see a vision in which he would show me different things. My friend introduced me to a Pentecostal church. I would call up the pastor and tell him the vision. He used to come and explain to me from the Bible exactly what I had seen in my vision." One such example she gave was about baptism. She narrated a dream on baptism: "In that dream, I saw myself under the water and was coming out. Something like a rubber stamp came and hit me here [showing her forehead]. I called up the pastor and he explained to me about baptism. Then I asked him to give me baptism. But he said, 'No, no, wait. You are going very fast; take time. No, no, you wait. You think about it.' He was telling me about baptism and what it means. After a week—no, after three/four days—I had the same dream. Then I knew in my heart that I had to take it. By then I knew what baptism was." Sania learned many things about her newfound faith through such religious experiences.

Kushbu went through a difficult time practicing her newfound faith, as she was from a Muslim family. She had a dream in which Jesus appeared as a woman and encouraged her to hold on to him: "Once in my dream I saw a woman dressed brightly. She was not an ordinary woman; I could see a motherly love in her. She asked me for food and I offered her, then she encouraged me by saying, 'Good, take care, and I am glad about you . . .'. She was not looking like a woman. She was talking to me as a mother, but the voice was like that of Jesus. Then I awoke and felt very happy." Kushbu felt happy and encouraged with this dream. Such dreams gave her the needed inner strength while she struggled alone to practice her newfound faith.

Devaraj claimed in his interview that his business trips were guided by his dreams: "If I had to go to Mumbai, the Spirit of the Lord would reveal to me one week before or the previous day through dreams. He would tell me what would happen, like missing a train, or missing my luggage, or falling sick. Taking this into consideration, I changed my plans. Sometimes, when I had gone despite these warnings, I had faced serious problems. Now that I have had such experiences, I take these warnings seriously." Dreams not only lead people to experience conversion, but also enable them to continue in their newfound faith. The content could be about the beliefs and practices of Christianity or guidance in daily life. These kinds of dreams strengthen converts in their faith and guide them in life situations.

Religious experiences of visions, hearing voices, and dreams make the converts feel that they have a special relationship with Jesus who communicates with them regularly and takes care of them. Converts believe that the visions, auditory experiences, and dreams are given to them to correct them, to encourage them, to guide them, and to teach them the beliefs and practices of Christianity. These experiences give them an assurance that Jesus is with them always. Converts feel that they are not alone; Jesus is with them always to guide them and help them.

Converts have constant interaction with the divine in everyday life. Such religious experiences reinforce their faith in Jesus. Kushbu narrated how Jesus guides her in handling a crisis:

Kushbu: The Lord speaks to me clearly about how to face a problem and handle it. The Holy Spirit instructs me how to do things. For example, when my husband comes from the office in an angry mood, the Lord instructs me not to argue or fight with him, but provide him something to eat, like that. I started reading the Bible and praying regularly. He gives me strength in my spirit, and by the counseling of Jesus I can overcome many difficult situations. He advises me in handling my problems ... He is a great counselor to me.

Q: How do you understand that he is speaking to you?

Kushbu: Yes! I can feel his voice—a motherly voice. I can also hear the other voice, of Satan. I am able to differentiate between the voices:

this is the voice of Jesus, and that is the voice of Satan. So I follow Jesus; at the same time, I bind Satan in my prayer.

The interaction between converts and Jesus is an ongoing religious experience in converts' lives. It shows the intimacy they have with Jesus, and the confidence that he is guiding them in every situation makes them feel closer to the divine.

In response to a question to describe God's qualities based on their conversion experience, converts described God as "real, a person, Spirit, eternal, creator, source of life, holy, truthful, light, salvation, immanent, awesome, unchanging, almighty, living, loving, merciful, compassionate, kind, gracious, good, one who does not expect anything in return, trustworthy, possessive, stronghold, wonderful, and beautiful." Even though they claimed that these descriptions are based on their experience of the divine, we cannot construe that they are purely based on their experience. Their understanding of God would have grown over time. Their involvement with a church and the influence of the religious authorities in shaping their perception of God cannot be ignored. However, they claimed that religious experience is a regular feature in their lives since the divine–human encounter. These descriptions of God are based on their reflections on their experiences.

They also described God based on what he did in their lives or how he related to them. God, for the converts, is a person who "loves, communicates, transforms, teaches, delivers, forgives, understands, blesses, guides, saves, cares, protects, comforts, helps, provides, honors, convicts, sees, gives strength, gives peace, gives joy, gives eternal life, reveals himself, seeks the sinners to save them, sacrificed his life, removes loneliness, removes ignorance, and is present always." Jesus is perceived as a companion in life who meets their emotional needs. He is also perceived as a superman who is always ready to respond to their extraordinary as well as small needs. These descriptions indicate constant interaction between converts and Jesus.

By having Jesus on their side, they feel that they have unlimited power to face any situation in life. The underlying perception is that God controls everything and takes care of everything in their lives. This confidence was not there before the divine–human encounter. Their confidence in Jesus has altered their perception of life and crises. Many who converted from Hinduism used to perceive their gods as unpredictable, not knowing whether a deity would bless them or bring a curse on them, but they are confident that Jesus is good. Even if critical situations arise, they are confident that they need not be shaken because Jesus will handle it, irrespective of them pleasing him or not. They have a strong feeling that they are not alone in facing any crisis because Jesus is with them. He has unlimited power to do anything and he always seeks their welfare. Furthermore, their confidence that Jesus responds to their prayers is not a one-time event but a regular experience.

Many who had never felt sinful earlier did feel sinful at the divine–human encounter. Some former habits were considered normal and acceptable, but after the divine–human encounter they consider them as sins. Some claimed that their sensitivity to sin dramatically increased since the divine–human encounter. Some said they did not have any bad habits, yet they still realized how sinful they were. Some of their thoughts and attitudes appeared sinful to them at the divine–human encounter. Bakht Singh explained how he felt when he read the Gospels:

Bakht Singh: I have never felt so ashamed as I felt then, because all the blasphemous words I had uttered against Christ came before me. All my sins from school and college days came before me. I learned for the first time that I was the greatest sinner and I discovered that my heart was wicked and filthy. My petty jealousies against my friends, my enemies, and my wickedness were all clear before me. My parents thought I was a good boy, my friends regarded me a good friend, and the world considered me a decent member of society, but only I knew my real state. Tears were rolling down my cheeks and I was saying, 'Oh Lord, forgive me. Truly I am great sinner.' (Singh, n.d. p. 5)

Similarly, Selvi described how she was convicted of her sins while having a vision of the crucifixion: "That day all my sins from my childhood days came to my mind like a movie. I could see the cross and all my sins. Sins did not mean big sins, but small things like arguing with my parents, disobeying them, and things that grieved Jesus, etc. My tears wet my pillow as I was crying and praying." These excerpts point out that converts were not struggling with sin before the divine–human encounter. They were quite normal, like anyone happily enjoying life. They did not seek a solution to address the problem of sin in their lives, because they never felt sinful. But their religious experience at conversion made them feel like great sinners and ashamed of their past. The presence of the divine imparts the consciousness of sin to converts.

Some felt sinful when they were exposed to the teachings of Christianity. They began to view their lives in the mirror of Christian teachings and felt they were sinful. That required them to look for a solution. Allavi, as a small boy from a Muslim family, after reading a tract, felt miserable about his sinful life. Krishna Pillai, a famous Tamil poet, read the Bible and realized that he was accountable for his sins. Similarly, a college student said, "One day [in a Bible study] they were talking about sin, and a fear gripped me." Ganga said that before she never had any fear of sin or sense of accountability for her sin: "Even if I knew they were wrong, there was no fear . . . Only now I have the consciousness of sin. The fear of God that I have now was not there earlier." Conversion experience made converts feel accountable for their sins.

Conversion makes converts feel guilty of their sins. Inban described his guilt: "Before I accepted the Lord Jesus Christ, I was like everyone—watching movies, reading novels, chatting with my friends unnecessarily, etc. But I did not feel guilty about [doing these things] because everyone was doing them, so I also did. I never felt guilty about any of those things . . . Since my conversion, if I commit any sin or misbehave, I feel so strongly guilty about it that I cannot even sleep." Converts' sensitivity to sin is increased and they feel guilty of even for small things that earlier they would have brushed aside as nothing. Most converts never felt sinful or wicked before they had their divine–human encounter or were exposed to the teachings of Christianity, but during the conversion process they felt guilty about their past. They also began to feel more guilty after the divine–human encounter.

The divine–human encounter leads converts to confess their sins. Converts claimed that when they confess their sins, they received a sense of being forgiven of their sins at once. Surya recalled, "When I accepted Jesus Christ as my God, I got peace and joy in my heart. I got the assurance that God has forgiven my sins." Surya was one of the few who had been struggling with his sins before conversion. He was searching for an answer to his sinful life in Hinduism, the religion of his birth. He tried various religious practices, but could not find any solution. His friends presented the gospel, and he was terrified by the message of the gospel that the wages of sins is death. He became all the more concerned about his sinful life.

Then he thought to himself, "Why not try Jesus?" He confessed his sins and claimed that he received forgiveness of sins at once. For many years, he had tried various ways and means, but in vain. When he tried Jesus, he felt his sins were forgiven.

Selvi and Bakht Singh claimed that during their religious experience all the sins they committed came flashing into their minds. At the divine–human encounter, their sins were brought back to their memory and made them feel how sinful they were. There was no argument or any attempt to justify their position as righteous; they never had any hesitation in accepting themselves as sinners. Their only response was to confess their sin and plead for mercy from the divine.

When they confessed their sins, they felt that they received forgiveness of sins at once. They felt that they were made clean or their sins were washed away, and they were freed from guilt. They felt clean in their inner life. Converts claimed that they were set free from sinful habits and no longer had the urge to continue the same things that they had enjoyed earlier. In their conversion experience converts adopted a new system of measuring morality: comparing with Jesus. Their conscience became sharpened to consider some formerly accepted attitudes, thoughts, and pleasure-seeking habits as sins.

James (1902/2004, p. 171) described conversion in this way: "a self hitherto divided, and consciously wrong, inferior and unhappy, becomes unified and consciously right superior and happy, in consequence of its firmer hold upon religious realities." This definition is not suitable for all converts to Christianity. Only some experienced the sense of a "divided self" or struggled over sin or felt miserable about their addiction or sinful life before conversion. Many never had consciousness of sin and were living a normal life, as we have seen above. But their religious experience interrupted this and brought in a sense of sin. The divine–human encounter brought the sense of a divided self in the presence of the divine, but then at once it brought the sense of being unified through being accepted by the divine. In their conversion experience converts are startled with a sense of sin, even though the sins were not grave in nature. They confess their sins and seek forgiveness from the divine, and they instantly feel they receive forgiveness and acceptance, which results in unspeakable joy. Converts gain a new desire to be holy and experience a sort of revival in their lives. They feel that they become more religious and spiritual. They feel that all their former years were wasted for not knowing Jesus earlier.

Converts do experience a divided self—not concerning their sin, but about leaving the religion of their birth. Converts struggle to leave their religion to adopt Christianity. Bakht Singh expressed his struggle in kneeling down while attending worship in a ship on his way to the USA. He did not conceal his biases against Europeans and Christians: "'these people do not know anything about religion. They have exploited my country and I have seen them eating and drinking. What do they know? After all my religion is the best religion.' So my national, intellectual and religious pride prevented me from kneeling and I wanted to go out" (Singh, n.d. p. 4). This is the kind of attitude people in India have toward Christianity. Krishna Pillai, a well-known Tamil poet, felt hurt when his brother converted to Christianity. Then, when the missionary under whom he was working asked, "When is your turn?," Krishna Pillai was so offended that he submitted his resignation. The missionary pleaded with him and promised him that he would never speak to him about religion. Krishna Pillai kept himself from even talking about Christianity with anyone. Later, however, when a friend told him about his conversion, Krishna Pillai had a religious experience—a spark of spiritual insight that he was a sinner—and confessed his sins and became a Christian (Appasamy, 1966).

The divided self over leaving one's own religion and accepting Jesus is unified by the divine–human encounter in the conversion process. The unique feature of this study, moving from other religious traditions to following Jesus, is unparallel to other conversion studies as the context here is multireligious. A religious change is possible without a religious experience, but in Christian conversion where the divine–human encounter is central that unifies the divided self over leaving one's own religion to follow Jesus.

Another spiritual effect of conversion is the hope of eternal life. The idea that this life is temporary and that life after death is permanent came to converts in conversion. They claimed that Jesus forgave their sins and assured them of eternal life. They visualize a life with Jesus in eternity. Kareem, a Muslim convert, felt that his religion did not give him the assurance of life after death. He found this assurance only in Christianity and he repeatedly emphasized this factor in his interview: "In Christianity, the moment people accept Christ, their sins are forgiven and the eternal life is assured . . . Christianity gives the assurance of eternal life, so I started following Christianity. This motivated me to follow Jesus." Mohan, from a Brahmin, family accepted Jesus as a teenager and echoed a similar view: "I did not have any assurance of life after death when I was a *Pujari*, but now, even, if I die today or if the Lord comes now, I have a hope that I will be in his kingdom. Even if I die tonight, I will reach the Father in heaven—*Parameshwaran*. I have this unshakable assurance. Assurance of life after death is strong and the hope of eternity is unshakable for me." Willayat Ali, a Muslim convert, died as a martyr during the Indian mutiny in 1857. He faced death boldly, without any regrets for his conversion, with a hope of entering eternal life (Paul, 1967).

The hope of eternal life in Christianity is for life with Jesus after death. This hope gives converts the confidence and courage needed to face any crisis in the present life. They talked with absolute certainty that they will be in heaven or with the Lord the minute they die. Mohan recalled an incident in his life: "A group of people came to burn me to death. I did not have any fear of death; rather, my zeal increased. Earlier I had a fear of death." He was ready to die for his newfound faith. Kumar said, "When I close my eyes [die], I will open my eyes in heaven. So why should I fear death? The fear of death is gone." The hope of eternal life gives converts confidence and sets them free from the fear of death. It gives them a new sense of purpose and meaning for this life, which gives them courage to face any crisis. One convert expressed her confidence by saying, "If I follow this God, he can solve all my problems. He has eternal life for me. Even if I suffer here, I have eternal life. I accepted the Lord Jesus for this reason." The hope of eternal life is one of the binding factors that keeps converts firm in their newfound faith.

Converts to Christianity experience a sense of gaining new power over evil or witchcraft. Sakunthala narrated her struggle against witchcraft:

Sakunthala: Everything used to be normal until my husband returned home by 9:00 p.m. But when he [husband] came home, there would be blood everywhere and it would smell. [It was not that he brought in blood, but while he was at home this happened. She said that literally there used to be blood in the house, not simply the appearance of blood.] I used to wash it off, but the smell of the blood lingered. I used to find blood, lemons, and *kunkum* [a sacred red-colored powder] around the house. [These are the materials used in witchcraft to cast a spell on enemies.] We had many plantain trees around the house and there would be turmeric and *kunkum* under each tree. I myself dug these out many times from under the trees. Once, for sixteen consecutive days, sixteen lemons were found. They were placed

Transforming Effects

there so that our family might be destroyed. Many times I found dried lemons inside the showcase. I did not know how they came in. Many things happened like this. But God helped me gather those lemons and burn them.

Sakunthala felt that only with the power of God could she handle these kinds of situations. She explained that these experiences were not dreams or hallucinations but real incidents in her life. In rural India, people still do such practices as witchcraft or black magic against their enemies. People face real struggles to fight against these evil forces. This is not unique to converts. Others seek the help of sorcerers to neutralize the evil forces, but converts to Christianity try to handle witchcraft through prayer, either by themselves or by calling a pastor or preacher to pray and cleanse their premises of the evil forces. Converts feel that with Jesus they have a power greater than the power of witchcraft. They feel they can use the name of Jesus to defeat these kinds of evil attacks.

Involvement in ministry is another spiritual effect of conversion. Converts develop an interest for active evangelism. They feel that what they have experienced ought to be spread to others. They are excited and filled with zeal to share their conversion experience so that others might have a similar experience. Some of them have dedicated themselves to be evangelists or to be actively involved in Christian ministry. Kushbu said, "My ministry is only among the Muslim women like me [following Jesus secretly]." She felt obligated to support Muslim women who follow Jesus secretly. Selvi, who had a vision of the crucifixion, went to college and actively spread the message of Jesus, though she was restrained by the college authorities. There were twenty-six conversions in Sania's college within a year of her conversion. Converts from the tribal religions became active members in their villages to promote Christianity.

The sense of experiencing the truth drives converts to share about their experiences. Converts are eager to tell others about their experience. They do this owing to their concern that others should also experience the truth. They began to present their religious experience and transformed life as proof that Jesus is real. Many are ready to accept converts' claims because they know how their lives changed after their conversion.

The *psychological effects* of conversion are: joy, peace, and happiness; a sense of reassurance with the divine presence; a positive self-image; and precognition. Mohan expressed his feelings about the first time he prayed to Jesus: "I cannot describe it in words. I had joy, and there is no word to describe this joy. As the psalmist says, 'Taste and see that the Lord is good,' and this cannot be described in words. Everyone who opens his heart to Jesus only can experience and feel the same. I accepted Jesus on the same day I received the Bible." He also mentioned that he experienced ineffable peace. Surya described his feelings: "When I accepted Jesus, I got joy and peace that the world could not give . . . I got joy that money could not buy. God has given me freely this joy and peace that the world could never offer. I have great joy. I was searching for it here and there, but I did not get it. But now God has given me peace and happiness freely." Surya felt that this joy is incomparable to any other pleasures. Vinitha reported, "We [she and her friend] were kneeling down and started praying. Suddenly, I felt a kind of peace engulfed me. I was crying for no reason. I did not have any particular reason to cry at that moment. I was crying because of joy. I did not know what it was really." Vinodha said, "I had visited many temples and offered many things, but I did not get peace of mind. But now I have gotten it [from her conversion]." Bakht Singh said, "The first change that I noticed in me was that a great joy was flooding my soul." Karan recollected his feelings after making a confessional prayer to mark his conversion: "I knew that my sins were forgiven on the spot. And the joy that I received at that time, you know, it is still lingering in my life. That gives me great joy even now." Rekha claimed that she found "true and inner joy." Sadhu Sunder Singh, after having a vision of Jesus, felt peace remain with him even after his vision ceased. Sarala, who lost her husband, felt that she was happy in spite of the tragedy. Selvi, after having a vision of the crucifixion, experienced great happiness and incomprehensible joy. She said, "I do not know how to express it! I received great happiness and peace on that day."

Converts' feelings of joy, peace, and happiness are not transitory, but permanent. However, fluctuation of these states may occur. Converts differentiate joy from happiness; joy is a state received at the divine–human encounter, and happiness is induced by activities. Pleasures are temporary, but the feelings of joy and peace are lasting states that are not altered by external circumstances. Converts feel inner joy and peace despite troubles and crises.

After the divine–human encounter, converts feel relieved or freed from a heavy burden. One college student said, "I felt as if a burden were lifted from me. Like a baby, I began a new life. I could not control the joy within me." In her interview, Ganga expressed, "I felt very light in my heart, as if all my burdens were removed from my heart. I felt I was a new creation." Mohan described his feelings after conversion with the phrases, "a burden was lifted," "relieved of the burden," and "sigh of relief." A century ago, Pandita Ramabai (2001, p. 32), a great reformer of India who converted from the Brahmin priestly caste, expressed her inability to describe her feelings: "Only those have been convicted of sin and have seen themselves as God sees them under similar circumstances, can understand what one feels when a great and unbearable burden is rolled away from one's heart. I shall not attempt to describe how and what I felt at the time when I made an unconditional surrender." Converts felt freed from the many burdens they were carrying. Mohan interpreted this as the fulfillment of Jesus's promise to give rest to those who come to him with heavy burdens.

Converts gain a new hope in their lives as they feel reassured by the presence of the divine. They gain a sense of hope that life will be different by having Jesus with them. The assurance that someone is with them and there for them make a difference in their lives. Old or young, converts feel that they are not alone and that Jesus is in control of their lives, so they feel bold and courageous. Hameetha, a Muslim woman, experienced her conversion at fifteen. She felt reassured by God's promise in Isaiah 41:10: "'Do not fear, for I am with you; do not be dismayed, for I am your God. I will strengthen you and help you; I will uphold you with my righteous right hand.' I felt how nice it is to have his righteous right hand supporting me always. I felt his power within me. Even now, whenever if I feel dull, immediately I can feel his right hand supporting me." She wanted some kind of support and feels she now gets it from Jesus. Such feelings are not a one-time experience, but an ongoing feature in converts' lives.

Converts' self-confidence is increased by the assurance of the divine presence. Inban said, "I could feel his encouragement; I could feel his strength; I could feel his intimate fellowship. I could feel the presence of God." Kamal talked about gaining self-confidence:

Kamal: [I feel] somebody is there for me, who holds my hand closely, who never leaves me in any situation. That is how I feel God is with me and has not left me. Many situations in my life made me so depressed, but I felt that he has not left me. The thought of his presence in my life is so real all the time . . . I gained a great confidence that I could even change the world. Christ will never let me down. He is there with me and I can do anything. No one can stand against me. I got great peace and great hope that after death I will be with Christ. Now I have everything.

During his school days, Kamal had to stay in the home of one of his relatives because his father was working elsewhere. His childhood days were not happy days for him. He did not get enough attention, love, and care. Since his conversion experience, he feels the presence of Jesus with him always. Now he feels that Jesus is holding his hand and is with him always. This gives him such enormous confidence that he can even think of changing the world. Mala, while studying in medical college, was struggling with loneliness; she did not have any close friend in the hostel where she was staying, as she comes from a low caste. She said, "Earlier, I had lots of uncertainty, fear, hopelessness, and loneliness. I did not have anyone as a close friend. But now it is not like that. Now I am not alone; I have a God who takes care of everything." Mala was searching for a friend who could love her and be with her. She could not find any friends, but she experienced Jesus as her close friend. Nambiar, a doctor, felt that in his conversion he was reassured by the presence of Jesus: "I can face difficulties with the faith that I have in Christ. Earlier I did not know what to do in difficult situations. Now I pray and he helps me in difficult situations in my family and professional life. That was a remarkable change in my life." Sarala needed some support and strength after her husband died. She perceived Jesus taking control of her life. She said, "For me, everything is God only. With that feeling, I was bold." Converts no longer feel lonely or depressed. They feel that Jesus is with them always, loves them, and takes care of them. This feeling enables them to have positive emotions.

When crises are resolved after their religious experience, converts feel that the turnaround is due to Jesus. This perception that Jesus brings about a change of situation in their lives enables converts to face life's realities with new strength and boldness. Their conversion experience changes their perception of reality. When converts face crises, they display hope, whereas they despaired before the divine–human encounter. Chitra said, "After accepting the Lord I faced lots of problems, but in all those problems the Lord's hand was with us. He used to comfort me through visions. He used to assure me by talking to me." Daily life throws many opportunities for converts to experience the presence of Jesus and be comforted by him like this. Janaki went through many difficulties. She recalled, "He [Jesus] made me strong. Whatever happened to me—however much he [my husband] scolded me, however many problems I faced in the family—the Lord was with me." Kamal described that his family situation did not change after conversion, but that he was able to face it: "After coming to Christ, I have gotten the confidence that I can overcome any crisis but not earlier. The situation has not been changed, but I have some hope that God will open a way and I am confident that Christ will definitely bring a change of situation." For Kamal, conversion did not bring a change of situation as others experienced, but it gave him new hope and confidence to face his situation. Even when their situations do not change, converts have the confidence that Jesus is with them. They feel that they are not alone in their struggles. Though they face crises and struggles, they do not seek another conversion to resolve them. This is noteworthy because some conversion studies portray crises as the cause of conversion. If crisis is the cause of conversion, then converts have to convert back to their former religion or to another religion when they face a new crisis, but we find that converts hold on to Jesus instead of seeking another conversion because of new crises.

Converts find prayer and the Bible as resources to solve crises in their lives. Their inner peace in the face of crises is a sign of Jesus's presence with them and demonstrates their assurance that he is in control of their situation. Kavia narrated her struggles:

Kavia: I have gone through a lot of difficulties; I mean so much. When I had my first baby there was no one to help me; I was facing financial difficulty. I had gone through many troubles, but I never felt alone. I was at peace because I had the assurance that Christ was with me. This was my personal experience and I do not know how to describe it in words . . . I take everything to the Lord . . . I just take it to the Lord in prayer. Then I am at peace. I do not know—sometimes it turned out in my favor, sometimes not in my favor, but the Lord gave me the grace to accept it and come to terms with whatever happens to me. So I was at peace . . . Even today, I am always at peace.

Kavia found prayer as the channel to take her concerns to God. The most interesting factor in her statement is that despite all her difficulties she felt inner peace. Normally, peace is associated with the absence of trouble or crisis. But Kavia claimed that she was peaceful despite all her troubles. This factor made her hold on to Jesus instead of returning to the religion of her birth.

Before conversion, Ramesh's father was running a business of printing wedding cards with pictures of Hindu gods. After his father's death, Ramesh decided to discontinue printing pictures of Hindu gods because he and his brothers felt that as Christians it was not right for them to do so, so they had to start a new business from scratch. He describes how they initially struggled in their new business:

Ramesh: I do not know how we managed those three years. I cannot tell you how we managed; it is a real surprise for me that we could manage those three years! We had a terrible time. All my brothers were studying. One day my mother asked me for money to buy some meat. I did not even have 100 rupees to buy some meat for the family; I told my mother to buy some greens to cook. In 1997 we were under a debt of 70 to 80 lakhs rupees [US$ 130,000 to 140,000]. I even told my brothers that it was better to sell [the machines] and settle the debts and lead a simple life. But we have not sold anything; instead we paid back all our debts. Those days we used to pray and claim the promise, "You do not borrow, but you will lend to many." Every Sunday we come to the office for prayer. We used to pray, "Lord make us to lend money to others." Today we do not have any debts.

For converts, prayer is one of the means of handling a crisis. Sometimes prayer works in their favor, as with Ramesh, but sometimes it does not. However, they can accept the situation and find the strength to manage the crisis. Converts never had this attitude towards crises prior to their conversion. They feel reassured in prayer that they are not alone in facing hardships. They feel the presence of the divine with them always.

Fear, for the converts, is no longer something to be reckoned. They claim that Jesus has set them free from all kinds of fears. The hope of eternal life liberates them from the fear of death. Their conscience is clear and they do everything honestly. They are no longer self-conscious because they gain confidence in conversion. Their conversion experience sets them free from all kinds of fears.

Converts acquire a positive self-image in conversion. Those who suffered from an inferiority complex no longer feel inferior but accept themselves. They used to be self-conscious and afraid to speak to people, but they became friendly with others after the divine–human encounter. They were shy but are now bold enough to make friends. Converts described their personality with the expressions like, "I was an introvert, shy, reserved, timid, and coward." But the divine–human encounter transformed them. They lost the fear of talking to people or in public, and they became bold and outgoing, easily making friends.

A sense of being fortunate or blessed is evident in converts' self-image. They feel that they are chosen by Jesus and that he came in search of them. Though they did not seek the love of Jesus, they felt that Jesus came in search of them. Considering themselves fortunate, converts consider others who have never encountered Jesus as unfortunate or unlucky. Converts are able to shed their self-consciousness, discover new talents, develop wisdom, and view themselves as chosen.

Converts' encounter with Jesus and subsequent relationship with him give them a new identity. Earlier, their family, caste, education, and rural or city context were the major factors in forming their self-image. After conversion, all those factors lost their significance. They consider those things worldly and not part of their true identity. They come to see themselves and their life in light of their newfound relationship with Jesus. This new identity gives them self-confidence and a positive self-image, which helps them foster good relationships with others. Thus, making friends becomes easier for converts.

Converts gain self-control. They can regulate their emotions and behaviors and at times are self-critical. They assess themselves in light of Christian values and the Bible. Converts become gentle in nature. Where they were hardhearted or stubborn or rough, they become tender-hearted. Converts view Jesus as their role model and they try to imitate him in every way. The qualities of Jesus influence them greatly as they come to know more about him, and they also became more like him. Nambiar said, "It is a transformation—an internal transformation, what the Bible calls 'the new man.' Everything is new—vision, aspiration, future, present—everything is a new perception." A sense of new identity and a feeling that "I am different" guide their thoughts, attitude, worldview, and actions. They also develop a sense of being a blessing to others, and they draw great satisfaction in helping others.

The divine–human encounter imparts new talents and wisdom to converts. Some have discovered new talents or redirected their talent for Jesus. Janaki, who could not go out to church for about thirty years, developed a new talent of writing songs and composing tunes. She could never go out to learn Christian songs and she claimed that the Lord taught her the music she wrote. She wrote songs based on Scripture verses; she felt the Lord had spoken to her in this way. Krishna Pillai, a great Tamil poet, was believed to have written his first poetry when he experienced conversion (Appasamy, 1966). Since then, he became a famous poet, known for his work *Ratchanya Yathriham* ["Pilgrim Progress" in Tamil]. Mala was good at writing poetry. Earlier she wrote about nature but after her conversion about God.

The sense of being new makes converts successful in life. Some claimed that they were poor or average students before conversion, but since then could perform very well in their studies. Balan shared about his success in his studies: "After I accepted Christ, the first blessing I got was that I became a very good student. I could learn subjects and write examinations well; these were signs of good transformation. My grades were increasing semester by semester. I would only say that it was not by my effort or anything like that. I prayed and I still do. I got good marks. I came out successful. I was one of the toppers in my college."

Converts also find success in business. Arun narrated his success: "Earlier my monthly turnover was between 70 to 80 lakhs rupees [US$130,000 to 140,000], but now it is double that amount. My business has multiplied. So God will never leave us. As it is written in the Bible, he will bless us a hundred-fold. I never believed that he would do this, but he is taking care of everything. I believe nothing is in our hands; everything is in his hands." Devaraj claimed similar success: "My turnover is doubling every year. I can see that with my eyes. By looking at my life, many have accepted the Lord." This obvious change gives converts confidence to be more firm in their newfound faith in Jesus. Though Arun never believed that God would bless him a hundredfold, to his surprise, he found that God had indeed blessed him.

On the other hand, the road to success is changed in conversion. Converts do not aspire for success by any means necessary. Devaraj walked out of his family business, since he wanted to be fully transparent in his business dealings and keep records straightforward with the government. Arun's dealings became transparent and he is sincere in paying all his taxes. Balan became convinced that scoring good grades by copying or getting a leaked question paper before an examination is wrong. Despite such stands, converts experience success. Now, success with God's approval is the mark of transformation in their lives.

Some have even changed their ambitions and career plans since conversion. Hameetha, mentioned earlier, told me that her husband broke the tradition of playing *Nathaswaram*, an Indian musical instrument similar to clarinet, in Hindu temples. This is a unique Muslim family in South India that plays this instrument in Hindu temples. Though they are Muslims, for about thirty generations they have been doing this. Hameetha's husband became a Christian due to her influence and broke the tradition. She said, "They [her husband's family] have been in this profession for about thirty generations. Thirty generations! My husband is the first one to break this tradition. After accepting Christ, my husband decided, 'Instead of playing before the Hindu gods . . . I will use my talent for the true God.' Initially people ridiculed him. However, he started playing for the Lord and I always encouraged him by saying, 'Do not worry; God will bless you abundantly.'" Converts adopted such types of new direction in their lives.

Behavioral effects of conversion include transformation of attitudes, interests, and behaviors. Converts admit that they were proud, jealous, dishonest, impatient, and violent before the divine–human encounter, but the conversion experience transformed them to be loving, patient, humble, thankful, trustworthy, responsible, and truthful. They became a source of encouragement to others. Converts are liberated from some addictive habits like smoking, consuming liquor, reading bad books, going for movies, and watching television. Converts' interests, circle of friends, ambitions, and career plans change because of conversion. They became God-centered; their focus in life is pleasing God and doing only what pleases Jesus.

Physical effects of the divine–human encounter include physical healing. Beemsingh Bai was on his deathbed due to tuberculosis and heavy drinking. He prayed to Jesus, challenging him to heal him if he is the true God. Instantly he felt a power flowing through him and experienced complete healing. You might recall the story of Susila, who claimed to have miraculous healing from cancer. The doctors told her that she would live only ten days, so her husband left her to die. Due to the medical bills, her mother cursed her that she was still alive. But someone told her that she could pray to Jesus and he would heal her. She claimed that she was healed miraculously after praying to Jesus. These converts owe their very lives to Jesus. They are convinced that, but for the power of Jesus, their lives would have ended. Converts claimed they received divine healing.

Social effects of the divine–human encounter include converts being enabled to love and forgive others. Devaraj said, "I could forgive those who were against me." Another businessperson, Durai, expressed a similar attitude: "I felt I should not have enmity with my brothers, though they had cheated me . . . I am reconciled with all of them." Converts developed love for others and life became "other-centered" since their religious experience. This does not mean they became totally selfless, but they became thoughtful of others compared to their earlier state. They are sensitive to others' needs and are eager to help others. Mohan said, "I was living for myself . . . But now, with Jesus, I started loving others. My selfishness, bitterness, and pride were cleansed." One convert described her transformed attitude in her daily chores. In some places, water supply to homes is not available. Women have to go to the common taps at the street corners to collect drinking water. Usually, when someone cuts the queue, quarrel breaks out. This woman pointed out her change of attitude in such a situation and said, "Earlier I used to quarrel with everyone who cuts the queue to collect water at the common water pipes on the streets. But now, even if two or three cut the line, I do not make a big issue of it and I let them go." Aruna said, "I never realized the meaning of loving others, or helping others. But since my conversion, whenever I get a chance, I help others." Nithya said, "Now I can relate to others better, whether they are rich or poor, beautiful or ugly. And I have developed a sincere love for others."

Converts are able to accept others and relate to them better. They began to treat others with love and respect and pray for others. Some who had been short-tempered found that they became able to control their temper. Ranjan said, "Earlier, at home, I used to get angry quickly, but now I am changed. My relatives have noticed that I have changed." Some converts said that they stopped using bad language. Others claimed that they were easily offended before, but now they are tolerant. These kinds of changes in the lives of converts make them successful in cultivating, restoring, and maintaining good relationships. Converts are transformed to be more patient, forgiving, accepting, and understanding.

Converts gain new recognition in the family and in society. Initially, they saw Christianity as a religion of the low caste, and they hesitated to consider following Jesus. Their family members and close associates looked down upon them when they converted and reacted sharply and violently sometimes. However, over a period, the same people began to look up to converts for advice and seek their prayers. Ganga felt that earlier people used to treat her without any respect, but "I have a better identity now . . . Earlier people would see me as *cheap*, but now they see me as my Daddy's

[Jesus's] child. I am proud of that." Ramesh expressed, "All our relatives are Hindus. Whenever we went to attend any family functions, they never respected us because we became Christians. They talked at our back and it was very painful for us . . . Now the situation is changed." Some converts went through a period of being despised or humiliated by others; however, sooner or later they commanded recognition and respect.

Converts are inspired by their conversion experience to take a stand against social evils. In India, especially in Tamil Nadu, demanding huge amount of cash and jewelry as a bride price (dowry) from parents is a common practice, despite a law against it. But converts are determined to marry without getting or giving dowry. Some converts are firm in breaking the caste barrier in marriage and stop categorizing people into low and high caste.

Their conversion experience motivated some to get involved in philanthropic activities. Actor Jayasudha started a charitable trust to help the poor get medical treatment. She wanted to emulate Mother Teresa in her contribution to society. Narayana Wamman Tilak, a Marathi poet, a convert from a Brahmin family, was ready to do any menial work in taking care of the poor and those who were affected by a plague during the nineteenth century. Once, Tilak and his wife carried the bodies of those who died of plague to bury them, as the staff in the relief camp were on strike. Normally, a Brahmin would consider himself defiled from coming into contact with a dead body, but Tilak could do that because of his conversion (Tilak, 1956). The conversion experience freed Tilak and his wife from the Brahminical mindset, so they could perform a needed service at a tragic time. Pandita Ramabai was another person who dedicated her life to the emancipation of destitute women and girls. She was against the discrimination of women in the religion of her birth (Ramabai, 2001). This kind of involvement in society is one of the effects of transformation due to conversion experience.

Economical effects of conversion involve converts' experience of God's abundant blessings, God meeting their financial needs, and their change of attitude toward money. Some reported financial blessings in their lives due to conversion. Others find that money has lost its allure in their lives. Converts feel that Jesus provides for all their needs. They do not mean that the church or some people help them financially; they receive God's support, sometimes in answer to their prayers. The experiences of divine providence are considered part of their religious experience. They trust Jesus for their needs.

Transformative Religious Experience

We saw how businessman Ramesh struggled to meet his end and how God brought a turnaround in his business. Arun, another businessman, claimed that his turnover had doubled since his conversion. Sarala told me, "Even though we earn very little, without borrowing money from others, we are living by God's grace." Sania's father stopped supporting her financially when he came to know that she became a Christian. She was in the hostel studying engineering. She recalled an incident and claimed that it was a miracle:

Sania: Once, I did not have money to buy a pen to write my examination and I told God, "I do not know what to do." I went out for a meeting or a class and came back. The warden called me and gave me a curious look, saying that there was a money order for me . . . She said, "The seal was missing. Who has sent it? Where did it come from?" My dad never sends money orders; he always transfers money through banks. I did not say anything to her. I just took it and went back to my room. The money order slip was there, but there was nothing on it—no stamp on it. The slip was absolutely clean. She also told me that the mailman who came was new and came at an odd time. He came only for this money order and gave it and went away. I took the money and went to my room, amazed: "Who could have sent it?" Nobody even knew that my father had stopped supporting me. I did not tell anyone [that I needed money].

I told my roommate that I got a money order but there was nothing on the slip. She was doing chemical engineering—a Brahmin girl. She was against all these things [conversion and Christianity]. She said, "What you say is impossible." She took it up as a challenge and went to the post office to verify. There was no record of the MO at the post office and no one knew where it came from or who had sent it. That made such an impact on her that she became a Christian. These kinds of miracles I have seen. Till today I do not know where it came from.

Sania perceived this as a miracle. So did her friend who got this verified at the post office. However, her dad himself could have made this arrangement to deliver the money through someone, as he was very rich and influential, so that she might not suffer financially. At the same time, he would have wanted her to know that he was firm in his opposition to her conversion. Nevertheless, Sania prayed to Jesus for her need and the need was met at the right time. That increased her faith in Jesus. No matter how the money came, for Sania it was an answer to her prayer. This gave her the confidence that Jesus is concerned about her welfare. This fact gave her enough confidence and strength later to face troubles due to her conversion. Ganga, a professional singer, said, "Actually, I was not getting any concerts and we suffered financially. But from the fourth day since my conversion, I started getting lots of programs and our financial situation improved." These things could be coincidences, but the prayer factor convinced converts that what had happened to them was in answer to their prayers.

Converts become generous in giving to the poor or to Christian ministry. As we have seen, Devaraj did not consider money a covetous thing in his life. To give away 51 percent of the profit from one's business is not easy. However, he felt that the Lord really blessed him and his business, therefore, it was easier for him to be generous towards Christian ministry.

In a world of greed and cutthroat competition in making quick money, for converts money has lost its allure. Ramesh narrated an incident in his business:

Ramesh: Since 1965, we were doing a family business of printing wedding cards with pictures of Hindu gods. We distributed them all over India. In 1995 we decided to stop this and started praying about it. If we stopped this, we might run out of business. But on the other side, we thought, "We are carrying the Bible and going to church, but daily selling lakhs of cards with pictures of Hindu gods." We felt that we were promoting them and felt guilty about it.

One day, we prayed and decided to stop this and destroy all the films used for printing the wedding cards. The cost of the films alone would be about 8 to 10 lakhs rupees [US$ 15,000 to 18,000]. We thought, "Even if we sell the films, it will continue to be circulated by other printers." So we destroyed everything on a single day. We wanted to print something different and decided no more printing pictures of Hindu gods. We did not tell anyone. Others thought that we had left the business of printing wedding cards. They thought neither we did the business of printing wedding cards nor did we let others do by selling the films. They did not know that we had burned them altogether.

We were looked down on by others for this. They commented that we would ruin ourselves and thought that we became mad after starting to go to church. We went through very difficult times for three years and even struggled for 100 rupees. No one knew our real condition; others thought that we were wealthy. But since 1998 there was a turnaround in our business, and it was a total transformation of the business. Overnight we stopped our family business and started a new one. We went for export printing. It took three years for us to learn and come up.

Ramesh and his brothers did not regard money as the most important thing in business. They were interested in pleasing Jesus; their business life revolved around Jesus. They trusted Jesus and had great confidence that God controls not only their lives, but their business as well. Now they feel vindicated. Their monthly turnover at the time of the interview was 1.5 crores (US$ 300,000). Since the divine–human encounter, converts began to value money less. While people are crazy for money, converts have a different attitude towards money, and money is not the center of their lives. They are ready to forego any sum of money to please Jesus.

As we have seen above, converts experience transformation in every aspect of their lives. Converts experience both sudden and gradual transformation. They begin to see their life as a "new creation," a "new man," and a "new heart." The divine–human encounter triggers transformation, and it continues as an ongoing process. Family members, relatives, neighbors, and friends came to know about their conversion by the transformed lives of converts. Their transformed lives help some families to experience conversion.

Converts' claims of "total change" or "complete change" are not meant to suggest that they become perfect in every sense. It only indicates, as we have seen above, that all dimensions of converts' lives are changed after the divine–human encounter in conversion. In Christian theology, justification is an event in which people are made right with God and God declares them righteous, whereas sanctification is a lifelong process. In conversion to Christianity, justification takes place at the divine–human encounter, where converts are convicted of their sin and at once are accepted by Jesus and made right with God by having an assurance of being forgiven and transformed. Sanctification is the process that begins at the divine–human encounter and is sustained by continued interaction with the divine. Transformation in conversion encompasses every dimension of converts' lives and is not restricted only to the religious aspect alone. In the next chapter we will see the hostilities faced by converts in India.

9 Hostilities

Every man going out of the Hindu pale is not only a man less, but an enemy the more.

—Swami Vivekananda (1907)

If the mystical truth that comes to a man proves to be a force that he can live by, what mandate have we of the majority to order him to live in another way?

—William James (1902/2004, p. 366)

Hostilities refer to the persecutions faced by converts owing to their conversion to Christianity in a multireligious society of India. The Indian family is a close-knit unit in which the head of the family still wields authority to make any important decisions affecting members of the family. In such a context, changing one's religion of birth causes a great tremor not only in one's family, but also in the larger community. In this chapter, we will discuss the reactions of families and communities when a member converts to Christianity. Many times, hostile reactions are not confined to one's family, but extended to relatives, to friends, and sometimes even to the larger community. This chapter will consider questions such as: How did family and friends react to conversion? What were the problems faced by converts because of their conversion? How did converts manage such situations? How did they find the needed strength to face hostilities?

Converts know that conversion to Christianity invites many troubles in India. Despite this, they decide to follow Jesus. Many converts were not eager to follow Jesus by leaving the religion of their birth. However, they eventually started following Jesus because of the divine–human encounter. Their religious experience gives them a certainty of knowing the truth that enables them to face any hostile situation due to their conversion. Family members react with shock and tears. The immediate response of families is to persuade the converts to renounce their newfound faith. When this fails, they resort to various pressure tactics to bring converts back.

Spouses of the converts react extremely. For example, when Thulgan Banu's mother and her siblings converted to Christianity from Islam, her father walked out of the house reacting to their conversion. He returned only after two years. The Tamil Poet Krishna Pillai's wife threatened to commit suicide if he took baptism. Narayan Waman Tilak's wife contemplated committing suicide when she heard that Tilak had adopted Christianity. In some families, the members felt ashamed to relate to the converts, as Christianity was perceived as a religion of the low castes. Some were perplexed how people could change their religion! Family members and friends reacted with shock, anger, irritation, hatred, unhappiness, mockery, and worry. Family members began to blame the converts for any mishap in the family. The family accused the converts as the cause of any tragedy or crisis in the family, by saying that the family deities were displeased. Some converts were mocked and publicly humiliated.

Some considered the converts insane. Sania was given electric shock treatment to cure her mental illness. Nambiar reported a similar reaction in his family when his brother converted. His parents treated his brother for mental illness by subjecting him to electric shock treatment. In other cases, the converts were forced to practice the religion of their birth. Some parents threatened and a few withheld financial support to their children for their studies. Some extended family members resorted to witchcraft against the converts and their families. Converts had to face physical threats repeatedly from family members and community members.

Some converts were disowned by the family and forced to leave the house. We discussed Sania's vision in the first chapter that led her to follow Jesus, leaving Islam. She was from a very rich and devout Muslim family. She was pampered by her parents as she was a single child till she was ten. In Indian families, boys enjoy more freedom than girls. Unlike other girls, Sania enjoyed much freedom, her dad's love and affection. But after her studies, she was never allowed to leave the house or contact any of her friends or seek a job. She was confined to her house because of her conversion. She narrated her ordeal:

Sania: Ours is a very religious family, so my father never even wanted to listen to the reason for my conversion. He said, "No! You cannot be a Christian and be my daughter. It is impossible." I stayed indoors for one and half years and they tried lots of things to change me. I was given electric shock, thinking that I was mad, and it was very painful. All those things . . . those things were very painful. Even now, if I think of them, they are painful. Now it seems like a story, but when you go through it, you feel as if there were no end.

One thing I realized: that I could not have gone through those troubles but for Jesus. I would have had a mental or nervous breakdown. I do not know where the strength came from! I was never a bold person. I was very fearful. All fears had left me. No fear! Absolutely no fear! Earlier, I was so fearful that I could not go from one dark room to another. I mean so fearful. But now there is no fear; it simply left. I do not know how. I have no fear. I was not afraid of anyone.

I had no Bible with me and no fellowship—nothing. For one and a half years, nothing happened. Absolutely nothing, God! Every night, after everyone went off to sleep, I would pray. And Jesus would simply speak to me. A lot of things happened.

My father never raised his hands on us. He is such a [loving] person that he has never even raised his voice over us; he was so gentle. But one day, he got so angry that he tried to strangle me to death. While he was strangling me, my mother came and took him away [voice trembling]. I had a ligament tear at my back. That night . . . I was crying. I could not understand why my father behaved in that manner. I was only twenty-one. I could not understand why he was doing this. I did not understand anything. I was hurt. I did not know . . . I was telling God that night, "I feel like dying," and I cried.

I heard someone singing the entire Psalm 23. Then, I did not know it was Psalm 23. Now I know, because I have read it. The entire psalm somebody was singing in my left ear. No music . . . one male voice . . . no music and nothing . . . I never heard the song again. When it came to "Surely goodness and mercy will follow me all the days of my life," I said, "I do not believe this that goodness and mercy will follow me." It was like . . . the song was going on and I was calmed down. I felt peace. Then the Lord said, "Forgive your dad." I said, "You must be crazy [laughs]; I cannot forgive. How could I! He has never done something like that." But I kept hearing, "Forgive your dad. Forgive your dad." I came to a point and I said, "Okay fine. I don't know how to forgive. Tell me how to forgive. I don't know . . . if you want, I will forgive." When I said, "Okay I will forgive, but you have to actually help me" . . . the pain in my back simply went off.

As I look back now, I think God did that to me, to explain to me the essence of who he is and the meaning of forgiveness. I understood how much he has forgiven me! He was on the cross to take away the pain, the pain that comes from sin. I felt that he was teaching me in this way, so I would never forget. I really understood, but I cannot explain in words how I got the message. His forgiveness is such a powerful thing.

I learned these things in that one and a half years. Maybe if I went to seminary to study theology, I do not think I would have learned all these things. Practically I learned these things.

Meanwhile, they brought one fakir, a Muslim holy man, a kind of folk Muslim. I was asked to vacate my room and stay in the guest room [to accommodate him]. I asked, "Why should I vacate my room and go to the guest room?" I was very upset. "Why doesn't the guest stay in the guest room?" But he occupied my room. I was very restless. I had no idea of spiritual warfare or anything. Nothing I knew. I really, very, very . . . [wanting to say that she did not know many things about spiritual life]. What would I say? I did not even know the order of the books; what comes after [in the Bible].

But that night—no, the second night—when that man was still there, I had a dream. I saw something, like, as if I were praying over . . . I was praying in my room over every door and window. I was praying over by putting my hand and praying over. So the next day, when I got a chance, when he was not there, I prayed over everything, whatever I saw. That evening the man disappeared. He never came back. [Laughs.] He simply left the room. My father was also surprised. He went out of the house and never came back. I did not know these things, what it was, but I was just doing whatever he [Jesus] was telling me. I think it was good that I did not know much. Now I would have questioned, "Why?" That time it was new, new things. But I did what Jesus told me to do. So many things happened.

Q: What happened after one and a half years?

Transformative Religious Experience

Sania: I was not allowed to go out. After one and a half years, my friend started applying for a job for me because they knew my condition—that I was like a prisoner in my own house. I got a job offer, an appointment letter. I showed it to my dad and said, "I want to work," and asked him how long I could be like this. Then my dad said, "If you are leaving the house, you should never return. Do not ever return. If you are leaving the house means, you sign off all the papers required, and then you and I have nothing to do [with each other]. He said one thing: "Everything which starts has an end. This one, I know it will come to an end. And I will do everything that I can to make sure you return to me and ask me to take you back." In our family, the elders are respected so much that no one talks back. I was also not bold enough to answer him. But that day, I replied to my dad. I did not know if what I said was from the Bible or not, but I said, "Dad, if you are fighting against me, you will win anyway, because in every way I am weaker than you—physically, materially, and in every way—you will definitely win. But think about it: what if you were fighting against God? Then you will never win." I just said that [loudly and triumphantly]. He did not know how to react. He simply kept quiet. I never talked to him like that, because I never talked to him [in this manner] or because he would not have expected that from me. I did not know what had happened!

In India, an unmarried girl walking out of the house is culturally a very sensitive issue. In a traditional family, a girl is under the custody of her father until her marriage, then under her husband. Sania narrated how she had to leave the house, as her father was planning to marry her off:

Sania: The next day there was lot of apprehension. As I was packing my things to leave the house, he [my father] said, "Do not take anything. If you are leaving, do not take anything. Everything you have belongs to me. I have given them all to you. So you cannot take anything." So I did not take anything. I was wearing a jean and a shirt, and in my pocket I had 10 rupees. I simply left the house. I would not say it was very easy or . . . but I was crying, and it was difficult. But I knew either I had to walk out or face the consequences. They were trying to marry me off. I had to ... I had to decide what to do. It was very tough and it was very difficult. But I had to leave.

I did not know where I was going. I went out and called my friend working in the same city and told her what had happened. I did not have money also. She told me to wait in one place. Another family friend, a Hindu, helped me. They knew what was happening in my family. He escorted me from [the city where she was] to [another place].

On the way I asked him, "You are doing this. Do you know if my dad comes to know what will happen?" He said, "Yeah, yeah, I know. I would not tell him, and nobody knows." I asked him, "Why are you helping me?" He is like my *Bhaiya* [brother], but a Hindu. He said, "Having seen you for the past one and a half years—all the turmoil that you went through—I know one thing: that you were not a person like this. You had never been so bold, but now you are fearless, so whomever you believe in must be someone great who has done this to you. Because of that I am helping you." Look at it! [Laughs.] He knew me since I was a child. He said, "You are completely different now. There must be something that made you different." He helped me reach ...

Sania's father started giving troubles to those who gave her shelter and supported her. She described her flight:

Sania: I started working. Then also my dad did not leave me. He is quite well known in business and political circles. He did everything possible [to make me return]. Wherever I worked, CIDs [Criminal Investigation Department staff] would come in search of me. Since I was an adult, they could not do anything to me, but they made life miserable for the people around me. My bosses were threatened [wherever she worked]. He did everything against my church. He gave a lot of trouble to the pastor and accused him with false charges. He did this to cut off the support system for me. So I had to move to twenty-six places, week after week shifting to different places. Because wherever I went, people around me were getting affected. Despite this, the church stood with me, and this had in fact unified the church as well. After some time, I felt that I should not tell my parents any longer my whereabouts. I stopped informing my parents where I was. Otherwise, I used to tell them of my whereabouts. Because he was doing this, I stopped informing them.

Then I got a job in a Christian [workplace] and did not inform my parents about my location. That time my father did not know where I was. My conversion became a very big issue in [the city where she was from] and this was covered by the newspapers. The church was united and all the pastors in that city together stood with me by not disclosing my location. All of them stood with me. My friends struck their neck out for me. Some of them lost their jobs; still they stood with me. After a few months, they traced my whereabouts because my dad was very influential. The police were also working for him.

Once, he came to the place where I was working. Two of my colleagues handled them and never allowed them inside. If he had come inside and spoke to anyone, they would have told my dad that I was there because none of them knew my situation. Since my colleagues were not sure whether my dad came with a search warrant or not, one of my colleagues came inside and told me to hide somewhere. Another colleague somehow managed . . . but my dad must have known that I was there; that is why he came. That was just a beginning.

I did not know where else I could go. I had gone to so many places already. Like a criminal, I was running from place to place. For me, if he were trying to do something to me, it was okay. But he was not attacking me, but others [whoever supported her] were getting affected. He was bringing trouble to those who were standing with me. So I did not know what to do. I did not know where to go. What to do? I was feeling very helpless. One of my colleagues called someone in another mission, in another city [far away], and told him about my case and asked him whether he could help me. He agreed to help me. My colleague told me that I would be leaving by tomorrow night, but he did not tell me where I was to go. I did not know what to do. He said, "I will get back to you tomorrow and tell you whether you will leave or not."

I prayed, "I do not know what to do. You [Jesus] have to tell me. This man is trying to help me, but unless you tell me to go, I will not move." He [Jesus] spoke through the word of God, "Trust the people whom I have put around you." So I knew that I had to go. The following night, it looked like no one knew where I was going. I was to leave from the rear gate and another person came from a nearby city by bus. He was an army man, a Christian. He was asked to escort me wherever I was going. By that time, the police surrounded the area and were searching house to house. I was in a Jeep [SUV], and by the SUV's indicators the bus was made to stop for a few seconds outside the city. Only before the bus stopped did my colleague tell me the city name where I was going and the name of the person who would meet me. [Till then] I had no idea where I was going. The bus stopped for half a minute and the army man took me in. This is how I left. We traveled all the way to another city by bus, as we could not travel by train, fearing that we would be caught by the police. Then from there, we took a bus again, and then a local train. Then we reached our destination after a few days. One couple took us to their house.

It happened ten years ago [1995] . . . I never went in searching for someone [to help me]. I had no relatives [in that city], no distant connection, and no blood connection, and not even friends' connection . . . Even for holidays we never visited this city, and I was a stranger. I did not look for anybody, but God brought many families to me as my guardians and I was protected. I never felt lacking for anything. When I left home, I signed off all kinds of papers [agreeing not to claim her rights as an heir] . . . I signed off all the papers when I left home [speaking in a low voice]. I did not even think twice. Maybe I was very young then and very idealistic. I did not think that I would not inherit all these. I simply signed off. However, I do not lack anything now.

After I left [that city], my father had a search warrant and got my friends and colleagues arrested from [the place she worked]. I had to do something to stop them. Therefore, I sent an affidavit to the police in [that city] that my conversion to Christianity was my own choice, therefore, the case should be closed. Then it was closed . . . I could not continue in [the place where she was working], because my father traced my affidavit with the help of police and came to the city where I was working. However, he could not locate me. Again the church stood with me.

However, God helped me start my own business without anyone's help. I started my business and did so well. After some time, 150 people started working [in my business]. [Laughs.] How could I be [like this]?! That is why I say, "God is no one's debtor." Wherever I go, he [Jesus] will go before me. I saw one thing: if you stand for Christ, he stands for you. I saw that happening in my life. He stood for me wherever I went. In every situation, he stood for me; in every situation . . . he was there to meet every small need. Amazingly, I never struggled in all the ten years. Since that time, ten years of my life, I have been alone. I never struggled. Now I am married. I never, never even once lacked anything . . . I always had food to eat, shoes to wear, a place to sleep, enough even to give to others. Never lacked, never lacked anything. And my business started doing very well.

Q: Haven't you ever thought of returning to your dad?

Sania: I became weary. Anyone would feel weary, you know, because of me so many problems [for others]. Why is my life like this? Why these struggles? Why am I struggling? Many times I felt that I should not live—I felt like that. Many times I also felt like going back, as I missed my mom and dad. Whatever it is, I love my dad a lot. He was very close to me. I miss my sister; the best years of my life were with her, because of the ten-years gap between us. When I left, she was a kid and she did not know anything. I felt she would never forgive me. On the other hand, when I see people around me, the support system was very good. I always, I always had to go back to . . . back to Jesus. It was the closest thing that I had and I felt energized.

Now I am saying this, and it is easy to say it in a story form. But when you go through that, living daily, it was hard. Especially those days were hard when I had to leave [the place she was hiding]. Even after moving far from my city, when I did not know where I was going, shifting many times, moving to new cultures, new friends, it was very tough.

Having gone through a life like a criminal pursued by the police, Sania had to constantly flee from one place to another to evade her father's pursuit. She had to accept the help and shelter of strangers at every move. Being a young girl, she went through a cruel ordeal. Sania was surprised that she could manage such difficulties. She continued:

Sania: I knew one thing: that it was not by my strength, because I knew myself. I knew that it was because of some supernatural intervention. I was not the kind of person [bold enough to face such situations]. So I guess some kind of strength was inside me; something was saying "Go on, go on." I tell this to many of my friends. Sometimes you stand and look back; you see bridges burning, and you cannot do anything about it. It is just burning, still up in flames. You cannot . . . you just stand and watch; you cannot do anything. I burned the bridges; I know I have to build the bridges also. God will help me build the bridges. But once it is burned, it is very painful, very hard. You almost feel like an orphan at times, because you feel nobody is there for you.

Definitely this experience has changed my life. Looking back, I have no regrets. I do not remember anything to cherish about the life that I led before I met Jesus, though I never had any problem, and I never did anything wrong. I cannot remember that phase of my life so well. But I would say in this phase of my life, there are lots of things to cherish.

Q: You seemed very close to your dad. What did you find in Jesus that you did not have with your dad? What made you leave the house?

Sania: The difference between my father's love and Jesus's love is that I never had to do anything to please Jesus. Although my father loved me, I always felt that I needed do something to please him; there is a requirement to meet. But with Jesus it is nothing like that. Even if I am depressed or I am feeling so dirty . . . I was so vulnerable, but he never condemned me. But with dad I could never be vulnerable; I could never show my weakness. Even though I love him, there was always a strain.

I really cannot express it. I just knew it. This is who I am; I belong to him [Jesus]. This is as if . . . I really believe as if the creation knows the creator—that kind of attachment I have with Jesus because I am created by him. So I really understood in my mind or heart . . . [struggling to express in words] I understand the feeling because he is the creator. The sense of belongingness I felt when I came to know that he is my creator is more than [the attachment she had] with my dad. I just say that I cannot pinpoint and say what it is.

Q: What is exceptional about Jesus?

Sania: When I found Jesus, I have my way of praying. I close my eyes and talk to him—just talking... The biggest difference is that I can hear him speak. I speak to him; I hear him speak back. I speak to him and hear him speak back.

Sania was only twenty-one years old when she left the house not knowing her next step in life. She also mentioned that her father got her to sign papers declaring that she would never claim her share of inheritance later. She was haunted by her father wherever she went. He troubled everyone who helped her in order to make her return home. However, he did not harm her physically but did everything possible to dislocate her. For many years she had to move from place to place to be out of reach of her father. She had to go through very painful experiences for the sake of her conversion. All these troubles she underwent because of the divine–human encounter she had, and she felt that she had experienced the divine contrary to her religious tradition. Now Sania is connected to her parents. Another convert from Islam, Kareem, was not given food and was tortured by his family because of his conversion to Christianity. Mohan, a Brahmin convert, was denied food and was forced to leave the house. He narrated his family's reaction to his conversion:

Mohan: I did not tell them [his family members about his conversion]. During 1988 to 1992 I was a secret Christian; till the day the trouble broke, no one knew [that he was a Christian]. Even the pastor of the church where I attended did not know that a Brahmin boy was attending his church. In 1992, one day, when I was in the church, where approximately five thousand people were attending, my brother came inside and dragged me out of the church. Since then, persecution and troubles started. Many even spat on my face. My parents came to know about my conversion in 1992. I was seventeen years old when I came out of my house. I have taken it as a privilege; to suffer for Christ is a privilege. I did not feel bad or murmur, "Oh, why did I become like this?"

I was not even given food. They went around telling others that I got converted, and I had changed. Even some nominal Christians came and counseled me that I should go back [to his former religion]. I feel pity for them. Only those who do not know Christ could say that it was okay [to return to Hinduism]. I could have told them about my experience, but . . .

My parents and my friends were watching my every move: Where I was going? With whom I was talking? They were monitoring me every time. I was involved in sports and there also I was followed. Whenever they [his family members] came to know that I had gone to a church or met a Christian friend, they used to beat me harshly. I could not predict who would beat me; anyone in the family would beat me, to any extent. Many times there was no spot on my body where there was no bleeding . . . I considered that God permitted those things. They offended me verbally, wounded physically, and denied my basic needs. I was not worshiping a dead God but the living. Jesus promised, "Neither I will leave you, nor will I let you down." This was true in my life. "Even heaven and earth will pass away but my words will not." This verse is true not only for me but for everyone.

The word of Christ strengthened me. From Genesis to Revelation, the words—loving words—comforted me. Through pastors, sermons, and the counsel of God's people I was comforted. The Bible says, "Clouds of witnesses are there." Stephen [in the Book of Acts] spread the truth; instead of garlanding him, he was stoned to death. I meditated on these incidents from the Bible with the help of the Holy Spirit. This is how I strengthened myself. It was beyond any man's capacity to bear the torment. Even today I am surprised that I could bear all those things! The Bible says, "Even if a mother forgets her child, I will not." He carried me like a father carries a child. He was with me all 365 days of a year. As a hen cares for her chicks, God's presence covered me. God's words were my comfort; God's presence was my comfort, and God himself was my comfort.

Similar to Mohan's experience, many converts are beaten up and threatened. Kishan Singh, a Sikh boy, became a Christian, and his father attempted to kill him because he would not return to Sikhism. He shot Kishan twice, but missed due to the commotion in the house, as others were trying to prevent him from killing the boy. However, his father beat him severely and ordered the servants to throw him on a train track so that he might get run over by a train. But the servants, instead of leaving him on a track, put him on a train. Later, he was treated in a mission hospital and was saved. Willayat Ali, one of the early martyrs of the Indian church during 1857, could not escape a violent mob. The mob tortured him and dragged him on the roads of Delhi asking him to recite the *Kalima*, but he refused, so they murdered him. His wife was hiding behind a tree watching this gory scene. Before he was caught by the mob, he gave firm instructions to his wife and children that they should not deny Christ at any cost. She held on to her faith despite witnessing the brutal murder of her husband, and later she faced many troubles for her newfound faith (Paul, 1967).

Mohan also narrated an attempt on his life by his own friends and how Jesus saved him miraculously:

Mohan: In 1992, when I was seventeen, a group of people came and told me, "You are a Brahmin; why are you preaching Jesus? Why are you going to the church?" They were very angry. They came to kill me, because they thought, if they left me [alone] I would convert many . . . They poured kerosene over me to burn me to death. Before doing that, they abused me with vulgar words and dirty words.

But I was comforted by Jesus's words, because he said, "What the world has done to me will be done to you. Be strong; I am with you." I did not reply and say anything to them. Isaiah says, "When he was beaten, he did not open his mouth." Christian life is not simply singing, preaching, giving offertory, or doing ministry. Christian life is displaying Christ—his qualities and his likeness. Earlier, I used to fight; I was short tempered . . . Since I accepted Jesus, who even embraced Judas, I have his likeness. A fraction of Christ-likeness enabled me to keep quiet while I was being attacked. They were surprised. One of them asked me, "What is this? We have said so many things, but you have not replied a single word! Are you a stone that cannot speak?" . . . My friends who knew me earlier were surprised that I could be so quiet!

Earlier, I had the fear of death, but then I was not afraid of death; instead, my zeal for Christ increased. Similar to the story of David and Goliath, I faced them in the name of Christ, and they came with kerosene and matchbox. But I was facing them in the name of God. I was worshiping God, and I was not afraid of death at all. I did not think that God would leave me or they would burn me to death. I thought, "Anyhow, death will come to everyone; it could be today or some other day. I will die for Jesus rather than denying Jesus." I was zealously holding on to Jesus.

Then I saw a heavenly vision. He [Jesus] opened my inner eyes and I saw Shadrach, Meshach walking in the fire . . . I saw the scene literally, face to face. I got the assurance that the one who saved Shadrach, Meshach . . . in 500 BC, is alive to save my life. He [Jesus] encouraged me and strengthened me. I have heard about and read this incident, but that day I saw the vision face to face. I wish they should try another attempt, so I could feel the presence of God! [Laughs.],

I saw Jesus face to face at seventeen and it was a miracle. He gave me the grace. They saw a bright light and realized that I had some supernatural power. They could not come near me and were terrified and ran away. As the Bible says, "Those who come against you will run away by seven ways." Only then had I seen Jesus face to face. I could feel the presence of Jesus since I had the vision of Jesus. I was convinced of what the truth was. They were very violent, but they ran for their lives. I knew them all. They could kill anyone.

Mohan claimed that he knew that the people who came to attack him were cruel and capable of killing anyone. However, he found that he was protected supernaturally. His vision gave him the assurance that Jesus is real and was there to protect him; it was worth holding on to Jesus. He talked about his former associates of Hindu fundamentalism and their reaction to his conversion:

Mohan: We have highly educated, committed, and dedicated people for teaching *Vedas*, *puranas*, and *yoga* in RSS [Rashtrya Swayam Sevak, a right-wing Hindu organization]. They are sacrificial and well disciplined. *Yoga* was good for physical body, but for the soul it was not helpful. No one told me to leave Hinduism or RSS. I decided to leave because Jesus gave salvation freely to anyone who calls on him. He gave his life. What else can we expect?

They opposed me and were trying to persuade me. Some knew my sincerity in my former devotion to Hinduism. I was better than the elders [he was only a teenager then]. Many were wondering,

"Even at this young age, he is like this! How will he be when he grows?"

So they were shocked to hear me saying that Jesus is the true God. They came to persuade me and tried to brainwash me. God's grace [sustained me]. One of the leaders even said, "You used to teach us when and what mantra to say, but now, if you say that Jesus is the true God, then it must be true." Nowadays, they come to me for prayer and not to oppose me.

Converts often face far greater crises since conversion than the crises they had before conversion. Though conversion resolves preconversion crises, in the Indian context it can also result in new, life threatening crises to converts.

Marriage is a burning issue in the families of converts because of their conversion to Christianity. If a convert is single, then it becomes a tussle between the family and the convert in choosing a life partner. Converts insist on marrying a Christian, but this means crossing the caste barrier against the family's wishes. Often converts do not insist on crossing the caste barrier; however, they insist on finding a Christian within the same caste. Rekha could not convince her parents to support her commitment to marrying a Christian, therefore, she had to walk away from her home, and she married Mohan, a Brahmin convert whose story was presented above.

Some converts did not insist on marrying a Christian. They obeyed their parents and accepted their choice of a person for marriage. They did not even object to their marriage ceremony being conducted according to their former religious tradition. After marriage, either they followed Jesus secretly or they discussed with their spouses their belief in Jesus and sought permission to follow him. Converts were quite comfortable with this arrangement, then slowly, over a period, they influenced their spouses and the entire family in some cases. Janaki had to wait for about thirty years to get her husband accept Jesus. Selvi went through very difficult times at home because of her faith. She felt guilty that she was not faithful to the Lord. She expressed her distress by saying, "I have betrayed his [Jesus] love. I am experiencing all this [troubles] owing to my sins. I have gone through painful times cursing myself, that I have betrayed the Lord . . ." At the time of the interview, Selvi's husband was more open to her beliefs and practices and started reading the Bible.

If a convert is elderly, then their children's marriage becomes a big issue. Relatives exert a lot of pressure on converts to marry off their children to a person who follows their religion; however, converts are firm in delaying the marriage, waiting and hoping for a suitable Christian match. Many traditional Christians in South India practice caste and choose marriage partners within their caste, so it is rare for traditional Christians to marry a convert. Converts to Christianity suffer because of these kinds of cultural practices within the church. Relatives and friends ridicule converts for taking such a stand that delays the marriage; however, converts claim that their stand is honored by Jesus, and they will find the right match eventually. The same people who ridiculed them expressed surprise in the way some weddings took place.

Some parents disowned or threatened to disown their children who converted. Such converts had to suffer financially when their parents stop financial support. Converts were also denied access to the Bible, Christian fellowship, and even to contact friends. Some families did not react to conversion; some converts also did not feel the need to inform their family about it. Some families accepted the conversion; they did not support or openly encourage it, but they accepted it as a reality and were even indirectly supportive. Some accepted it with some restriction, telling converts not to practice their newfound faith publicly.

Converts to Christianity in India have to face various kinds of troubles: losing friends and family, hunger, poverty, fear of future troubles, being disowned by parents, difficulty in finding a suitable life partner, and public humiliation. Some were pushed to a situation where they even contemplated suicide. Life can become far more difficult due to conversion. Conversion in India means added problems and sometimes even life-threatening situations. However, converts find extraordinary strength to go through these situations despite all these troubles.

Converts adopt different strategies to tackle situations in the family. Some converts practice their newfound faith secretly; they are scared to come out openly and declare their change of religion. Such converts are always under fear that they might be caught following Jesus. They do not inform family members of their conversion or baptism. Some avoid situations where they would have to participate in religious rituals. Some have courage to resist the pressure to practice the rituals of the religion of their birth. Some converts take part in both religious practices. Balan reported that he would take part in *pujas* [prayers], but in his heart he would pray to Jesus. Some women converts follow the same strategy. One teacher said,

"My father called me to the temple. I went there, but I was praying to Jesus." Another teacher said, "When *prasad* [sacred food] was offered, I just prayed and ate it because I did not want to hurt my family members." In spite of these circumstances, converts follow Jesus secretly. One of the women in her forties said, "I do not tell others about going to church or Bible study because people would look down on us." Another woman said, "We hide the Bible and go." Janaki described how she was not allowed by her husband to practice her faith publicly for thirty years:

Janaki: My father was a Hindu and he used to go to the Hindu temple, but my mother was a born-again Christian . . . so I had seen my mother as a Christian woman who always read the Bible and prayed to Jesus. My father was not a staunch Hindu, but on his way to the office he would go to the temple and pray. But he never opposed us for praying. My mother was regularly going to church, attending Tuesday fellowships and prayer meetings, etc., but she never took us. Only at home we read the Bible and prayed.

In Indian culture, a boy and his family make a formal visit to a prospective bride's home to meet her. The girl, dressed in her best, serves coffee or tea to the boy and his family members. If they like the girl, then further talks will be held, which include negotiation of the dowry. If they do not approve of her, they will simply say that they will inform the girl's father later. I asked Janaki how she could agree to marry a Hindu when they came to see her for marriage. She said:

Janaki: I did not know, as a believer, that I should not marry a Hindu. When I heard that he was coming to see me in my home, I just prayed that he would agree to marry me. I just went into the kitchen and prayed because I knew his mother was a Christian. My mother and his mother were very close relatives. When his sisters came to see me without *bindhi* [a sacred dot worn by married Hindu women] on their foreheads, I assumed that the entire family was a Christian family . . . I never thought he was a Hindu.

Q: What was your feeling when you heard that he was a Hindu?

Janaki: I felt very bad. When he asked me to wear *bindhi*, I thought that it was only for the wedding, but he wanted me to wear it always. Before marriage, I never had *bindhi* on my forehead. When I entered my mother-in-law's house after our wedding, the first thing my husband did was buy a *bindhi* and ask me to wear it. I felt very bad. My mother-in-law encouraged me by saying, "You don't worry! He wants you to wear; so you simply wear." I was afraid of him, so I used to keep quiet and never question him.

Q: How did you sustain your faith in that atmosphere?

Janaki: My mother-in-law and I would pray together. I had a daily devotional book called *Palaivana Neerodai* [Streams in the Dessert]. I asked my mother to get me a Bible, and she gave me one. I would hide the Bible and read. Mostly he [her husband] would be at the office. When he is at home, I don't read the Bible. All four of my sisters-in-law are also believers, so whenever we meet we have good time of fellowship.

Q: Did your husband object you reading the Bible?

Janaki: From the beginning, he made it very clear that I should not do anything Christian. He told me, "You should follow me and you should do what I say." I do not argue with him; I simply obey him, and that is my nature. Whenever he was away, I was completely free. I was on my own.

Q: What made you follow Jesus rather than your husband?

Janaki: God's abundant love made me follow Jesus. At my time of distress, Jesus wipes my tears, he consoles me, and he gives his words. He always talks to me through his verses, and I keep noting them down. He shines his light on me. I praise him for he is the light. I have come across many hurdles in my life, but he had given me the strength to hold on to him. I also received the anointing of the Holy Spirit. He made me strong.

I don't mind whatever my husband says . . . because he does not fight with me, but he would stop talking to me for weeks together. I cannot be happy without him talking to me, so I do not argue with him; I cooperate with him to maintain peace in the family. Even if he calls me to the temple, I will go there and stand behind him. If he gives me something to eat that was offered in the temple, I take it. Sometimes I throw it out, sometimes I put it in my mouth and then spit it out later. Something like this has happened now and then.

Q: When did you take baptism? Was it before your marriage?

Janaki: No, no, my mother never took us to church. So it was only after marriage. I never had the courage. My fourth daughter was sick when she was three. Then I prayed to God, "I do not like to go to the temple. If you heal my child, I will stop going to the temple." Even otherwise, only twice in a year would he call me to the temple. I thought that when we expect some blessing from God we need to give up something for the Lord, so I prayed that if my daughter was healed, I would go to church. By then, I was married for fifteen years and gained some courage to tell my husband, "All these days I have obeyed you, but hereafter I will obey God." During Christmas vacation, I went to my mother's house and took baptism.

Q: When did you start going to church?

Janaki: I started going to church very recently—a year before, only after he became a Christian, since January 1, 2004.

Q: All these years you never had church fellowship?

Janaki: Some of my family members follow Jesus. Whenever we go home or we come together, we talk about spiritual things. We ask one another, "What did God speak to you? What did you say to Jesus?" We pray together. My brothers will talk to my children, saying, "If Jesus comes now, he will take us; what are you going to do?" . . . My second sister-in-law taught me many songs, and I love singing them. My fourth sister-in-law would pass on audio cassettes and books to me. I could not go out freely because people would inform my husband, and he would not like that, then that would lead to unnecessary problems for me. I never went to church without his permission. Only when my child was healed did I go to church and I shared that as a testimony . . . Once, I took my daughter to [a preacher who prays for healing]. At home, we [she and her children] pray together; we believe that when we pray directly to God, he answers us . . . We did all these things in his [her husband's] absence. [Laughs.] Some people informed my husband that in his absence I was conducting prayer meetings at home. He inquired from my sister-in-law's children. The children were also supporting me. [Laughs.] God favored me a lot by providing me with such support from others and his support as well.

Q: How do you pray?

Janaki: The moment my husband goes for a walk, I would lock the door and pray for forty minutes. Then I would start doing the household works. Around 9:00 a.m., he would leave for the office, then I would refresh myself and start reading and meditating on the Bible till 11:00 a.m. While cooking, I praise and worship God. At noon, I would go around my house; as I walk, I praise him and claim his promises, like, "I will satisfy you with long life and I will show you my salvation." Then I pray with thanksgiving. God has blessed me with the gift of tongues; I pray and praise him in other languages. When my husband was expected, I would sit on a dining chair near the window and pray with my eyes opened because I was scared of him. Even if I delayed for a few seconds to open the door, he would question me, "What were you doing?"

Once I was caught. By mistake, I left the daily devotion book on the sofa. He saw that and asked me about it. I lied to him, saying, "I do not know what it is. Your sister came and left it." He told me to return it at once. Then immediately I went to her house and returned it. She felt very bad about her brother's act. Her son was feeling all the more shocked that his uncle made a big issue of a small book. Because of this, in the afternoon I would open my eyes and pray, so I could see him coming through the window and open the door at once. This was how my prayer life was during those days. God has given me the gift of writing songs also.

Q: Do you write songs?

Janaki: Yeah! I have written many songs. We sing those songs. In the evenings, the Spirit of God helps me write songs. Daily he speaks to me through his words. He comforts me and encourages me through the verses. He gives me the tune also. His ways are different. Children would return from school and I would sit with them. At 8:00 p.m. we have our family prayer and I make my children be part of it . . . In the night I pray with my children, then we have our dinner. Then children would pray alone and go to bed; I would also go to bed. That was how my prayer life was. God would constantly speak to me. He was leading me always. Because I was praying, I could understand his voice. Sometimes I would hear him calling me.

We saw in the previous chapter, how Janaki hears the voice of God audibly. Sometimes she thought that it was her husband calling her and went to see him, but found him fast asleep. Then she understood that it was God who called her. Her intimate relationship with the divine sustained her without a church fellowship all those years. I was curious to know how she was able to lead her husband to follow Jesus.

Q: How did your husband come to follow Jesus?

Janaki: A well-known preacher wanted to visit my family to condole the death of my son-in-law. [He died in mysterious circumstances. It was not clear whether he died in an accident or was murdered. Her husband was shattered by his sudden death]. First my eldest daughter got separated and then my second son-in-law died suddenly. So I agreed to invite the preacher who wanted to visit us to pray for my family as we were in trouble. He came and for the first time we prayed together in our house in front of my husband. Since then, my husband removed all the idols from our house. I threw out all those things related to previous religious practices from our house. I felt these things were hindering the blessing for my family.

I prayed, "Lord, hereafter I will glorify you alone." I fully submitted my life to him and said, "Many things have happened in my life. Father, I trust you alone. Lord, you are everything to me. Lord, I will glorify only your name." From the temple people used to come for donation. I would give them money because I was afraid of my husband, but since then I discontinued all those things. The whole family was in a state of shock due to the tragic death of my son-in-law. Many questioned, "Why is this tragedy happened in your family?" The situation was distressing.

But the Lord encouraged me through his words, "The Lord is with you always; he is at my right hand; I will not be shaken." But I felt that I did not glorify my Lord fully, so I prayed and promised him that I will glorify him alone. After the death of my son-in-law, my husband handed over the temple keys to others. [He was the elder who took care of the affairs of a particular temple in the town, as he was a wealthy man. The festivals were organized under his leadership all those years. But at this point he stopped all his involvement with the temple.] Within a month, our neighbor brought things that were offered in the temple for us. Our watchman came at 6:00 in the morning and gave them to me. I was wondering what to do. Our watchman said, "If you do not want it, I will take it." First I thought, "Let him take it," because I did not want it. Though that year we did not participate and did not contribute anything to the temple festival, he brought this. I thought to myself, "If I tell my watchman to take it, this practice will continue next year also. So I told my watchman to return them." Very boldly I did something for the Lord for the first time.

I surrendered fully to the Lord saying, "I trust you alone, Lord, and you take care of our children and us. We do not have anyone. You are our shelter." Since we do not have sons, we love our sons-in-law very much, but . . .

My husband would cry a lot, thinking of our children. He would always blame himself; that because of his sins the children were suffering. He used to say, "I only spoiled the lives of my children." During those days, God helped me to tell him that together we could ask the Lord to lead us. I showed him Isaiah 51:11, "Everlasting joy will crown their heads. Gladness and joy will overtake them, and sorrow and sighing will flee away." My sister also showed me the same verse. For the first time, I told my husband about Jesus; that he should call on him and then the Lord will listen to him and do favors to our children. Since then, he knelt and prayed and he started reading the Bible with interest and listening to the messages from the television. Almost for a year he was at home; he did not go out much. As the Lord said, "Consecrate yourselves, for tomorrow the Lord will do amazing thing among you." Since then, the Lord has been leading us about what to do and what not to do. Daily he tells me something and I obey him completely.

My husband was invited to a Christian meeting meant for businessmen, and he attended the meeting. The next day he agreed to go to church. God worked in his heart for a year. He heard his prayer and cry. That one year was like a training period for us; the first six months we went through a lot of troubles, but at the end of the year our daughter had peace in her life. God helped him call on Jesus. He was slowly changing; he started reading the Bible and praying. God had a plan for our family. Then he accepted Christ as his savior and the next day he came to church.

    I was little hesitant to take him to my church because it is a Pentecostal church. People shout "Hallelujah" while worshiping. They make us stand and kneel down. The preaching is very forceful. Whenever my pastor preaches, it comes with authority. However, my husband liked it. When God works, he makes everything beautiful. God has blessed him with salvation and fullness. He was joyful. God removed all his sorrows and tears from his eyes. He gained confidence that the Lord will take care of our children and he believes that the Lord will never let us down. Within three months, by God's grace he also took baptism.

Q: How do you feel about it now?

Janaki: I am so glad. My children are so happy that the Lord has done a great thing, though we went through lots of struggle. On the same year, my first son-in-law came to take my daughter. Earlier she was refusing to go, but God helped her to join her husband. God has changed my son-in-law to love his wife and children. God has blessed her family also.

    Janaki found some fellowship and support from her mother-in-law, a follower of Jesus, and sometimes from her sisters-in-law, but she was not allowed to attend church for about thirty years. Nevertheless, she held on to her faith in Jesus through prayer and meditating on the Bible. Her husband, who treated her poorly for her faith, eventually became a follower of Jesus. She waited patiently all those years, and when a suitable time came—a time of tragedy—she took courage to invite her husband to seek Jesus for peace, as he was shattered by the death of his son-in-law. Her husband tried and felt it worked in his life too, so he converted. In spite of these difficult situations, after thirty years Janaki was able to lead her husband to follow Jesus. Similar to Janaki, Kushbu, a Muslim convert, followed Jesus secretly. She narrated her difficulties:

Kushbu: When I took baptism, nobody in my family knew that I had become a Christian, but only when I started going to church they started watching me and catching me. They troubled me; my brother and family members and my husband would surround me and corner me, saying, "Why do you have to follow Christianity? What is there that is not in Islam?"

I told my husband, during the first night after our wedding, "I am a follower of Jesus Christ and I love him more than anything else." When he confronted me later, I reminded him of those things. This was another occasion to share my testimony for the glory of God. I questioned my husband, "I have told you about my faith on the first day itself; why are you ganging up my family members against me now?" He replied, "Your family members are making me do this." He further said, "You are spoiling my name by going to church and your relatives are telling me that I am a fool to let you do this. So I want to be strict with you now."

But I could not keep myself away from the fellowship. I tried different routes every time to go to church because my brothers were following me whenever I went. I took a roundabout route to reach the church that was close by. I went secretly because I did not want to hurt my husband. But I wanted to satisfy my spirit also. I was rejoicing in my spirit despite this.

As a convert, it was very difficult for me to go to church. We [Muslim converts] go to church very secretly. So I put on an ordinary dress as if I were going to a market, so my husband would not notice and my relatives would not know. And I would go to any church that was open and nearby. I cannot go to church on Sundays.

But after ten years, I had a vision to go to [a particular church nearby]. For two years I did not have any problem. My husband did not say anything. But after two years my relatives and my neighbors who saw me going to church told my husband that I was spoiling the name of our community. My husband, hearing them, beat me. All this turmoil went on for some time, but I decided to follow Jesus anyhow and continue to read the Bible. He would also abuse my family members to make me angry. Initially, I would pray to Jesus to punish my husband for his behavior, but my pastor counseled me not to do anything against the wishes of my husband and to remain at home to be a Christian. Initially, I was annoyed with my pastor for his advice, but later I understood that it was the correct way to follow Jesus in my situation. I tried, but it was very difficult to keep myself away from the church. Sometimes I was able to go to church. The Lord protected me, counseled me, and led me.

My husband tried witchcraft against me. It did not work, but it affected my child, who was admitted to a hospital. She was under treatment for one and a half years. People were blaming me for the sickness by saying that it was a punishment from Allah. I poured out my heart and prayed to the Lord, and the Lord visited the hospital and touched my daughter and she became alright. The Lord did not put me to shame in front of my people.

At one point, all these problems stopped, for the glory of Jesus Christ. Now I tell my children, "These kinds of torment I went through, so you must be strong enough to hold on to Jesus." When my husband was not at home, my children and I would pray together. We would pour out all our needs to the Lord. Once my husband told me, "You have spoiled yourself and your life. Why are you spoiling my children too?" But the Lord gave me the strength to tell him gently that I was not spoiling our children; I was giving them good teachings only.

At times, after much prayer, I have shared with him about problems solved through prayer. But I do not tell him directly that Jesus is the true God and that he should accept him. I know that in God's time he will make all things beautiful. I was very particular that through deeds I should show him that Jesus is the true God and a loving God and Jesus will do everything.

Q: What made you hold on to Jesus despite such difficulties and problems?

Kushbu: Jesus takes care of all my problems. Whenever I am in need, I pray and get things done. He is my provider. Whenever someone speaks ill of Jesus, I get upset and it is unbearable to me. But Jesus will talk to me through verses written on the walls of a church or through some paintings or wall hangings, like that. The Lord comes to me and speaks to me and that is a real comfort to me. Especially during difficult times, he leads me and takes care of me.

I love to attend the worship on the first day of every month in our church. I cook on the previous day to spare time to attend church in the morning. I tell my family as if I were going out to get milk. Then I go to church in the morning during 5:00 to 6:00. When I go,

I pray, "God, you send an angel before me to protect me so I will not get into any trouble [for attending church]." God has answered me.

God also communicates through visions. He tells me what is going to happen in advance. He has taught me how to handle problems, how to pray, and how to handle witchcraft, etc.

God called me to do his ministry. A genuine call came to me while attending a church service. Since then, I started doing the ministry. My ministry is among Muslims, especially among women like me [who follow Jesus secretly]. I support and encourage them in their struggles and counsel them and share the Word of God with them. I also train them how to carry on with Jesus and how to be a secret believer and how to read the Bible secretly.

Q: How do you read the Bible secretly?

Kushbu: In the initial days, I would cover the Bible inside the saris. Later, I used to collect old Bibles and tear apart each book and keep it under old newspapers or inside boxes meant to store groceries, because I was longing to read the Bible. Unlike some women followers of Jesus who never had a chance to read the Bible for months together, I could always read the Bible this way. If I do not read the Bible for a day I feel bad. The only drawback I had was that I could not go to church for Sunday worship, but I came to reckon with it. On January 1, 2001, I prayed, "Lord, everyone is rejoicing, but I am not given a chance to go to church for the all-night prayer. Why Lord?" But the Lord spoke to me clearly, "You are called to be different and your ways are not to be like others. Do not compare your life with other believers." The Lord spoke to me according to my situation, so I felt it was God's word. Since then, I do not feel bad about not getting a chance to attend church on Sundays.

Converts were determined to hold on to Jesus despite the troubles and find ways to strengthen themselves, as Kushbu did. Despite opposition from their family and being accused of betraying their family and community, converts had a strong conviction that they have done the right thing. They were not willing to retract their decision to follow Jesus, except a few who thought of returning and felt suicidal. They were strengthened by prayer, reading the Bible, and support from a church or other believers. Some accepted their situation, reckoning that it was allowed by God, and such understanding gave them strength to bear everything for the sake of Jesus.

Converts were committed to love and forgive their family members in spite of the torture, suffering, and affliction caused by them. They were very intent to please their family members in every other way, without giving up Jesus. It was obvious that they had greater love for Jesus than for their family. Sania was clear that she loved her dad, but she could not give up Jesus because her love for Jesus was greater.

Some converts adopted a strategy of retaining their social identity as Hindus or Muslims in order to maintain peace in the family and the community, while claiming their spiritual identity as followers of Jesus. They were comfortable in maintaining multiple identities. Converts adopted this strategy to redraw the boundaries of religion by differentiating between religious identity and spiritual identity. They saw their conversion experience as a religious experience of Jesus while seeing Christianity as the institutional form of religion. In this way they deployed their religious identity as Hindus or Muslims while claiming to have a spiritual identity as followers of Jesus by virtue of their religious experience.

However, converts have the deep desire to bring their faith into the open and eagerly wait for an opportunity. Janaki, when a tragedy struck her family, asserted her belief in Jesus, which eventually led her husband to convert. When converts found solutions through prayer they invited their family members to try Jesus. Such crises gave them the opportunity to declare their faith firmly, which led to the conversion of other family members.

This phenomenon of following Jesus while not being part of an institutionalized church is not an isolated phenomenon, but is widespread in India and abroad. *Kristubakthas* (devotees of Christ), a movement in Varanasi, North India, initiated by a Catholic priest, is one of the movements that brings Dalits and OBCs (Other Backward Castes, which are the caste groups placed between the low castes and the high castes) together in the name of Jesus. They do not have any structured form of worship or rituals but devotedly read the Bible and pray to Jesus. However, they follow their traditions in social customs. In Tamil Nadu and in many places in the South India, the non-church movement is spreading fast. Dasan Jeyaraj (2010, pp. 26–27) identified four reasons for the growth of the non-church movement in Chennai:

1. To avoid rejection and exclusion from family.

2. Fear of losing one's role and identity in the community.
3. Fear of breaking family tradition or to avoid being named as a rebel.
4. Ignorance of the need to be part of a church.

Such movements are also growing in Islamic societies, not only in India, but worldwide; this is called the Insider Movement by missiologists. This strategy is adopted primarily by converts from Hinduism and Islam in India; they are of the view that this is the best way to follow Jesus in a multireligious society. Following Jesus while retaining their social identity is a self-initiated movement by converts in India.

Is the strategy of converts retaining their social identity as Hindus or Muslims while following Jesus a deceptive one? Marilynn Brewer (2001) claims that studies have pointed out that everyone derives social identity from more than one social group and manages multiple social identities according to different social contexts. She explains, "On an ongoing basis, the individual (either consciously or subconsciously) weighs and assesses available aspects of the self to determine which are activated or engaged as guides to behavior in the current situation. The individual may be aware that different identities have conflicting implications for behavior, in which case self-expression reflects some choice or compromise among different aspects of the self-concept. Actualization or enactment of different identities is influenced by the demands of the situation or social context, but the process is one of selecting from a repertory of identities or self-representations that reside within the individual" (p. 121). She observes that there are four strategies for an individual to handle multiple identities in a conflicting context. First, an individual may commit to one dominant group identification and ignore other group identities. Second, a person can insulate different group identities in different environments and be alert not to activate multiple identities simultaneously. The third strategy is to adopt an inclusive strategy, such as when group identities overlap, for example, African-Americans identifying as Americans. The fourth strategy, conjunctive, is adopted when multiple categories intersect.

Identity, whether personal or social, is not fixed. Personal identity changes in different life situations and social identity changes in different social contexts. Integration of multiple identities leads to well-being and smooth sailing in social functions. Integrated identities even draw elements from conflicting social groups in order to present a multifaceted self to negotiate conflicting contexts. Arthur L. Greil and Lynn Davidman (2007) claim that people creatively adapt traditional identities to new situations. This is very true in the case of converts in India. Although the boundaries between Christianity, Hinduism, and Islam are clearly marked, converts to Christianity create multiple identities so they can cross traditional boundaries. Converts articulated that they continue the religious practices of their religion of birth for social reasons, not for religious purposes. They create new meanings for the same religious practices that they have been following all along. When social boundaries are loosely marked, it is easier for them to move from one identity to another identity. Maintaining uniformity and cohesiveness is very important for membership in a social group. When invited by family to go to a temple or mosque, converts go with them and activate their identity as Hindu or Muslim; however, they try to maintain their new identity as the followers of Jesus by injecting new meaning into the practice of going to a temple or mosque; they go there, but they pray only to Jesus.

According to social identity theories, the self is enhanced by the positive image of the ingroup. Converts are members of two groups that are inherently in conflict: Christianity and Hinduism or Islam. They compare both groups based on social context and activate one identity over the other. In India, Christianity is viewed as a foreign religion or the religion of Dalits, hence, converts cannot enhance their self-image by activating only their Christian identity. On the other hand, because of their religious experience of encountering Jesus, they do not give up their Christian identity. Therefore, they juggle their two identities according to social context.

By continuing some of their former religious practices in conflicting or threatening situations, converts show that they are committed to the dominant group identification by activating their dominant identity as Hindu or Muslim while underplaying their identity in their newfound faith in Jesus. Following Jesus secretly falls into the strategy of compartmentalization or insulation of multiple identities. Converts are cautious that multiple identities are not simultaneously activated. In this instance, the social context determines which identity is activated. When they are with their families, they activate their identity as Hindu or Muslim, and when they are away from them they activate their identity as Christian. Converts adopt the inclusive strategy when they are among fellow converts to Christianity by identifying all converts as Christians in general, including secret Christians who have converted from Hinduism or Islam. However, in a larger social context converts may adopt the conjunctive strategy. Secret converts from Hinduism may identify only with other secret Christians converted from Hinduism, rather than with secret converts from Islam, or vice versa, even though the identity of "secret Christian" overlaps with the identity of "convert from Islam."

Geoffrey A. Oddie (1997, p. 6), in his study of conversion movements in South Asia, observed, "it was not a case of either/or but of striking the balance between the old and new, or perhaps of adopting an additional identity." Converts juggling different identities in different social contexts is not unusual but very normal, because we all juggle multiple identities in various social contexts. Managing multiple identities in conversion is not a deception, but a core element of managing oneself in a multireligious context.

Converts felt that their conversion experience was complete with the divine–human encounter. Initially they did not consider being part of a church or Christian community to be an essential element of following Jesus, due to hostile situations. Janaki could not attend church for about thirty years, but she held on to her faith. Balan was quite content with his experience of Christ for the first one and a half years without being part of a church; however, he later joined a church. Sania was under a sort of house arrest for one and a half years during which she could not attend church or read the Bible. She was able to manage her ordeal only through prayer. As for Bakht Singh, he did not participate in a Christian community for about a year, yet he was sure about his conversion. Rekha also did not attend church for about a year after her conversion. Vinodha was never able to attend church worship services. Rarely she was able to visit a Catholic church, but she was never able to be part of a church community.

Converts believe that their personal experience of Jesus is the essence of conversion to Christianity. Their perception of Christian spirituality is reduced to maintaining a personal relationship with Jesus. They consider all other requirements taught by the church as nonessential. It is only certain persons or the Christian community that create in converts a sense that their conversion is incomplete because they are not part of a church.

Over a century ago, William James (1902/2004, p. 39) argued for the definition of religion as: *"The feelings, acts, and experiences of individual men* [and women] *in their solitude, so far as they apprehend themselves to stand in relation to whatever they may consider the divine.* Since the relation may be either moral, physical, or ritual, it is evident that out of religion in the sense in which we take it, theologies, philosophies, and ecclesiastical organizations may secondarily grow" (Italics original). James argued that the heart of religion is feeling, not theology, philosophy, or ecclesiastical structure. Converts view Christianity from the perspective of their religious experience of Jesus. They do not consider being part of a church as an essential element of conversion, but they consider prayer and reading the Bible to be essential features of following Jesus because they are the channels of conversing with the divine. Converts sustain their intimate relationship with Jesus through prayer and reading the Bible.

James (1902/2004, p. 385) claimed that what makes religion alive is not theology or philosophy, but the feelings of people who experience the divine. He said, "What keeps religion going is something else than abstract definitions and systems of concatenated adjectives, and something different from faculties of theology and their professors. All these things are after-effects, secondary accretions upon those phenomena of vital conversation with the unseen divine." Converts' attitude towards dogmatic theology and systematic theology is similar. From the vantage point of the divine–human encounter, converts are able to redraw religious boundaries that would otherwise create division and conflict for them. When they are not allowed to attend a church and are forced to practice the religion of their birth by attending a temple or mosque, they comply, but they pray to Jesus. For many Christians, it would be an abomination to say that one is going to a temple to pray to Jesus, but for converts the essence of worshiping Jesus is talking to him, and this may be done in a church or temple or mosque. What makes Christianity alive in India is neither dogmatic theology that is preoccupied with metaphysics nor contextual theologies that promise liberation here and now, but religious experience that establishes an intimate relationship with Jesus. It is intimacy with Jesus that sustains people in following him.

During their struggles, converts find various factors that sustain them: divine presence, divine love, intimacy with the divine, divine strength, supernatural protection, hope of eternal life, conversation with the divine, and the Bible. Jesus's suffering is a model and inspiration to them to bear all their sufferings. A convert who is medical doctor reported, "Despite so many problems from my family, the Lord was with me, comforting and strengthening me." Mohan, who experienced supernatural protection when people came to burn him to death, recalled that "the word of Christ strengthened me." Similarly, Sania, while moving from place to place to escape her dad's pursuit, claimed that she would not have had the strength to go through all her struggles by herself. She said, "I knew that it had to be some supernatural intervention because I was not that kind of person [able to bear all those troubles]." Subsequent religious experiences sustain converts in times of trouble. Converts holding on firmly to Jesus despite their struggles is a striking phenomenon.

Converts are sustained not by their own strength, but by strength from the divine. Some factors that enable them to hold on to Jesus are the conviction that the presence of Jesus is with them always, the confidence that their prayers are answered by him, and the experience of Jesus speaking to them through the Bible. The love and care extended by the church or other believers are the other factors that sustain converts during persecution.

Converts' personal experience of Jesus, their continued experience of hearing him speak to them, and their intimate relationship with Jesus stand out as the major factors that bind converts to Jesus. Converts are fascinated by the love of Jesus experienced at the divine–human encounter, and the continued outpouring of his unconditional love and acceptance grip them tightly and persuade them to forego anything else, including any familial relationship, in order to hold on to the love of God. Their transformed life is taken as evidence of God's work. The sense of being saved, the assurance of being forgiven, and the hope of eternal life are some of the factors that enable them to be firm in their newfound faith. A sense of being "alive inside" since the divine–human encounter keeps them going. A new identity, a new purpose in life, and the experience of leading others to Christ also motivate converts to hold on to Jesus. A belief that God solves their problems and blesses and cares for them, a new level of self-confidence, and a sense of having God on their side are other factors that make converts fascinated with their newfound faith.

Not every convert in India faces hostilities from their family or community. However, converts live with the fear that problems might arise in the future due to their conversion. In some converts' families there was opposition initially, but after seeing converts' transformed lives their family members' attitude toward their conversion became positive. The transformation in converts' lives also has great influence among their friends and is considered proof of the divine power operating in them. Converts encourage people to try Jesus when they face crises. When their prayers are answered, family members or friends also began to follow Jesus.

Converts use prayer as a channel to talk to Jesus at anytime and anywhere. It is not restricted to a religious site, nor are any religious authorities required to mediate. This makes converts feel that they have easy access to the divine. Inban said, "I can talk to him like talking to a friend . . ." Nithya said, "I would always talk to him, even for very small things." They feel prayer comforts them and gives them peace during times of trouble. Deensha said, "I pray and immediately get relief." Prayer reassures them that Jesus controls their life situations. Komala reported, "Even though we went through lots of problems, I was feeling peace at heart because I felt that I have prayed about this and the rest he will take care of." Converts experience the divine presence during prayer. Prayer enables them to resolve crises and gives them strength and peace to handle difficult situations. The experience of prayer being answered by Jesus validates their conviction that Jesus is true and works in their daily lives.

Some converts claimed that prayer gave them power over sins. Others began to see their lives transformed as they prayed. Kushbu claims, "I just pray to God to help me be quiet. My character has changed almost 90 percent." Nithya prays, "Make me more like thee." Converts sometimes see a vision or hear God's voice during prayer. The confidence that their prayers are answered by Jesus is the key factor behind their unshakable faith in him. When their prayers are not answered, some converts offer the explanation that it could be due to their sin, while some hope that their prayers will be answered later. However, a few unanswered prayers do not make them lose their faith in Jesus.

Prayer is one of the key factors that enables converts to stick to Jesus. Prayer gives power and peace, prayer transforms life, and prayer induces religious experience. William James (1902/2004, p. 400) claimed, "Prayer . . . is the very soul and essence of religion." Converts are fascinated by this new channel for interacting with the divine. Auguste Sabatier defined prayer as: "No vain exercise of words, no mere repetition of certain sacred formula, but the very movement itself of the soul, putting itself in a personal relation of contact with the mysterious power of which it feels the presence,—it may be even before it has a name by which to call it . . . this prayer rises and stirs the soul, even in the absence of forms or of doctrines, we have living religion" (quoted in James, 1902/2004, p. 400). This definition shows the essential nature of prayer through which people can connect to the divine. Through prayer converts sustain the intimate relationship with the divine that began at the divine–human encounter. Prayer is no longer a mere ritual for converts to Christianity.

Converts claim that Jesus speaks to them through the Bible. They believe that the Bible speaks appropriate to their situations, has answers to their questions, and offers solutions to their crises. Nathan realized that God spoke to him when he read the Book of Acts and from this he decided to continue in his newfound faith. Balan was able to grow in his newfound faith only by reading the Bible at the early stage of his conversion. Kareem left his house after his conversion, as it was not safe for him to remain there due to opposition from his family. He was without food and money and claimed that the Word of God sustained him. Converts draw strength by reading the Bible to deal with life situations and crises. The words of the Bible are comforting to converts during their troubles.

Converts find that reading the Bible transforms their lives. The Bible convicts them of their sin and enables them to have a better understanding of the Christian faith. The Bible shapes their ideas of God, worship, sin, salvation, faith, etc. The idea of God speaking to them through the Bible is not restricted only to opening the Bible and reading it. Converts feel that sometimes Bible verses written on a compound wall of a church or displayed on a car or autorickshaw, or statements or Bible verses heard in a sermon, are meant for them and given to them from Jesus. Every day they look for a Bible verse to sustain them. This gives them an assurance that he is with them, concerned about them, and speaks to them. This assurance increases converts' faith in Jesus. By such experiences they come to perceive the Bible as the Living Word or God's Word.

Personalized reading of the Bible is not peculiar to converts in India. Luhrmann (2012), in her study of the Vineyard Fellowship, observed that members read the Bible from their own context or situation with an expectation that God will speak to them. She explains, "they describe reading as if they were conversing: they look for the way God answers, inspires, consoles, enlightens by changing the way that the text reads. God is understood to be communicating when, as one congregant put it, 'a verse just jumps out at me,' or when you have a powerful bodily feeling—you feel peace, or intense joy, or suddenly you feel very tired, as if a burden has been lifted and now you can sleep" (p. 59). A physical and emotional response is attached with the reading. They are not concerned about the historical context but with what God is telling them now. She observed, "The emphasis is upon reading the text for what it says, as if you can read it straight, for its truth. There is no sense that texts from the past hide from us behind authorial intentions we can no longer understand, or that they were written for a social and economic community we do not live in now. On Sunday mornings and in house group, we would read the most obscure and historical texts—Judges, for example—as if they were written for us, to help us understand how God wanted us to be with him" (p. 12). Similarly, converts' reading of the Bible is always personalized to their situation. They do not read the Bible as a religious ritual only to be done in a religious gathering, but they read it whenever they feel like reading. It helps them experience the presence of Jesus. They love to read the Bible. They have a strong feeling that the divine converses with them through the Bible every time they read it. The messages they hear from the Bible are apt for the day or the situation as they seek help from the divine. Thus, converts perceive the Bible as God's Word, true and consistent.

What is the role of social factors in supporting the converts in the conversion process, especially during persecution? Rambo (1993, p. 1) claims, "All conversions (even Saul's on the road to Damascus) are mediated through people, institutions, communities and groups." Lofland and Stark (1965, p. 871) first suggested the idea of a social relationship in their "world-saver" model at the stage of a cult affective bond. They observed, "conversion frequently moved through *pre-existing* friendship pairs or nets" (italics original). This idea was developed further by other scholars (Bainbridge, 1992; Downton, 1980; Long & Hadden, 1983; Rambo, 1993; Richardson, 1985) who observed that a social relationship is required for a potential convert to become part of a group. Social agents played a key role in starting the process of conversion and sometimes in the consolidation of the conversion process. Such agents might be the divine or also in the categories of kinship, friendship, leadership, or strangers. Kinship agents include immediate family members and relatives. Friendship agents include friends and colleagues. Leadership agents refer to teachers, religious authorities, and leaders in society. Strangers are those who come in at a particular situation in a convert's life. For some the conversion process begins suddenly with the divine–human encounter. In such instances, a human agent is absent at the beginning stage, though later someone helps the convert in his or her spiritual journey. However, converts, while acknowledging the role of human agents, give all the credit to the divine by highlighting the centrality of the divine–human encounter. They claim that it was entirely an act of God's grace that they experienced Jesus personally.

Human agents presented themselves as a source of help and encouragement to the converts. Agents' availability in times of need and their comforting words attracted converts. Converts began to feel that they have someone to listen to them. The agents offered moral support, introduced Jesus, and invited them to try Jesus. Converts did not accept Jesus immediately. They try their own way, and only when they experience the divine–human encounter do they go all out to follow Jesus. In other instances, converts persuaded the agents to help them move forward. Nevertheless, for some, church authorities were not helpful. In some cases a stranger influenced the conversion process. Narayana Wamman Tilak, a well-known Marathi poet, was disillusioned with the religion of his birth and wanted to start a new religion. During a train journey, he conversed with a European who was a Christian. After listening to Tilak about his plan of starting a religion, this person told Tilak that he would become a Christian in two years and gave him a New Testament. Tilak did not even ask his name and neither did the European ask Tilak's name. Just as the European stranger predicted, within two years Tilak became a Christian after reading the New Testament (Tilak 1956).

Though generally there is an influential relationship with an agent that helps one experience conversion, nevertheless, an emotional attachment between a potential convert and an agent is not necessary for starting the conversion process. The process may be initiated spontaneously by the divine at the divine–human encounter.

The role of a church or other group of believers is vital in understanding the conversion process. Some claim that they went just for fun to Christian gatherings and that led to conversion. Some went in search of a solution to their crisis. When they first attended the Christian gathering, many converts felt attracted by the atmosphere, songs, sermons, and so on. Converts were impressed with the love and affection shown to them by the group members. Participation in the Christian community enhances the transformation process in the lives of converts. Christian community provides a supportive role to converts in facing hostilities due to their conversion. It teaches converts the beliefs and practices of Christianity. Being part of a Christian church or a fellowship enables converts to hold on to Jesus in times of trouble. Without such community support, converts' zeal for the newfound faith can easily diminish. However, many converts who were unable to attend church continued to keep their newfound faith. In the next chapter we will discuss the Step Model that explains the conversion process.

10 The Step Model

> Various types of beliefs can be implanted in many people, after brain function has been sufficiently disturbed by accidentally or deliberately induced fear, anger or excitement.
>
> —W. Sargant (1957, p. 132)

> A person cannot experience Christian conversion without an encounter (in one way or another) with Jesus and a turning to him.
>
> —Richard V. Peace (1999, p. 87)

The first six chapters of this book discussed the varieties of religious experience associated with conversion to Christianity. The chapter on the mystical turning point analyzed the divine–human encounter in the conversion process and showed the centrality of it in the conversion process. Chapter 8 discussed the transforming effects of conversion in various aspects of converts' lives, which led to their integrated well-being. The chapter on hostilities shed light on the persecution unleashed on converts by their families and communities for leaving the religion of their birth. It also showed how converts endured these hostilities and held on to their newfound faith. Despite their persecution, many converts were even able to eventually convert their family members to Christianity.

Based on the analysis of the various types of conversion experiences from a phenomenological perspective, we can say that a transformative religious experience or religious conversion is both a complex process and an event—the divine–human encounter—which triggers personal transformation, an ongoing process that is sustained by religious practices and socialization, leading to integrated well-being and a change of religious beliefs. In this chapter I tie up the threads that emerged in the previous chapters with an interdisciplinary Step Model that explains the conversion process.

The Step Model gives due significance to religious experience in the conversion process, to which converts attribute great significance. Developing a comprehensive model for such a complex phenomenon is difficult. I have not adopted a particular theoretical position to develop this model, but I have developed an interdisciplinary model from a phenomenological perspective while drawing insights from the fields of psychology, sociology, anthropology, and theology. Flexibility is built into the Step Model. The conversion process is so complex that the steps cannot be precisely demarcated to a definite, clear beginning and ending. However, the steps enable us to make sense out of the complex reality of the conversion process. In light of the existing models of conversion, this chapter traces the steps of conversion and highlights the role of religious experience, religious practices, and hostilities attached to conversion in India.

Lofland and Stark (1965) sketched the process of conversion in the "world-saver" model with seven stages: tension, problem-solving perspective, seekership, turning point, cult affective bonds, extra-cult affective bonds, and intensive interaction. Tension is a felt discrepancy within the self in comparison with imagined ideals. In the stage of the problem-solving perspective, a person may choose to seek the help of a psychiatrist or other expert to solve one's psychological conflict, but converts choose a religious problem-solving option. In the seekership stage, converts explore religious alternatives to resolve their tension. At the turning point, a crisis-like situation leads converts to consider new possibilities. In the stage of cult affective bonds, a relationship with a member or group becomes influential in leading one to encounter the group. In extra-cult affective bonds, either converts already lack affective bonds to society, or their emotional attachment to others outside the cult becomes neutralized by the group. In the final stage, intensive interaction, converts' interaction with the group leads to their "verbal conversion," and they reach "total conversion" when they dispose themselves to the group. One becomes an active agent in this final stage. These steps are cumulative in nature; one needs to go through them in order to experience conversion. This model was tested by Kox, Meeus, and Hart (1991), who found it to be inadequate to explain the process of conversion. They found that these conditions or steps are independent, not cumulative. Richardson (1992) observed that conversion in Christ Communal Organization (CCO) differs in terms of the extra-cult affective bond. In this situation, potential converts had affective bonds with their parents that resulted in conversion, as the parents were already members of the group. Moreover, the world-saver model fails to accommodate religious experience and religious practices in the conversion process.

Brauer (1978) identified a different set of seven stages in the conversion process: indifference, dissatisfaction with self, new understanding, beginning of changes, sudden conversion experience, sense of new being, and the beginning of the path of transformation. Downton (1980) laid down ten stages of conversion experience: disillusionment, seeking spiritual solutions, determination to move forward, personal futility, contact with the religious community, accepting the claims, initiation, surrender, intensification, and gradual modification.

Tippett (1992) studied group conversions and developed a model of conversion from an anthropological perspective. He schematized the conversion process as the period of awareness, point of realization, period of decision, point of encounter, period of incorporation, point of consummation or confirmation, and period of maturity. In the period of awareness one must be aware of the alternative options before conversion. This awareness could be stimulated by natural development, pressure from outside, personal crisis, and direct advocacy. The point of realization, unlike a period, it is a definite moment. At this point, the period of awareness ends and the period of decision begins. The alternative option becomes a possibility at this point. The period of decision is one's response to this realization. This response may be rejection of the alternative option, total acceptance, or modified acceptance. The point of encounter is the climax in the decision-making process, where there is a decision to accept the alternative option by rejecting the old belief system. The period of incorporation involves consolidating the new context through instruction, training, and finally with a ritual. The point of consummation or confirmation involves moving further in deepening one's experience in the new belief system and then moving to the next stage, the period of maturity, which is a continuous process. As with others, Tippett's model does not deal adequately with religious experience and the role of religious practices in conversion, nor does deal with hostile reactions to conversion.

The Step Model

Rambo (1992, 1993) developed yet another seven-stage model: context, crisis, quest, encounter, interaction, commitment, and consequences. Context refers to the environmental factors that contribute to having a conversion experience; these could be personal, cultural, historical, sociological, and theological. The next stage, crisis, brings to light the limitations of the present state and opens a door to consider new options. The crisis may be personal or social or both. In the quest stage one actively seeks solutions to the problems or crisis. In encounter, the potential convert meets the agent who presents the new option. Interaction is the stage in which intense learning takes place. In commitment, one makes a decision to adopt the new option and establishes a link with God and the religious community. The stage of consequences involves the transforming effects of conversion. In spite of incorporating various perspectives on conversion, Rambo's model fails to elaborate the religious experience in the conversion process.

The quest in Rambo's' model is similar to Richardson's (1985) "active" convert in the conversion process. The stage of interaction is in line with social psychological theories of conversion (Bainbridge, 1992; Downton, 1980; Lofland & Stark, 1965; Long & Hadden, 1983; Richardson, 1985). Rambo's seven-stage model brings out the social psychological process in conversion vividly, yet, though it acknowledges the role of religious experience and religious practices in the conversion process, it does not give due significance to them, as converts would attribute. Furthermore, Rambo has not elaborately dealt with the reactions to conversion by family and community and with the strategies of converts to manage these hostilities.

Gooren (2010) has identified contingency factors, personality factors, institutional factors, and social factors as vital in the conversion process. His conversion career model traces different levels of religious participation: pre-affiliation, affiliation, conversion, confession, and disaffiliation. This model explains the denominational shift within Christianity in the Latin America, but it does not capture the intricacies and intensity of religious change that involves moving from one religion to another. Gooren also has not captured the role of religious experience and religious practices in the conversion process.

As mentioned above, the world-saver model (Lofland & Stark, 1965) approaches conversion from a social psychological perspective and incorporates the antecedents and the role of a group in the conversion process. For Tippett (1992), conversion is a continuous process. Rambo's (1992, 1993) stage model brings out the consequences elaborately. Gooren's

(2010) model highlights the dynamics of denominational shift within Christianity. However, none of these models highlight the centrality of religious experience and the vital role of religious practices in the conversion process. They also do not address conversions that take place in isolation, without a group setting at the initial stage.

Batson, Schoenrade, and Ventis (1993) attempted to incorporate the divine element in the process of personal transformation. They suggested four stages: existential crisis, self-surrender, new vision, and new life. In existential crisis, one finds that the present cognitive structure does not answer the following questions: What is the meaning of my life? How does one handle death? In self-surrender, one is helpless to find a solution to the existential crisis. At this point, there is a loss of consciousness and the present cognitive structure loses its grip over the individual. New vision gives a person a new perspective that comes "from a transcendent realm outside oneself" (Batson et al., 1993, p. 104). The new vision resolves the existential crisis. In new life, the shift in reality results in a new way of life as one begins to see life with the new perspective and with a new assurance. It gives the power to be positive and effective in approaching life. They claim that the new vision gives a person a new perspective that comes from outside of oneself, that is, from the divine.

Similarly, James (1902/2004) and Bulkeley (1999) claim that interaction with the divine occurs at a realm beyond the conscious mind. They indicate the possibility of interaction between the conscious mind and the beyond through the mystical states of consciousness. Batson et al. (1993) incorporated this dimension of religious experience in personal transformation, however, they failed to consider the social psychological factors in personal transformation. Each discipline should consider the divine factor in understanding conversion, while incorporating the various perspectives of other disciplines. The Step Model proposed here incorporates both the religious and social psychological aspects in conversion.

Gordon (1967) pointed out that parents react to their children's conversion to cult groups; however, he did not address hostile consequences for converts, probably because there were few in the context of individualized Western society. Lofland and Stark (1965) made only a passing remark on reactions of family members while discussing the extra-cult affective bonds. Rambo (1993) mentioned the reactions of the Hindu community to Ambedkar's conversion to Buddhism. However, the existing models have not elaborately dealt with hostilities to religious conversion and converts' response to these hostilities. There is a need for a model that addresses the hostilities attached to religious conversion in a multireligious society.

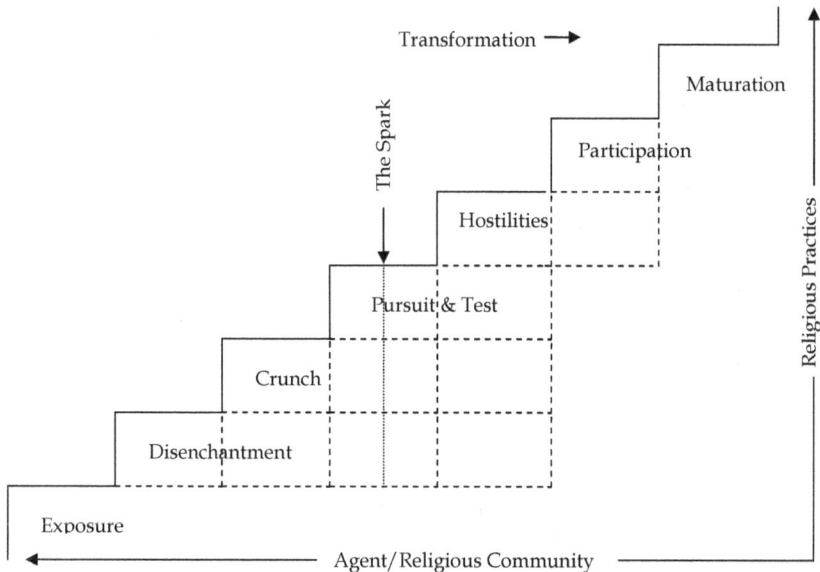

Figure: Step Model of Transformative Religious Experience

The Step Model of transformative religious experiences has seven steps: Exposure, Disenchantment, Crunch, Pursuit and Test, Hostilities, Participation, and Maturation (see the figure above). They indicate different phases in the conversion process and are generally sequential; the dotted lines of the steps indicate the possibility of skipping some of the steps in the conversion process. The downward arrow indicates the Spark—the divine–human encounter. Unlike the periods, it is a moment and the central *event* in the conversion process.

This model has two axes that provide the supportive roles in the conversion process. The *x* axis indicates the social psychological dimension and the *y* axis indicates the religious dimension. These two axes provide the context for conversion or an interface between the social and religious dimensions. These factors have constant interaction throughout the process and cannot be restricted to a single step. The horizontal arrow on the top, pointing towards the step of Maturation, indicates the transformation that begins at the Spark.

Exposure is the first step in the conversion process, in which one gains basic knowledge of the symbols, beliefs, and practices of another religion. In India, children learn about different religions in school. In a multireligious society, people are aware of beliefs and practices of other religions through their daily interactions with others. This step of Exposure is in line with the period of awareness in Tippett's (1992) scheme of conversion. He claims that there is no conversion without awareness. The exposure to a new religion plays a vital role in the later stage in understanding the religious experience. This is especially vital for conversions in which no human agent or religious community is involved in initiating the process. Converts identify the symbols in their religious experiences based on prior knowledge, but not based on their prior religious belief.

In the step of *Disenchantment*, one is disillusioned with the religion of one's birth. The reasons for this could be spiritual, theological, and social. Some explore other religions to satisfy their spiritual thirst, feeling that their religion is inadequate to meet their spiritual needs. Some compare and analyze the beliefs, practices, and theologies of religions and feel dissatisfied with the religion of their birth. Some are dissatisfied with their religion due to social discrimination and exploitation by religious authorities. Lofland and Stark (1965) also claimed that potential converts found that the religion of their upbringing was inadequate to solve their crises. Gordon (1967) observed that religious change begins with dissatisfaction with the religion of one's upbringing. In this period potential converts begin to search for alternative religious option, or at least they are open to considering a new religion.

Crunch refers to a difficult situation in one's life prior to conversion. It is the step in which a person experiences difficulties and finds the present cognitive system inadequate to offer a solution. Converts face various kinds of crunch prior to conversion. They could be psychological, existential, behavioral, financial, or other practical crises. These factors may be independent, but may be cumulative in some instances. Crunch is a context in which conversion occurs, but is not the cause of conversion because not everyone does face Crunch prior to conversion. This step is parallel to crisis in the stage model (Rambo, 1993) and to tension in the world-saver model (Lofland & Stark, 1965). I affirm Rambo's (1993) claim that crisis might play the role of a "catalyst initiator" but cannot be the cause of conversion.

Pursuit and Test is a two-dimensional step in the conversion process that involves a passion to explore the new religious option and a desire to

The Step Model

test its claims. At this phase, a convert searches for an alternate solution to a crunch, or may passionately seek to know more about another religion in their spiritual quest. As they seek to increase their knowledge of a new religion, they also test its workability. Some do not search for alternative options due to the absence of a crisis, or because they remain satisfied with the religion of their birth even if they do have a crisis. In such an instance, the Spark—the divine–human encounter—occurs spontaneously and sets ablaze a passion to know more about the new religious option.

Contrary to the classical paradigm of conversion in which the convert is passive, Richardson (1985) found that converts were active in the conversion process. Similarly, Rambo (1993) claims that converts seek to enhance the meaning of their lives. The step of Pursuit and Test is similar to the stage of seekership in the world-saver model (Lofland & Stark, 1965) and to the quest in the stage model (Rambo, 1993) in terms of search, but it differs from these models in terms of potential converts testing the new option. It is a significant factor that potential converts test the claims of the new religion before accepting it. This stage may proceed or follow the religious experience that I call the Spark.

The *Spark* is the divine–human encounter in the conversion process. Unlike the steps, the Spark is the *event*—the turning point in the conversion process. Classical studies on conversion gave more importance to sudden conversion experiences and considered the same as an event. This is also known as Pauline paradigm or classical paradigm. Recent studies view conversion as a process. Now conversion is understood more as a process than an event (see Richardson, 1985; Spilka, Hood Jr., Hunsberger, & Gorsuch, 2003). Contemporary studies on conversion have become reductionist in their approaches and do not emphasize the significance ascribed by converts to the divine element in their conversion experiences. Sudden conversion cannot be considered unreal. We have discussed earlier the mystical turning point in detail and found that the religious experience is central to the conversion process, especially in Christian conversion.

The Spark could be a supernatural experience with sensory elements or a mild experience of a realization, a flash of spiritual insight, or an awareness of the divine presence. The Spark generally occurs during the period of Pursuit and Test, however, it is not restricted to this step alone. The dotted line of the Spark in the Step Model (see the figure on p. 239) indicates the possibility of it occurring at any step—Crunch, Disenchantment, or Exposure—because the divine–human encounter occurs spontaneously. The Spark triggers the step of Pursuit and Test instantly.

Earlier we have identified the features of the mystical turning point as revelatory, conversational, and intimate, in addition to the features James (1902/2004) identified: ineffable, noetic, transient, and passive. The Spark in the conversion experience is revelatory because, contrary to the previously held religious belief, converts encounter a new figure altogether in their religious experience. Irrespective of their religious background, converts identify the figure in the religious experience as Jesus. At the encounter a gentle conversation takes place between the divine and the convert that makes the encounter personal, not generic. Further, the encounter sets up a loving and intimate relationship between the divine and the convert. Though the divine is invisible, after the encounter converts relate to the divine as if to a loving human companion. This bond of love lasts and converts experience the divine as a close companion. However, converts are often unable to explain the turning point. While the conscious mind is preoccupied with the struggle to leave the religion of one's birth, the solution sometimes arises out of the mystical states of consciousness. Once the Spark occurs, the convert is convinced that it is *the truth*. All preconceived ideas and negative attitudes towards the new religion vanish. There is a moment of passivity and an element of noesis is present. This encounter gives the convert a sense of experiencing the truth. A convert feels that this experience is something personal with the divine. It is incomparable to any other experience and is ineffable. The passivity and the ineffability of the encounter concur with James's assertion that it occurs at the mystical states of consciousness. The divine–human encounter is also transient, therefore, what converts are able to narrate about the experience is limited to what the conscious mind perceived at the time.

As we have seen in chapter 7, the divine–human encounter is the turning point and central to the conversion process. The Spark initiates the transformation in the conversion process. This concurs with Batson et al. (1993) that a new vision arises from the transcendental realm. Tippett (1992) and Rambo (1993) have also acknowledged this factor, but Lofland and Stark (1965) and Gooren (2010) have not addressed this dimension. No model of religious conversion can afford to sideline this factor as converts attribute great significance to it. From a phenomenological perspective, the Step Model designates a significant place for the religious experience in the conversion process, unlike the other models.

The *Line of Transformation* in the Step Model indicates the transforming effects of conversion. The horizontal line with an arrow pointing towards the step of Maturation indicates the movement of transformation.

It begins when the Spark occurs and moves towards the step of Maturation. The Step Model does not restrict this movement of transformation to a single step; it is an ongoing process. Transformation is not a completed act, but only begins at the Spark and moves towards maturity. This is parallel to the consequences in stage model, where Rambo (1993) identified the consequences or effects of conversion as sociocultural and historical, psychological, and theological. I have argued elsewhere (Iyadurai, 2009) that conversion leads to both self- and social transformation. As we have seen in the previous chapter, the effects of the conversion experience transform the spiritual, psychological, behavioral, physical, social, and economical dimensions of a person's life. The fruit of the conversion experience is the integrated well-being of a person.

Hostilities is a period in which a convert faces hostile reactions from both family and community. Generally, this period starts after one adopts the new faith; however, sometimes it begins at the step of Pursuit and Test. The reaction of a family varies from verbal persuasion to verbal abuse, mockery, physical assault, rejection, denial of financial support, being chased out of the home, public humiliation, murder threats, and ultimately even murder. You would have noticed the intensity of persecution reported by converts in the earlier chapters.

In conversion research, only a few (Gordon 1967; Lofland & Stark 1965; Rambo 1993) have made a brief mention about reactions to conversion from a family or a community. However, they have not elaborated the extent of the hostility faced by converts and how converts respond to such situations. Other studies rarely emphasize or elaborate on this issue, as the samples are from the West, where the individual's rights are respected and families might not be as likely to react as harshly. In a community oriented and multireligious context like India, conversion is viewed as a serious offence against the family and the community. The Step Model highlights this aspect of hostilities and shows that sometimes conversion creates far more crises than it resolved.

This phase of the conversion process challenges the problem-solving perspective. Here conversion creates far more stress and crises. I strongly support the claim of Rambo (1993) that crisis is not the cause of conversion. If stress and crisis are the causes, then in response to hostilities there should be another conversion, but converts often endure hardships to hold on to their conversion experience and sometimes eventually convert their entire family.

Prayer, reading the Bible, and the support of the religious community are the sustaining factors during this period of Hostilities. Prayer is the most important of all these three. When access to the Bible or the religious community is denied, converts find the strength needed to handle the hostilities through prayer. Subsequent religious experiences are the other factor that sustain converts in the newfound faith during hostilities.

In the step of *Participation*, a convert joins the religious community. Participation might be in the form of active involvement by taking baptism, or participation in community activities without taking baptism, or simply attending worship. Converts find participation in the religious community enhances transformation and supports them to hold on to their newfound faith. The religious community plays the role of a family to converts when they are faced with opposition from their family and friends.

This step is parallel to cult affective bonds in the world-saver model (Lofland & Stark 1965), the period of incorporation in Tippett's (1992) scheme, interaction in the stage model (Rambo 1993), and different levels of religious participation in the conversion career model (Gooren 2010). However, Lofland and Stark emphasize that the cult affective bond is necessary, but fail to explain conversions where there is no such bond.

Converts acquire a new identity in conversion; however, some of them retain the social identity based on the religion of their birth. They believe that the conversion experience is spiritual and personal, but not necessarily religious. Converts differentiate between institutionalized religion and spirituality. They consider taking baptism and participation in the religious community as external rituals that are not essential to the conversion experience. However, the religious authorities and the religious community reject this idea and impart a sense of lacking in their conversion experience, saying that without their explicit participation in the religious community and rituals, their conversion is incomplete or not real. Though the religious community is open to new converts, the community asserts its definition of conversion.

Though participation in the community enhances transformation due to socialization and other factors, it is not a prerequisite. This factor challenges the existing social psychological theories of conversion (Bainbridge, 1992; Downton, 1980; Lofland & Stark, 1965; Long & Hadden, 1983; Richardson, 1985), which claim that socialization leads to transformation. How can a convert sustain his or her conversion without participating in a religious community? In such a situation, the family's influence is at its height, because the convert is isolated from any contact with the religious community. The only social influence possible is from the family, to bring the convert back to the religion of his or her birth. Contrarily, converts are sometimes even able to influence their family members over a period to adopt the new religion. Therefore, social influence is not the only means of effecting transformation. Malony (1998) and Heirich (1977) pointed out that socialization alone cannot explain religious conversion. Therefore, I assert that transformation is a result of the divine–human encounter and is enhanced by socialization. Irrespective of one's participation in the religious community, transformation is an ongoing process.

Maturation is the step in which a convert proceeds from one level to another in the path of transformation. Transformation is not complete in the conversion experience; it only begins at the Spark and is a lifelong process. Tippett (1992) speaks of maturation as a continual process in his scheme of conversion and Rambo (1993) views conversion an ongoing process. The Step Model gives due place to ongoing transformation in conversion.

The two axes in the Step Model provide the broad context for the conversion process. The x axis represents the role of agents and the religious community in the conversion; the y axis represents the role of religious practices. These two axes are the interface between the social psychological and religious dimensions in conversion.

Agents are the ones who introduce the new religion to converts and play an active role in activating the step of Pursuit and Test. The agent could be from the circle of kinship, friendship, leadership, a stranger, or the divine.

Conversion may take place without any affective relationship. Though an affective relationship plays a role in the interaction between an agent and a convert (Lofland & Stark 1965), but it is not the only factor that leads someone to experience conversion. Heirich (1977) and Malony (1998) claim that conversion is not just due to friendship. A social network could be a facilitating factor in initiating or sustaining the conversion process; however, it cannot be the cause of conversion.

Socialization is activated when a potential convert is in the step of Crunch or in the Pursuit and Test period. In the case of the divine–human encounter that initiates the conversion process, the converts would then search for an agent or a religious community to further the conversion process. The religious community plays an active role in leading a convert towards maturity in the transformation process. When a convert undergoes persecution, the religious community provides support.

The y axis represents the role of *religious practices* in conversion. Converts believe that prayer and reading the Bible are the most essential religious practices for their spiritual sustenance. They are the channels through which converts maintain the intimate relationship with the divine that began at the divine–human encounter. Prayer is the constant factor that facilitates interaction with the divine and sustains transformation.

Converts pray and read the Bible not as rituals, but as means to relate to the divine. When a convert faces persecution and is isolated, these religious practices are the only sustaining factors. Converts do other religious practices like baptism, Eucharist, and corporate worship when the situation is conducive for them to declare their conversion openly. Studies have rarely discussed the significant role of prayer and reading of sacred texts in conversion explicitly and comprehensively.

In summary, the Step Model of transformative religious experience has identified seven steps in the process of conversion: Exposure, Disenchantment, Crunch, Pursuit and Test, Hostilities, Participation, and Maturation. The Step Model accommodates the role of religious practices and social psychological factors in the conversion process. It incorporates the divine–human encounter in conversion to which the converts attribute great significance. Hence, it views conversion as both a process and an event. This study also brings to light the hostilities to conversion in a multireligious context, where converts are ready to pay any price, even to lay down their lives. This particular dimension needs further exploration. Future research can apply the Step Model of transformative religious experience in other contexts and assess its applicability to other cultural or religious contexts and to group conversions.

For converts to Christianity, conversion is an encounter with Jesus that initiates an intimate relationship with him. Converts relate to Jesus as if to a close friend. Jesus becomes a close companion to converts and they talk to him at any time for any reason. Converts to Christianity resemble the participants of Luhrmann's (2012, p. 312) study in their relationship with Jesus, as she describes, "This personlike God can comfort, like a friend, and respond directly, like a friend. He can be a real social relationship for those who make the effort to experience him in this way . . . that social relationship lacks so many features of actual human sociality—no visible body, no responsive face, no spoken voice." This is true of converts' experience of Jesus, but converts differ from Vineyard Fellowship members, who are trained by the church to orient their minds to experience the presence of God. Converts to Christianity in India are not trained in this way, and some do not even belong to a church, but they experience Jesus and learn to relate to him in a similar manner after the divine–human encounter. Luhrmann (2012, p. 313) also talks about the privacy of this relationship with the divine: "The more intimately someone comes to feel connected to God in this style of spirituality, the more sharply he or she feels that God speaks uniquely to each. Those who seek God in this way come to deeply respect the way God is different with each person: and with this respect grows an understanding that all people reach for God through the thick density of their own thoughts and feelings. And since minds are private from each other, no Christian can have full knowledge of any other Christian's relationship with God." In conversion to Christianity, converts find a lifelong companionship with Jesus that is private and mystical.

Bibliography

Ambedkar, B. R. Statement by Dr. B. R. Ambedkar on Gandhi's Fast. Online: http://www.mulnivasibamcef.org/pages/page3q.asp.
Appasamy, J. A. (1966). *Tamil Christian Poet*. London: United Society for Christian Literature.
Ayer, A. J. (1952). *Language, Truth, and Logic*. New York: Dover.
Bainbridge, W. S. (1992). "The Sociology of Conversion." In *Handbook of Religious Conversion*, edited by H. N. Malony & S. Southard, 178–91. Birmingham, AL: Religious Education Press.
Batson, D. C., P. Schoenrade, and L. W. Ventis (1993). *Religion and the Individual: A Social-Psychological Perspective*. New York: Oxford University Press.
Brauer, C. J. (1978). "Conversion: From Puritanism to Revivalism." *The Journal of Religion* 58:227–43.
Brewer, M. B. (2001). "The Many Faces of Social Identity: Implications for Political Psychology." *Political Psychology* 22/1:117–21.
Bulkeley, K. (1995). *Spiritual Dreaming: A Cross-Cultural and Historical Journey*. New York: Paulist.
Bulkeley, K. (1999). *Visions of the Night: Dreams, Religion, and Psychology*. SUNY Series in Dream Studies. Albany: SUNY Press.
Bulkeley, K. (2003). "The Study of 'Big Dreams': Critical Connection between Religion and Neuroscience." In *NeuroTheology: Brain Science, Spirituality, Religious Experience*, edited by R. Joseph, 427–46. San Jose: University of California Press.
Bulkeley, K. (2005). *The Wondering Brain: Thinking about Religion With and Beyond Cognitive Neuroscience*. New York: Routledge.
Clarke, S. (2003). "Conversion to Christianity." In *Religious Conversion in India: Modes, Motivations, and Meanings*, edited by R. Robinson & S. Clarke, 285–90. New Delhi: Oxford University Press.
Das, B. (1980). *Thus Spoke Ambedkar*. Vol. 4. Bangalore: Ambedkar Sahitya Prakashan.
Downton, J. V. (1980). "An Evolutionary Theory of Spiritual Conversion and Commitment: The Case of Divine Light Mission." *Journal for the Scientific Study of Religion* 19:381–96.
Edison, T. A. (n.d.). Quotes by Thomas Edison. QuotationsBook.com Online: http://quotationsbook.com/assets/shared/pdf/author/2228.pdf/.
Emerson, R. W. (2008). Essays, First Series. Project Gutenberg. Online: http://www.gutenberg.org/files/2944/2944-h/2944-h.htm#link2H_4_0002/.
Freud, S. (1914/2010). *On Dreams*. Translated by M. D. Eder. New York: Cosimo.
Freud, S. (1932). "Lecture XXXV: A Philosophy of Life." *New Introductory Lectures on Psycho-Analysis*. Online: http://www.marxists.org/reference/subject/philosophy/works/at/freud.htm.

Bibliography

Gandhi, M. K. (1999). *The Collected Works of Mahatma Gandhi*. Vol. 70: 21 October, 1936—24 February, 1937. Electronic book. New Delhi: Publications Division, Government of India.

Gooren, H. (2010). *Religious Conversion and Disaffiliation: Tracing Patterns of Change in Faith Practices*. New York: Palgrave Macmillan.

Gordon, A. I. (1967). *The Nature of Conversion*. Boston: Beacon.

Greil, A. L., and L. Davidman (2007). "Religion and Identity." In *The Sage Handbook of the Sociology of Religion*, edited by J. A. Beckford and N. J. Demerath, 549–65. Los Angeles: Sage.

Griffith-Dickson, G. (2000). *Human and Divine: An Introduction to the Philosophy of Religious Experience*. London: Duckworth.

Hardy, A. (1979/1984). *The Spiritual Nature of Man*. Oxford: Clarendon.

Heirich, M. (1977). "Change of Heart: A Test of Some Widely Held Theories about Religious Conversion." *American Journal of Sociology* 83/3:653–80.

Hume, D. (1902/2011). *An Enquiry Concerning Human Understanding*. Project Gutenberg. Online: http://www.gutenberg.org/files/9662/9662-h/9662-h.htm.

Iyadurai, J. (2009). "Religious Conversion: Self-Transformation and Social Transformation." In *Transforming Religion: Prospects for a New Society*, edited by F. Wilfred, 196–212. Delhi: ISPCK.

James, W. (1902/2004). *The Varieties of Religious Experience*. New York: Barnes & Noble Classics.

Jayasudha. (2000). "I Hated Every Minute of It." Online: http://www.rediff.com/entertai/2000/may/13jaya.htm/.

Jeyaraj, D. (2010). *Followers of Christ outside the Church in Chennai, India*. Zoetermeer: Boekencentrum Academic.

Johns Hopkins Medicine. (2006). "Hopkins Scientists Show Hallucinogen in Mushrooms Creates Universal 'Mystical' Experience." Online: http://www.hopkinsmedicine.org/press_releases/2006/07_11_06.html.

Katz, S. T. (1978). "Language, Epistemology, and Mysticism." In *Mysticism and Philosophical Analysis*, edited by S. T. Katz, 22–74. New York: Oxford University Press.

Kleber, H. D. (2006). "Commentary on: Psilocybin Can Occasion Mystical-Type Experiences Having Substantial and Sustained Personal Meaning and Spiritual Significance by Griffiths et al." Prepublication proof. *Psychopharmacology*. doi: 10.1007/s00213-006-0461-9.

Kox, W., W. Meeus, and H. T. Hart (1991). "Religious Conversion of Adolescents: Testing the Lofland and Stark Model of Religious Conversion." *Sociological Analysis* 52:227–40.

Lofland, J., and R. Stark (1965). "Becoming a World-Saver: A Theory of Conversion to a Deviant Perspective." *American Sociological Review* 30:862–75.

Long, T. E., and J. K. Hadden (1983). "Religious Conversion and the Concept of Socialization: Integrating the Brainwashing and Drift Models." *Journal for the Scientific Study of Religion* 22/1:1–14.

Luhrmann, T. M. (2012). *When God Talks Back: Understanding the American Evangelical Relationship with God*. New York: Knopf.

Malony, H. N. (1998). "The Psychology of Religious Conversion." Online: http://www.religiousfreedom.com/Conference/japan/Malony.htm.

Malony, H. N., and S. Southard, editors (1992). *Handbook of Religious Conversion*. Birmingham, AL: Religious Education Press.

Bibliography

Moustakas, C. (1994). *Phenomenological Research Methods.* Thousand Oaks, CA: Sage.
Nieto, J. C. (1997). *Religious Experience and Mysticism: Otherness as Experience of Transcendence.* Lanham, MD: University Press of America.
Oddie, G. A. (1997). *Religious Conversion Movements in South Asia: Continuities and Change, 1800–1900.* Richmond, Surrey: Curzon.
Otto, R. (1923/1958). *The Idea of the Holy.* 2nd ed. London: Oxford University Press.
Paloutzian, R. F. (2005). "Religious Conversion and Spiritual Transformation: A Meaning-System Analysis." In *Handbook of the Psychology of Religion and Spirituality,* edited by R. F. Paloutzian and C. L. Park, 331–47. New York: Guildford.
Paul, D. R. (1967). *Triumph of His Grace.* Madras: CLS.
Peace, R. V. (1999). *Conversion in the New Testament: Paul and the Twelve.* Grand Rapids: Eerdmans.
Ramabai, P. (2001). *A Testimony.* 12th ed. Kedgaon: Pandita Ramabai Mukti Mission.
Rambo, L. R. (1992). "The Psychology of Conversion." In *Handbook of Religious Conversion,* edited by H. N. Malony and S. Southard, 159–77. Birmingham, AL: Religious Education Press.
Rambo, L. R. (1993). *Understanding Religious Conversion.* New Haven, CT: Yale University Press.
Rambo, L. R., and L. A. Reh (1992). "The Phenomenology of Conversion." In *Handbook of Religious Conversion,* edited by H. N. Malony and S. Southard, 229–58. Birmingham, AL: Religious Education Press.
Richardson, J. T. (1985). "The Active vs. Passive Convert: Paradigm Conflict in Conversion/Recruitment Research." *Journal for the Scientific Study of Religion* 24:163–79.
Richardson, J. T. (1992). "Conversion Process in the New Religions." In *Handbook of Religious Conversion,* edited by H. N. Malony and S. Southard, 78–89. Birmingham, AL: Religious Education Press.
Sargant, W. (1957). *Battle for the Mind: The Physiology of Conversion and Brainwashing.* London: Heinemann.
Singh, B. (n.d.). "How I Got Joy Unspeakable and Full of Glory." Online: http://www.brotherbakhtsingh.org/PDF%20files/How_I_Got_Joy_Unspeakable_a.pdf
Spilka, B., W. R. Hood Jr., B. Hunsberger, and R. Gorsuch (2003). *The Psychology of Religion: An Empirical Approach.* 3rd ed. New York: Guilford.
Tilak, L. (1956). *From Brahma to Christ.* London: United Society for Christian Literature.
Tippett, R. A. (1992). "The Cultural Anthropology of Conversion." In *Handbook of Religious Conversion,* edited by H. N. Malony and S. Southard, 192–205. Birmingham, AL: Religious Education Press.
Ullman, C. (1989). *The Transformed Self: The Psychology of Religious Conversion.* New York: Plenum.
Vivekananda, S. (1907). *Complete Works of Swami Vivekananda.* Vol. 5. Electronic book. Online: http://www.holybooks.com/complete-works-of-swami-vivekananda/
Wiebe, P. H. (1997). *Visions of Jesus: Direct Encounters from the New Testament to Today.* New York: Oxford University Press.
Wulff, D. M. (1995). "Phenomenological Psychology and Religious Experience." In *Handbook of Religious Conversion,* edited by H. N. Malony and S. Southard, 183–99. Birmingham, AL: Religious Education Press.

Bibliography

Yong, A. (2008). "Natural Laws and Divine Intervention: What Difference Does Being Pentecostal or Charismatic Make?" *Zygon* 43:961–89.

Zinnbauer, B. J., K. I. Pargament (1998). "Spiritual Conversion: A Study of Religious Change among College Students." *Journal for the Scientific Study of Religion* 37:161–80.

List of Personal Interviews by Joshua Iyadurai

Aravind. (2005, November 12).
Arun. (2005, November 14).
Aruna. (2005, October 16).
Balan. (2005, November 4).
Chitra. (2005, November 15).
Deensha. (2005, November 16).
Devaraj. (2005, November 15).
Durai. (2005, November 13).
Ezhil. (2005, November 15).
Ganga. (2005, December 1).
Hameetha. (2005, November 17).
Inban. (2005, October 21).
Janaki. (2005, November 14).
Kamal. (2005, October 7).
Karan. (2005, October 16).
Kareem. (2005, November 16).
Kavia. (2005, December 6).
Komala. (2005, December 1).
Kumar. (2005, November 14).
Kushbu. (2005, November 25).
Mala. (2005, November 27).
Mohan. (2005, November 4).
Nambiar. (2005, October 21).
Nathan. (2005, November 12).
Nithya. (2005, November 17).
Praveena. (2005, November 3).
Ramesh. (2005, November 14).
Ranjan. (2005, September 22).
Rekha. (2005, November 4).
Sakunthala. (2005, November 15).
Samsudeen. (2005, November 16).
Sania. (2006, March 18).
Sarala. (2006, June 27).
Selvi. (2005, November 15).
Surya. (2005, November 16).
Sushila. (2005, November 15).
Vinay. (2005, September 17).
Vinitha. (2005, October 30).
Vinodha. (2006, June 27).

Index

Ambedkar, B. R., 1, 238
anthropological model, 236, 240, 242, 244. *See also* Tippett
Aravind, 116–18
Arun, 161, 190, 194, 190
Aruna, 150, 151, 192
automatism, 13, 30, 147
   James, 30
Ayer, J. A., 120, 143

Balan
   Bible reading, 230
   Hindu rituals, continued, 213
   praying to generic God, 10, 108–12, 157
   purpose in life, 162
   secretly following Jesus, 227
   success in studies, 190
   turning point, 149, 150
Batson, D. C., 153, 154, 238, 242
Bible, reading
   comforts, 209, 231
   exposure to Christianity through, 121
   God speaking through, 9, 57, 72, 83–84, 106, 147–48, 150, 160, 229–31
   growing in newfound faith through, 231
   interaction with divine through, 3, 228, 232
   interested in, 70, 75, 95, 108, 124, 219–20
   intimacy with the divine through, 12, 228, 246
   Jesus as savior, leads to realize, 57, 90, 127, 150
   Luhrmann, T. M., 231
   personal experience, 139
   as religious experience, 153
   as religious practice, 3, 12, 246
   secretly, 129, 223
   sinner, leads to realization as, 57, 179, 231
   solution, brings, 83, 187, 230
   strength through, 11, 223, 231
   as sustaining factor, 231, 244
   transforms, 45, 63, 65, 231
   See also New Testament, reading
beliefs, 30, 142, 157, 163, 175–76, 212, 233–34, 240
   in act of God, 99, 229
   all religions same, 116, 133
   in atheism, 127
   change of religious, 3, 31, 116, 132, 141, 145, 158, 170, 212, 224, 235
   Christianity, in, 127, of, 175–76, 233
   comparison of, 142, 240
   contrary to their, 33, 155, 156
   general, 157
   in divine presence in real life, 55
   in God, 127
   in Jesus, 6, 30, 158–59, 169
   loss of, 145
   in miracles, 99
   Jewish, 158
   newfound, 158
   previously held religious, 6, 13, 30, 99, 108, 112, 132, 135, 142, 149, 154–56, 158, 169, 170
   questioning of religious, 108, 132
   in religion, 14, 101, 135, 142, 149, 240
   replacement of religious, 6, 30, 158–59, 169–70

Index

beliefs *(continued)*
   rejection of old system of, 236
   strengthening of, 30
boundaries, redrawn religious, 224
   crossing of traditional, 226
   social 226
bracketing, 4
   Moustaka, C., 4
   Rambo, L. R., 4
   Reh, L. A., 4
Brahmin
   caste, 127, 139, 141, 185, 193, 210
   convert, 63, 68, 127, 130, 141, 208, 212
   family, from, 9, 34, 108, 136, 145, 181, 193
   friends, 25, 27
   Namboodri, 70, 72
Brauer, C. J., 236
Brewer, M. B., 225
Buddhism, mentioned, 1, 238
Bulkeley, K.
   on conversion dreams, 55–56
   on dreams connecting sacred, 34, 153
   on interaction with divine, 238
   on mystical states, 161
   on waking ego consciousness, 143, 153–54, 163

career model, 237, 244
chanting, 9, 76–77, 82, 150, 157
Chitra, 174, 186
Christianity
   adopt, 33, 50, 54–55, 102, 144, 151, 181
   antagonism/animosity against, 6, 33, 143, 145, 149, 151, 162, 170
   beliefs and practices of, 175–76, 233
   British, brought by, 143, 226
   considered, never, 32, 42, 136
   conversion in, 2, 3, 238
   crisis resolved by, 144
   claims of, 120–21, 142, 150
   Dalits, associated with, 143, 199, 226
   enmity toward, 13, 24–26, 82, 121, 126, 143, 156, 164
   eternal life assured, 181–82
   exposure to, 42, 82, 99, 101, 108, 127, 132, 179
   faith in, 72
   following, 59
   hesitant to follow, 6, 8, 101, 104, 143, 192
   interest in, 33
   institutional as, form, 224
   know more about, 32, 63, 112
   knowledge on, 14, 20, 64, 116
   practice, 29
   prayer as proof of, 101
   prejudice against, 33, 112, 151
   sins forgiven in, 181
   test the workability of, 100
   tried, 99, 100, 144
   true, 127
   truth of, 85
   weighed suitability of, 121
Clarke, S., 2
cognitive restructuring, 159
   Batson, D. C., 153
   personal transformation, 153–54
   Schoenrade, P., 153
   turning point, 159
   Ventis, L. W., 153
community
   caste, 69
   Christian, 227, 233
   Hindu, 238
   link with religious, 236–37, 244–45
   role of religious, 11, 239 figure, 240, 244–46
   support of, 233, 246
consciousness of sin, 7, 10, 109, 152, 179, 180
conversion, defined, 3, 4
   James, W., 3, 180
   Rambo, L. R., 3
conversion as process, 3, 5, 6, 12, 127, 132, 143, 153, 164, 170, 235—42, 245–46
   agent's role, 232, 233, 247
   church or community's role, 233, 241

Index

crisis
　absence of, 25, 187, 241
　of addiction, 24
　in business, 89
　"catalyst initiator," 240
　cause of conversion, 187, 243
　Christianity resolved, 144
　confidence and courage to face, 182, 187
　dream answer to, 54
　dream, resolution through, 50
　energy to face, 55
　existential, 162, 238
　in family, 10, 94
　feeling of not being alone in facing, 178
　financial, 88
　gospel as solution to, 121
　help at the time of, 42
　Jesus guiding in, 176
　prayer, resolved by, 93, 94, 113, 148, 188
　Rambo, L. R., 243
　of sin in religious experience and resolution of, 32
　solution to, 83, 85
　solution to, not sought from Christianity, 31, 32, 99, 145, 233
　solution to, sought in one's religion, 42, 116, 145
　sought new religious option, 164
　in stage model, 237
　strength and confidence to face, 55, 182, 188
　vision, relief through 32
　See also crunch
crunch
　crisis in stage model, parallel to, 240
　as context, 7, 240
　kinds of, 240
　in Step Model, 6, 7, 239 figure, 239–40
　tension in world-saver model, parallel to, 240
　See also crisis
Dalits, 1, 2, 143, 224, 226
Davidman, L., 225–26

Deensha, 172, 230
Devaraj
　conversion narrative, 94–99
　forgiving others, 192
　generous, became, 195
　guidance through dreams, 176
　resolution of crisis, 148
　success in business, 190
disenchantment
　in Step Model, 6, 239 figure, 240, 246
　one's religion, with, 42, 132, 240
divine
　as close companion, 7, 242
　communication, 9, 57, 83, 147, 148
　conversation with, 3, 7, 9, 30, 154, 159, 160, 167, 172, 176, 197, 228, 232, 238, 242
　depend on, 54, 159
　experiential knowledge of, 161
　forgiven by, 7, 151, 180
　identified with Jesus, 6, 13, 34, 142, 147, 154, 167
　interaction between mystical states of consciousness and, 154
　intimacy with, 3, 7, 9, 12, 154–55, 165–67, 171, 177, 218, 228, 230, 242, 246
　interventions as proofs, 10, 85, 88, 99
　James on interaction with, 154
　love and acceptance from, 7, 9, 32, 70, 165–67, 228
　power, 145
　prayer answered by, 172
　prayer, channel of communication with, 101, 230, 246
　presence of, 3, 7, 32, 121, 142, 167, 185, 228, 230, 241
　present in real life, 55, 170
　relationship with, 55
　self-revelation of, 142, 158–59
　sinful before, 32, 179
　source of dream, 55
　support, 50, 55
　under power of, 164
　union with, 160

Index

divine-human encounter
  "alive inside," 229
  answered prayer, 108
  behavioral effects, 191
  being forgiven and, 7, 151, 165
  centrality of, 232
  consciousness of sin, 7, 26, 141, 170, 178
  confession, 151, 179
  contrary to religious belief, 156, 158–59, 164
  conversation with the divine, 7, 154, 159–60, 172
  conversion process begins with, 232–33, 245
  crying, 136
  divided self unified, 181
  divine love, 166
  dream, 147, 154
  economical effects, 193–96
  event 3, 6
  experience of Jesus, 12
  follow Jesus because of, 199, 232
  friendly, became, 189–90
  healing, 191
  imparts new talents, 189
  ineffable, 163
  intimate relationship with the divine, 166–67, 171, 230, 246–47
  James, W., 3
  Jesus, savior, God, true, 127, 155, 161, 167, 132, 141, 144, 153
  joy and peace, 136, 184
  justification, 196
  knowledge given, 6, 162, 165
  knowledge of God, gained, 6, 154, 161
  miracle, 99
  mystical experience, 120, 144
  mystical states of consciousness, 11, 154, 158–59
  never felt sinful before, 178–79
  noetic, 154, 162
  passive, 154, 164–65
  personal transformation, triggers or results in, 2, 12, 119, 144, 169, 196, 235, 245
  personal, 6
  physical effects, 191
  positive and pleasant, 144
  presence of the 'Other,' 83
  psychological effects, 183–91
  rational explanation, beyond, 146–49, 152, 158
  relieved of heavy burden, 184
  religious boundaries redrawn, 228
  religious change, 144, 152, 153, 156, 169
  revelatory, 31, 108, 154–56, 158–59, 162, 165
  sanctification begins at, 196–97
  sense of divided self, 180
  significance of, 10
  sins were brought back to memory, 180
  social effects, 192–93
  spark, 6, 12, 144, 239–41
  spiritual effects, 170–83
  spontaneous, 241
  Step Model incorporates, 246
  transient, 154, 164, 242
  truth, experience of, 161–62
  turning point, 6, 10, 121, 148, 154, 159, 170, 234, 242
  unparallel, 6, 154
  vision, 154
  waking consciousness, beyond, 153
  See also religious experience; spark; turning point
Downton, J. V., 236
dreams, 34–56, 147, 176
  Bulkeley, K., 34, 55–56, 153
  Hardy, A., 55
Durai, 192

Edison, T. A., 13
Emerson, R. W., 101
epoche. *See* bracketing
experience
  attending Bible study, 58
  auditory, 173, 176
  "born again" 144, 164–65
  in church, 18
  divine love, 165, 167
  divine providence, 193
  divine, 161, 177, 241

Index

God speaking to, 9, 57–84, 147–48, 231
God, 6, 10, 32, 84, 128, 167, 193, 147, 150, 167, 170, 193, 246–47
great change, 117
hearing a sermon, 63
Holy Spirit, 28, 94
intuitive awareness, 152
Jesus or Christ, 12, 21, 93–94, 111, 144, 147, 156, 184, 186, 224, 226–29, 232, 247
joy, 136
miraculous, 148
painful, 208
peace, 136
prayer, 10, 101–19, 148, 230
praying to Jesus and to other deities, 112
salvation, 59, 74, 133
sense of being forgiven, 164
sense of gaining new power, 182
sensory, 30, 31, 145, 153, 156
spiritual, 3
strange, 150
struggling with ultimate questions, 102
transformation, 196, 207
truth, 161, 162, 183
visions, 8, 13–33, 147, 176
exposure
  to Christianity, 82, 101
  to new religion, 240
  in Step Model, 6, 239 figure, 239–40, 246
Ezhil, 86–88
  answered prayer, 112 115, 157
  Jesus speaking to, 159–60

faith, 28, 39, 49, 69, 90, 212, 224
  change of, 10, 30, 143–44, 162
  Christian, 11, 28, 69, 72, 94, 144, 149, 231
  experiential, 99
  experimental, 99
  Hardy, A., 99
  intellectual dimension, 152, 161, 165
  intuitive dimension, 152, 165

James, W., 152
Jesus or Christ, in 73, 88–89, 94, 119, 138, 176, 195, 220, 226, 230, 231
journey, 9, 137, 175
Luther's 152
newfound, 3, 7, 11, 12, 83, 117, 119, 121, 132, 136, 139–40, 156, 160, 174–76, 182, 190, 199, 210, 213, 229–34, 244
nurtured in, 117
previous, 40–41, 98
Freud, S., 34, 57

Gandhi, M. K., 1
Ganga, 11, 184, 192, 195
  consciousness of sin, 179
  turning point, 145–46
Gooren, H., 237, 242
Gordon, A. I., 238, 240
Greil, A. L., 225, 226
Griffith-Dickson, G., 13
Gospel
  heard, 66, 153
  of Jesus Christ, 116
  John's 76, 77, 80, 82
  message of, 10, 147, 150, 152–53, 165, 179
  provided new identity and dignity, 1
  shared, 64, 75, 93, 133, 166, 179
  spread, 28
  as truth, 121
Group Conversions, 2

Hameetha, 185, 191
Hardy, A. 119
  on dream, 55
  on experimental and experiential faith, 99
  on religious experience, 32, 33
Hart, H. T., 235, 236
Heirich, M., 245

Hindu
  fundamentalism, 1, 128, 211
  priest, 10
  rituals, 29, 32, 78, 88, 113, 136

257

Index

Hindu converts, 1, 9, 10, 28, 89, 177, 225
  continued Hindu rituals, 49
  continued worshipping Hindu gods, 60
  made to practice Hindu rituals, 29, 32
  refused baptism to, 28
  stopped wearing *bindhi*, 38
  stopped worshiping Hindu gods, 28, 145, 149
Hindu woman
  as daughter-in-law, 29, 32
  flower on hair, 53
  marriage, 87, 94, 214
  wearing *bindhi*, 38, 214
Hinduism
  answer for sinful life in, 179
  belief in, 133
  caste in, 25
  devotion to, 211
  follower of, 9
  knowledge of, 139
  lost belief in, 145
  never believed in, 121
  religious requirements of, 145
  spiritual life in, 131
hostilities, 3, 198–233, 246
  in Step Model, 6, 239 figure, 243–44, 246
  manage, 237
  sustaining factors, 244
Hume, D., 85

identities
  Christians, 226
  community, 225
  dominant, 226
  followers of Jesus, 226
  group, 225
  integrated, 225
  multiple, 224–27
  new, 1, 162, 189, 226, 229, 244
  personal, 225
  religious, 214, 224, 226
  repertory of, 225
  secret Christian, 227
  social, 224–26, 244

  spiritual, 224
  theories of, 226
  traditional, 226
  true, 189
Inban, 9, 185
  conversion narrative, 58–62
  God speaking to, 63, 146, 147, 157, 159
  Jesus a companion, 170
  life after death, 163
  prayer, 239
  sin, 63, 179
individual conversion, 2, 8
integrated well-being
  divine-human encounter leads to, 3, 235
  fruit of religious conversion, 7, 11, 234, 243
Isalm
  belief in, 17, 19
  conversion to, 2
  converted from 8, 171, 199, 208, 225
interdisciplinary model, 5, 235

James, W., ix, 153, 154, 161, 165, 238, 242
  on automatism, 30
  on consciousness, 153, 154
  conversion defined, 3, 180
  on effects of conversion, 170, 198
  on faith, 152
  on interaction between divine and human, 154, 238
  on prayer, 101, 119, 230
  on religion, 227–28
  on religious experience, 120, 153, 154, 160–61, 163–64, 170, 242
  on transformation, 169–70
  on union with divine, 160
Janaki, 11, 212
  intimacy with the divine, 166
  new talents, 189, 190
  problems due to conversion, 186, 187
  secretly following Jesus, 174, 214–20, 227
Jayasudha, 85–86

Index

Jeyaraj, D., 224–25
Johns Hopkins Medicine, 169

Kamal, 147, 172
 gaining confidence, 185–87
 intimacy with Jesus, 171
Karan, 10
 Bible reading, 142
 conversion narrative, 121–27
 forgiven, 184
 hostilities faced by, 208, 231
 prayer, 151
Kareem, 181
Kavia, 163, 187
Katz, S. T., 155
Kleber, H. D., 169
knowledge
 authentic, 163
 certainty of, 162
 Christianity, 20, 116
 cultural, 158
 divine, 161–62
 experiencing the truth, 161
 gained, 6
 given, 6, 158, 162
 Hinduism, 139
 Jesus, 158–59
 prior, 13
 religious, 120
 revelation, through, 158
knowledge of God
 authentic, received, 155
 direct revelation, through, 6
 gained through religious experience, 156, 158
 growing in, 73
 newfound, real and true, 6, 151
 personal experience, based on, 6, 151, 154
 prevents idol worship, 60
 See also knowledge
Komala, 9
 conversion dream, 34–42
 Jesus speaking to, 159
 identifying Jesus, 156
 prayer, 230
 praying to generic God, 42, 112
 turning point, 147
 vision, 173–74
Kox, W., 235–36
Kumar, 88
 baptism, 94, 148
 conversion narrative, 88–93
 life after death, 182
 turning point, 148
Kushbu, 11
 dream, 175
 Jesus guiding, 176
 Jesus speaking to, 176–77
 prayer, 230
 secretly following Jesus, 175, 183, 220–23

Lofland, J., 232, 235, 238, 242, 244
Luhrmann, T. M., 83, 167–68, 246
 on God talking to, 57, 83, 84
 on miracles, 99–100
 on prayer training, 167
 on reading Bible, 231
 on relationship with God, 166–67, 247
 on sensory experience, 30–31

Mala, 150, 170, 186
Malony, H. N., ix, x, 245
marriage
 caste and, 107, 193, 213
 Convert's children's, 39, 51, 53, 54, 141, 212–13
 convert's, 29, 32, 39, 63, 67–69, 87, 94, 107, 111, 141, 202–3, 206, 212, 214
 crisis in, 48, 79
 giving or receiving dowry in, 51, 193
 problems due to conversion after, 42, 215
maturation
 in Step Model, 6, 239 figure, 242, 245–46
 Tippett, R. A., 245
Meeus, W., 235–36
mild experiences, 10, 120–42, 149, 153, 165, 241
miracles, 10, 84–100
 crisis resolved, 94–97

259

Index

miracles *(continued)*
  deliverance from danger, 85–86
  as evidences, 100
  healing, 88–91
  Luhrmann, T. M., 99, 100
  proofs, 94
  results in turning point, 148
  saved from suicide, 86–88
Mohan, 11
  conversion effects, 184–85
  conversion narrative, 128–31
  hostilities faced by, 182, 208–9, 210–12
  life after death, 181
  New Testament, reading, 129, 132, 142, 157
  prayer, 183
  secretly following Jesus, 208
mystical experience
  cognitive functioning in, 161
  differentiated from religious experience, 120, 160
  knowledge through, 163
  mediated by religious beliefs, 155
  union with divine, 159, 160
  See also religious experience
mystical states of consciousness
  Bulkeley, K., 161
  divine-human encounter occurs in, 11, 154
  interaction between divine and, 154
  interaction between the conscious and beyond, 238
  James, W., 154
  Katz, S. T., 155
  knowledge given through, 158–59
  religious experience in, 153
  revelation through, 158
  solution arises out of, 242
  turning point occurs at, 6
  See also rational consciousness; waking consciousness
mystical turning point. *See* turning point
Nambiar
  conversion narrative, 70–75
  difficulties, facing, 186
  God speaking to, 159
  hostilities, 199
  New Testament, reading, 157
  transformation, 189
Nathan, 10
  conversion narrative, 103–7
  Jesus speaking to, 160, 230
  prayer, 157
  prejudices against Christianity, 112
New Testament, reading, 70, 77, 104, 117, 128–29, 132, 134, 158, 233
  Beatitudes, attracted, 70
  Christian, makes one, 233
  confession of sin, 129
  desire to, 108
  John's Gospel, 77
  passionate in, 132
  realized as sinner, 77
  secretly, 105, 129
  someone within communicating, 157
  Supreme God found, 132, 142, 157
  transforms, 65
  urge to, 150, 157
  vision of Jesus, 71
  See also Bible, reading
Nieto, J. C., 120, 142, 160
Nithya
  falling in love, 11, 146, 152, 166
  intimacy with Jesus, 166
  love for others, 192
  prayer, 229–30
  turning point, 11, 146, 152

Oddie, G. A., 227
Otto, R., 142

participation in religious community
  enhances transformation, 233, 244
  explicit, 244
  as external ritual, 244
  in Step Model, 6, 239 figure, 244–46
  levels of, 237, 244
Paloutzian, R. F., 144
Paul, Saint
  conversion of, 6, 33, 159
  vision of, 30, 31, 158, 160
Peace, R. V., 30, 160, 234

Index

Phenomenological
  approach (methodology), ix, 4
  inter-disciplinary model, 235, 242
  perspective of conversion, 3, 4, 234
  psychology, 4
  Rambo, L. R., 4, 5
  Reh, L. A., 4, 5
  study, 4
  understanding, 2, 7
  Wulff, D. M., 4
practices, religious, 3, 5, 78, 226
Praveena, 9, 75–83, 150
prayer, 101–19
  answered by Jesus, 10, 29, 39, 58, 87, 89, 101, 108–9, 112–13, 115–16, 119, 131, 144, 147–48, 156–57, 172–73, 178, 195, 219, 229–30
  change of religion, leads to, 148
  commitment, 151
  confession of sin, 152, 184
  divine presence during, 36, 39, 159, 230
  Emerson, R. W., 101
  family, 39
  generic God, addressed to, 101, 102, 108, 112, 119, 156
  God's voice in, 83, 230
  Hardy, A., 119
  healing through, 89, 93, 115
  interaction with the divine through, 3, 83, 101, 172, 228–29, 246
  intimacy with the divine through, 12, 83, 172, 228, 230
  James, W., 101, 119, 230
  joy, happiness, and peace, gives, 112, 142, 157, 187, 229–30
  Luhrmann, T. M., 167
  meaning through, 119
  meeting, 28, 66, 89, 91, 105, 106, 214, 217
  power, gives, 119, 230
  problems solved through, 38–39, 87, 89, 93, 94, 148, 187–88, 222, 224, 230
  proofs, 101, 108, 119, 148, 229–30
  religious experience, 10, 102, 115, 119, 230
  religious practice, essential, 12, 246
  role of, 3, 12, 246
  Sabatier, A., 230
  Satan bound by, 177
  strength through, 11, 188, 223, 227, 230, 244
  success in business through, 97, 172
  sustaining factor, 230, 244
  training, 31
  transforms, 66, 230, 246
  unanswered, 116, 117, 119, 230
  vision in, 230
  witchcraft handled by, 183
pursuit and test
  in Step Model, 6, 239 figure, 240–41, 243, 245
  See also test

quest
  to know Christianity, 112
  quenched in reading New Testament, 128
  to read Bible, 127
  spiritual, 63, 241
  in stage model, 237, 241
  Supreme God, to reaching, 132, 142
  See also pursuit and test

Ramabai, P., 185, 193
Rambo, L. R. 3, 238, 240
  on conversion, 3, 232, 241, 243, 245
  on crisis, 243
  on intimacy with God, 166
  on phenomenological approach, 4, 5
  stage model, 237
Ramesh, 188, 195–96
Ranjan, 165, 192
rational consciousness
  accepts knowledge through mystical experience, 158, 162
  beyond, 158
  gaining knowledge aside, 163
  See also mystical states of consciousness; waking consciousness

Index

Reh, L. A. 4, 5
Rekha, 9
  conversion narrative, 64–69
  true love in Jesus, 70, 165
  truth, 161
religious consciousness, 142
  Otto, R., 142
religious experience, 30–33
  central to conversion, 2, 3, 5
  created a sense of sin, 32, 121, 141
  differentiated from mystical experience, 120
  dream, 9, 34–56
  event, 3, 10–11
  Hardy, A., 32–33
  James, W., 120, 153–54, 160–61, 163–64, 170, 242
  mild experiences, 120–42
  miracles, 85–100
  prayer, 101–19
  presence of the 'Other,' 63, 83, 142
  true love, 70
  vision, 8, 13–33
  voices of God, 57–84
  See also divine-human encounter; mystical experience; spark; turning point
Richardson, J. T. 236–37, 241
rituals, 42–43
  Christian, 244
  converts avoid, 213
  converts forced to practice, 29, 32, 65, 213
  converts voluntarily practicing, 49, 213
  Hindu, 78, 42, 43, 109
  prayer not, 230, 246

Sakunthala, 182–83
Samsudeen, 161, 171
Sania, 8, 11
  auditory experience, 30
  automatism, 30, 164
  Bibe reading, 17
  conversion narrative, 14–23
  hostilities faced by, 199, 200–208, 228
  identifying Jesus, 31, 155–56
  intimacy with Jesus, 21
  Jesus speaking to, 20, 30, 159
  miracle, 194
  prayer, 194–95
  praying to generic God, 112, 159
  purpose in life, 162
  sense of sin, 32
  visions, 14–15, 18, 155–56, 175
Sarala, 9, 51–54, 157
Sargant, W., 234
Schoenrade, P., 153–54, 238, 242
Selvi, 9
  auditory experience, 30
  automatism, 30, 147
  conversion narrative, 24–29
  hostilities, 29, 32, 212
  Jesus speaking to, 30, 159–60
  prejudiced against Christianity, 24–25
  presence of the Other, 151
  sense of sin, 26, 27, 32, 178, 180
  true love in Jesus, 70, 165
  vision, 24, 26–27, 30
Sensory experience
  cause of, 31
  hallucination, similar to, but not, 30–31
  identification of Jesus, 156
  kinds of, 31
  Luhrmann, T. W., 30
  replacement of religious belief, 30
Singh, B. 144, 156, 178, 180–81, 184, 227
Singh, Kishan, 209
Singh, Sadhu Sunder, 112, 156, 184
social psychological
  dimension/aspect, 6, 238, 239 figure
  factors, 238, 246
  perspective of conversion, 237
  process, 237
  theories, 237, 244
socialization, 3, 144, 235, 244–45
spark
  divine-human encounter, 239, 241–42
  event, 6, 241
  in Step Model, 6, 239 figure, 241

moment, 6
realization, 121
revelatory, 242
spiritual insight, 121, 144, 165, 181
transformation begins at, 6, 239, 242–43, 245
triggers pursuit and test, 241
See also divine-human encounter; turning point
spiritual dimension
  conversion, 2, 7
  life-changing dreams, 56
spiritual life
  in Hinduism and Christianity, 78–79, 110, 131
  in Islam and Christianity, 19
stage model, 237, 240–41, 243–44
Stark, R., 232, 235, 238, 242, 244
Step Model, 234–48, 239 figure
  hostilities in, 243
  interdisciplinary model, 5, 235
  flexible, 235
  line of transformation in, 242
  religious aspects, incorporates, 238, 246
  religious experience, significance of, 12, 235, 242, 245
  religious practices in, 12, 245
  transformation process, 243, 245
  seven steps of, 6, 239, 246
  social psychological aspect, incorporates, 238, 246
  spark in, 241
  x axis, 245
  y axis, 245
supernatural experience, 5, 241. *See also* sensory experience
Surya, 162
  change, 162
  peace and joy, 179, 184
  purpose of life, 162
  sense of being forgiven, 179
  struggling with sin, 179
Sushila, 113, 114, 157

test
  new religious option, 10, 241
  one's religion, 42
  prayer as acid, 101, 119
  prayer to Jesus as, 112
  workability of Christianity, 100, 164
  See also pursuit and test
Tilak, N. M., 193, 199, 233
Tippett, R. A.
  anthropological model, 236, 240, 242, 244
  conversion process, 237, 245
  maturation, 245
transformation
  attitudes, 118, 162, 191
  begins at the spark, 6, 12, 65, 239, 242–43, 245
  behaviors, 118, 138, 162, 191
  cognitive restructuring results in, 154
  divine-human encounter triggers, 2, 3, 119, 144, 196, 245
  inner, 117–19, 189
  James, W., 169–70
  line of, 239 figure, 242–43
  maturation and, 245–46
  meaning in life, 21
  participation in religious community enhances, 233, 244
  personal, 2–3, 11–12, 21, 65, 138, 154, 169, 238
  prayer sustains, 246
  process, 233, 238, 243, 245, 246
  social, 243
  socialization, and, 244, 245
  in studies, 190
  total, 66, 98, 196–97
transforming effects, 169–97
  behavioral, 191
  economical, 193–96
  James, W., 170
  physical, 191
  psychological, 183–91
  social, 192–93
  spiritual, 170–83
transformative religious experience, definition of, *See* conversion defined
turning point, 143–68
  answer to prayer brings, 147
  change of faith, 143

263

Index

turning point *(continued)*
  cognitive restructuring, 159
  consciousness of sin, 152
  conversational, 11, 159–60
  conviction: Jesus is true, 152
  conviction: one's religion of birth is false, 152
  divine-human encounter is, 6, 10, 121, 148, 154, 242
  falling in love, similar to, 146
  forgiven, 152
  ineffable, 11, 146–47, 149, 163–64, 242
  intimacy, 11, 165–67, 170
  miracles result in, 148
  mystical states of consciousness, occurs at, 6, 11, 151
  noetic, 11, 161–63
  passive, 11, 164–65
  revelatory, 11, 155–59
  sensory experience results in, 144–45
  spark, 241
  sudden realization, 144, 149
  transient, 11
  waking consciousness, beyond, 152
  world-saver model, 235
  See also divine-human encounter; religious experience; spark

Ventis, L. W., 153–54, 238, 242
Vinay, 10, 136–41
Vinitha, 132–36, 142, 157, 184
Vinodha, 9
  conversion dream, 42–50
  Jesus speaking to, 56, 156–57, 159
  loving relationship with Jesus, 9, 50
  peace, 50, 184
vision, 13–33
  auditory elements, 13
  automatism, elements of 13, 30
  cognitive restructuring, 153–54
  conscious during, 26, 31
  conversion, led to, 10
  convert passive, 13
  of crucifixion, 24, 147
  depression, relieved from, 22, 32
  divine communication, 159–60
  enmity against Christianity changed, 26
  happiness and joy, filled with, 27, 184
  Jesus as real, belief in, 211
  of Jesus, 9, 13–14, 20, 24, 32, 71, 102, 104, 147, 173–75, 184, 211
  Jesus, identified with, 13, 18, 20–21, 31, 33, 112, 147, 156
  liberation, instant, 24
  love of Jesus, 24
  new, 238, 242
  Paul's, similar to, 30, 31, 158, 160
  prayer, answer to, 112, 148, 156–57
  praying, someone within, 151
  prejudices and enmity against Christianity disappear, 13
  prior religious belief redundant, 13, 155, 158
  religious belief replaced, 30, 158
  sensory organs active, 13
  Shadrach Meshach, saw, in 211
  sinful not earlier but during, 16, 26, 32, 178
  struggling with sin prior to, 24
  transformed, 24, 30
  transient, 164
  troubled by, 9
  truth, knowing, 32, 63, 211
  turning point, 27
  voice speaking in, 30
Vivekananda, S., 198
Voices of God, 57–84
  accepted Christ, 57
  Bible, God spoke through, 9, 57, 83, 160, 230
  Luhrmann, T. W., 84
  sermons, God spoke through, 9, 57
  someone from within communicating, 57

waking consciousness
  beyond, 55, 147, 150, 152–53, 163
  Bulkeley, K., on, 143, 153, 163
  James, W., on, 153, 163
  knowledge not only through, 143
  negative attitude towards Jesus/Christianity, 158–59

misleading belief on, 163
new belief brought to, 151
other forms of consciousness besides, 153
returns to, 6, 13
suspended, 11
See also mystical states of consciousness; rational consciousness

Wiebe, P. H., 33, 157
world-saver model, 232, 235–37, 240–41, 244
Wulff, D. M. 4

Yong, A., 85

www.ingramcontent.com/pod-product-compliance
Lightning Source LLC
Chambersburg PA
CBHW071246230426
43668CB00011B/1615